THE OBLIGATIONS AND RIGHTS OF THE PASTOR OF A PARISH
ACCORDING TO THE CODE OF CANON LAW

The Obligations and Rights of the Pastor of a Parish

According to the Code of Canon Law

Msgr. Edward A. Sweeny, JCD, PhD

ST PAULS

Alba
House

Library of Congress Cataloging-in-Publication Data

Sweeny, Edward A.
   The obligations and rights of the pastor of a parish according to the Code of
Canon Law / Edward A. Sweeny.
      p. cm.
   Includes bibliographical references.
   ISBN 0-8189-0910-2 (alk. paper)
   1. Clergy (Canon law) 2. Parishes (Canon law)   I. Title.

   KBU2872.S93 2002
   262'.9'4—dc21

                                                                    2001046438

Nihil Obstat:
Rev. Msgr. George P. Graham, JCD
Censor librorum
January 25, 2002

Imprimatur:
Most Rev. William Murphy
Bishop of Rockville Centre
February 12, 2002

The Nihil Obstat and Imprimatur are official declarations that a book or pamphlet is free of doctrinal error. No implication is contained therein that those who have granted the Nihil Obstat and Imprimatur agree with the contents, opinions or statements expressed.

Vidimus et approbavimus ad normam Statutorum
Universitatis Sancti Pauli, Ottaviensis,

   Datum Ottavae, Dec. 5, 2001
   Roch Pagé
   Decanus

Produced and designed in the United States of America by the Fathers and Brothers of the Society of St. Paul, 2187 Victory Boulevard, Staten Island, New York 10314-6603, as part of their communications apostolate.

ISBN: 0-8189-0910-2

Printing Information:

Current Printing - first digit   1   2   3   4   5   6   7   8   9   10

Year of Current Printing - first year shown

2002   2003   2004   2005   2006   2007   2008   2009   2010

Copyrights and Permissions

Table of Contents

Introduction

The Second Vatican Council has infused new life into various Church institutions and that life generates a new light in which the theological and ecclesial elements of those institutions can be more clearly seen than before. Among those institutions the parish and the office of pastor of a parish, while retaining many of their historical features, are now perceived to be more dynamic, personal and communitarian than had previously been the case.

The expression *pastor of the parish* has been used deliberately in the title and often in the text of this study. This has been done in an effort to promote greater clarity. In English usage, in many countries the pastor of a parish (*parochus*) is called *the parish priest*, while in other countries the term *the parish priest* may indicate any priest assigned to a parish, whether as pastor or parochial vicar. In addition, the Holy Father and all diocesan bishops are often referred to as *pastor(s)* in Church documents.

Attuned to the ecclesiology of Vatican II, canon law now presents a parish as a Eucharistic community of the faithful, clergy and laity together, honoring God by celebrating the liturgy with one another, each actively participating according to his or her own proper role, all living their day to day Christian lives as witness of their faith and aware that their community is a vital part of a particular diocese and of the universal Church. The parish is seen to exist for the salvation of each and every person living within its boundaries.

The Second Vatican Council also focused on the facts that the pastor of a parish is, theologically and juridically, at the center of a parish community and that the lay faithful have abilities, experience, expertise, gifts and charisms which can and should be recognized, developed and utilized for the spread of the faith and the good of the parish, diocesan and universal Church.

The qualifications which c. 521 of the 1983 Code requires of a priest in order for him to be appointed pastor of a parish are substantially the same as those stipulated by c. 453 of the 1917 Code. The pastor of a parish is clearly understood to be especially conformed to Christ by priestly ordination in order to serve God's people. The pastor is expected to carry out his service by providing mutually respectful and cooperative leadership, in such a way that the lay faithful and the pastor may work together to carry out the threefold tasks of Jesus as priest, prophet and king. All participate in Christ's tasks in a general way through Baptism and priests also share in them in an essentially different manner through priestly ordination. The Code of 1983 places a great emphasis on the obligation of the pastor to lead by example and persuasion.

The members of the Pontifical Commission for the Revision of the Code of Canon Law had as their first guiding principle that the law should determine and safeguard the rights and obligations of each person in relation to the rights and obligations of other individuals in particular and to those of the community in general.[1]

During various formal and informal meetings with pastors following the promulgation of the Code in 1983, a good number expressed the opinion that the Code stipulated many, many obligations for the pastor of a parish and very few rights. Does that opinion have any basis in fact? Pursuit of that basic question has developed into this study, which has as its goal to provide a comprehensive overview of the obligations and rights of the pastor of a parish as they are expressed, both *explicitly* and *implicitly*, in the 1983 Code of Canon Law.

---

[1] See *Communicationes*, 1 (1969), p. 79.

Throughout this study the terms *obligation* and *right* will be used in a broad sense. This broad sense includes what might be termed *entitlements*, or *legitimate expectations*, which will be fulfilled if each person or group obeys the canons with respect to every other person or group, even in those cases in which a canon does not express a strict canonical obligation or right.

Some canons of the Code simply acknowledge and/or restate obligations and rights which have divine positive law, natural law, divine revelation or the authentic magisterium of the Church as their origin and ultimate authority. Other canons acknowledge and/or institute obligations and rights devised by human reason and are dependent for their binding power on the will of the supreme authority of the Church; in some cases even obligations and/or rights set down in local civil laws are also given canonical status. Still other canons are exhortatory, pointing to a goal which is to be sincerely and earnestly sought rather than absolutely and immediately achieved. As a result not every obligation or right expressed in the Code has the same binding power, can be enforced in the same way, or, in the final analysis, even has the same importance.

At times in the course of the analysis and interpretation, canonists may arrive at different and perhaps even irreconcilable conclusions concerning the meaning and/or application of one or another canon. In view of the number of canons considered in this study, it should not be surprising that various canonists have taken other positions in some instances. I have not annotated nor attempted to address every such disagreement; I have attempted to present accurate interpretations of the canons involved and clearly to detail the analyses and reasoning which have led to those interpretations.

In this study, obligations have been consistently placed before rights, first, because pastors exist in the Church to work for the good of souls, the *salus animarum*, which c. 1752 solemnly identifies as the Church's supreme law. Secondly, most of the rights of the ecclesiastical office of pastor seem to have come into being in order to enable the pastor to fulfill his obligations toward the Christian community.

All things considered, it is my view that the Code, reflecting the teachings of the Second Vatican Council, establishes *Service in the Form of Leadership* as the principal obligation and the principal right of the pastor of the parish. The pastor is obliged and entitled to teach the faith so that it produces dynamic Christians; together with the faithful he is to plan and celebrate the liturgies through which they will offer public worship to God as a Eucharistic community; he is to govern the parish in a consultative manner aided and advised by the faithful in a relationship of mutual trust and respect. Various canons indicate the Church's awareness that the pastor will need the help of the faithful in order to fulfill many of his obligations, and that, even though he should prudently share some of his authority with others, he cannot delegate away his leadership responsibility. It may also be noted that the parish has not lost its role as an almost indispensable administrative grouping in the Church, but that element is not especially emphasized or regarded as primary.

It is my hope that this work has provided some useful insights into the theological and juridical dimensions of the ministry of a pastor of a parish.

I wish to thank all those who have made it possible for me to undertake and complete this study, in particular the late Bishop John R. McGann and the late Bishop James T. McHugh, the second and third Bishops of the Diocese of Rockville Centre. I thank especially the several canonists who have reviewed the text and provided important advice, information and critiques. I readily express my appreciation to Dr. Eileen Kilbride for her careful consideration and critique of the text from a non-canonical viewpoint. Finally, but by no means of least importance, I thank my family, especially my cousin Alice K. Meier, and my friends who have helped and encouraged me to complete this study.

Abbreviations

AA   VATICAN II, Decree on the Apostolate of Lay People,
        Apostolicam actuositatem, November 18, 1965: *AAS*, 58
        (1966), pp. 837-864.

AAS   *Acta Apostolicae Sedis.*

AG   VATICAN II, Decree on the Church's Missionary Activity
        Ad gentes, December 7, 1965: *AAS*, 58 (1966), pp. 947-990.

AN   SACRA CONGREGATIO PRO CLERIS, General Catechetical
        Directory *Ad normam decreti*, March 11, 1971: *AAS*, 64
        (1972), pp. 97-116.

CCEO   *Codex canonum Ecclesiarum orientalium, auctoritate Ioannis
        Pauli PP. II promulgatus*, Romae, Typis polyglottis
        Vatcanis, 1990.

CD   VATICAN II, Decree on the Pastoral Office of Bishops in
        the Church *Christus Dominus*, October 28, 1965: *AAS*, 58
        (1966), pp. 673-696.

CIC   *Codex iuris canonici, auctoritate Ioannis Pauli PP. II
        promulgatus*, Libreria editrice Vaticana, 1983.

CLSA   Canon Law Society of America.

CP   PONTIFICIUM CONSILIUM INSTRUMENTIS COMMUNICATIONIS
        SOCIALIS, Pastoral Instruction for the Proper Implementa-
        tion of the Decree of the Second Ecumenical Council of
        the Vatican Concerning the Means of Social Communi-
        cation *Communio et progressio*, May 23, 1971: *AAS*, 63
        (1971), pp. 593-656.

CT   POPE JOHN PAUL II, Apostolic Exhortation, Catechesis in
        Our Time *Catechesi tradendae*, October 16, 1979: *AAS*, 71
        (1979), pp. 1277-1340.

DH   VATICAN II, Declaration on the Right of the Person and
        Communities to Social and Civil Liberty in Religious

Matters *Dignitatis humanae*, October 7, 1965: *AAS*, 58 (1966), pp. 929-941.

DV   VATICAN II, Dogmatic Constitution on Divine Revelation *Dei Verbum*, November 18, 1965: *AAS*, 58 (1966), pp. 817-830.

EN   POPE PAUL VI, Apostolic Exhortation, Evangelization in the Modern World *Evangelii nuntiandi*, December 8, 1975: *AAS*, 68 (1976), pp. 5-76.

GE   VATICAN II, Declaration on Christian Education *Gravissimum educationis*, October 28, 1965: *AAS*, 58 (1966), pp. 728-739.

GS   VATICAN II, Pastoral Constitution on the Church in the Modern World *Gaudium et spes*, December 7, 1965: *AAS*, 58 (1966), pp. 1025-1115.

LEF   *Lex Ecclesiae fundamentalis*

LG   VATICAN II, Dogmatic Constitution on the Church *Lumen gentium*, November 21, 1964: *AAS*, 57 (1965), pp. 5-67.

OE   VATICAN II, Decree on the Catholic Eastern Churches *Orientalium ecclesiarum*, November 21, 1964: *AAS*, 57 (1965), pp. 76-85.

OT   VATICAN II, Decree on the Training of Priests *Optatam totius*, October 28, 1965: *AAS*, 58 (1966), pp. 713-727.

PC   VATICAN II, Decree on the Up-To-Date Renewal of Religious Life *Perfectae caritatis*, October 28, 1965: *AAS*, 58 (1966), pp. 702-712.

PO   VATICAN II, Decree on the Ministry and Life of Priests *Presbyterorum ordinis*, December 7, 1965: *AAS*, 58 (1966), pp. 991-1024.

SC   VATICAN II, Constitution on the Sacred Liturgy *Sacrosanctum concilium*, December 4, 1963: *AAS*, 56 (1964), pp. 97-133.

SCDW SACRED CONGREGATION fOR DIVINE WORSHIP

UR   VATICAN II, Decree on Ecumenism *Unitatis redintegratio*, November 21, 1964: *AAS*, 57 (1965), pp. 90-107.

Three Technical Terms

Three terms used in the study of canon law and found in this book may be unfamiliar to various readers; concise explanations are therefore provided here:

Fontes is a Latin word for *wells* or *origins*. In the study of canon law *fontes* has historically come to refer to the sources of canons. The sources of canons are important because both the 1917 Code (c. 17 §2) and the 1983 Code (c. 17) indicate that the history of a canon can have a role in the legal interpretation of that canon and, at times, other canons as well. All of the *fontes* however, for both the 1917 and 1983 Codes are unofficial. That is, they are not established by the Holy See as the canons of the codes are. Although carefully elaborated, the *fontes* remain simply the private work of the experts who produce them. Many of the *fontes* cited for canons of the 1983 Code build on and expect the researcher to be aware of the existence of the canons of the 1917 Code and their *fontes*. Indeed, many of the canons in the Code of 1983 have sources extending far back well beyond the canons of the 1917 Code into the history of the Church.

Provision refers to the actions, decided upon and carried out in accord with canon law, by individuals and/or groups who have the right to select or propose a properly qualified individual, as they select and/or install an individual who will fill a vacant, or in certain cases a soon-to-be-vacant, ecclesiastical office or other administrative post.

In solidum, as it is generally used in reference to providing pastoral care in a parish concerns the assignment of more than one individual to work *together* or *jointly* or as a *team*; each individual being equally responsible to see to it that integral pastoral care is provided.

Chapter One

The Office of the Pastor of a Parish
In the Light of Vatican Council II

INTRODUCTION

On January 25, 1959, not quite three months into his pontificate, Pope John XXIII (1958-1963) announced his intention to convoke a General Council of the Catholic Church.[1] In that announcement the Holy Father explained why it was important for the Church that such a decisive step be taken. The Pontiff saw Christ's grace spreading its fruits through the world, but he also observed human freedom misused and denied, people fighting against the truth, pursuing worldly goods and material progress and distracted from searching for more important spiritual goals. The Pope also saw a relaxation of traditional discipline and good order.[2]

The historical achievements of Ecumenical Councils in the past led the Pope to judge that such a Council would once again provide the Church with a needed renewal of ecclesiastical discipline, contemporary and clear doctrinal affirmations, religious unity and increased Christian fervor.[3] In the Pontiff's prayers and

---

[1] Pope John XXIII, Special Allocution to the Cardinals *Questa festiva*, January 25, 1959, in *Acta Apostolicae Sedis* (=*AAS*), 51 (1959), pp. 65-69, here at p. 68. English translation in *The Pope Speaks*, 5 (1958-1959), pp. 398-401, here at pp. 400-401.

[2] *Ibid.*

[3] *Ibid.*

plans the crowning achievement of this Ecumenical Council was to be:

> ...the desired and long-awaited modernization of the Code of Canon Law... the practical application of the rules of ecclesiastical discipline, applications the Spirit of the Lord will surely suggest to us as we proceed.[4]

Since the documents of Vatican Council II are the sources of the pastoral perspective of the revised Code and provide the substance of many of its canons,[5] the importance of the Council for the renewed Code of Canon Law can hardly be overestimated.

> The pastoral emphasis [of Vatican Council II] on the deliberations and decrees directly affected church discipline and ecclesial activity.... The Commission [Pontifical Commission for the Revision of the Code of Canon Law] would have been foolish to begin any revision without awaiting the documents expressing the Church's pastoral teaching.... The process of revision was not simply a reformulation... but a redrafting and reform of ecclesial structures and norms.[6]

Concisely put, the Council had to explain *what we are as a Church* and *who we are as the People of God*, before Church Law

---

[4] *Ibid.*

[5] "Indeed, in a certain sense this new Code could be understood as a great effort to translate this same conciliar doctrine and ecclesiology into *canonical language*...." JOHN PAUL II, Apostolic Constitution *Sacrae disciplinae leges*, January 25, 1983, in *AAS*, 75 II (1983), pp. vii-xiv, here at p. xi. English translation in *Code of Canon Law, Latin-English Edition* (=CLSA *Code of Canon Law, Latin-English Edition*), translation prepared under the auspices of the Canon Law Society of America, Washington, DC: Canon Law Society of America, 1983, here at p. xiv. Unless otherwise indicated, English translation of canons of the revised Code will be derived from this source.

[6] J.A. ALESANDRO, "General Introduction," in *The Code of Canon Law: A Text and Commentary* (=*Commentary*), Commissioned by the Canon Law Society of America, J.A. CORIDEN, T.J. GREEN, and D.E. HEINTSCHEL (eds.), New York: Paulist Press, 1985, pp. 1-22, here at p. 5.

could be drawn up to guide us in living those realities in our everyday lives.

One of the hallmarks of Vatican Council II was its ecclesiology, which the canons of the revised Code mirror.[7] Significant elements of the Second Vatican Council's ecclesiology led canonists to provide in the Code "a redefinition of parish… and pastor…,"[8] which in turn changed the obligations and rights of parish pastors, increasing some, decreasing others, and reinterpreting still others.

As a result, for those obligations and rights to be studied they need to be both appreciated in the light of the Second Vatican Council's teachings and analyzed in their juridic expression in the Code.[9] As a first step, in Chapter I two questions will be studied: What did Vatican Council II teach about a parish? What did Vatican Council II teach about the ecclesiastical office of pastor of a parish?

1.1 — VATICAN COUNCIL II ON THE PARISH

1.1.1 — Preliminary Considerations

Parishes as we know them today, communities of the Christian faithful within a diocese and ministered to by a priest assigned by the diocesan bishop, began to come into existence in

---

[7] "The instrument which the Code is fully corresponds to the nature of the Church, especially as it is proposed by the teaching of the Second Vatican Council in general and in a particular way by its ecclesiological teaching." JOHN PAUL II, *Sacrae disciplinae leges*, in *AAS*, 75 II (1983), p. xi. English translation in *CLSA Code of Canon Law, Latin-English Edition*, p. xiv.

[8] J.A. JANICKI, "Introduction to Pastors, Parishes and Parochial Vicars," commentary on cc. 515-572, in *CLSA Commentary*, p. 414.

[9] Cardinal Felici noted that because of their different goals and manners of expression, conciliar teachings often had to be explicitated in the Code in juridic form. P. FELICI, "Norma giuridica e 'pastorale'," in *La norma en el derecho canónico, actas del III congreso internacional de derecho canónico. Pamplona, 10-15 de octubre de 1976*, vol. 1, Pamplona: Ediciones Universidad de Navarra, S.A., 1979, p. 19.

the fourth century. After the Emperor Constantine's Edict of Toleration (313) and the Emperor Theodosius' recognition of Christianity as the official religion of the Roman Empire (380), the Church and its communities could organize more publicly.[10]

The spiritual needs of Christians living in rural communities outside of the urban areas where the bishop and the priests of a diocese lived and ministered eventually led to the assignment of some of the priests to live in those rural communities and serve the faithful there under the authority of the bishop. The Council of Trent (1545-1563) *encouraged* the establishment of parishes as a better way to meet the needs of the faithful.[11] In the 1917 Code of Canon Law, c. 216 §1 *required* the division of the territory of a diocese into parishes in order to provide for the necessary care of souls.[12] The same c. 216 §4 did take note of the existence of parishes constituted in special circumstances, unified by some factor other than specific geographic boundaries. Such parishes were clearly exceptions; no new parishes of the sort could be established without a special apostolic indult,

---

[10] A.B. Mickells, *The Constitutive Elements of Parishes: A Historical Synopsis and a Commentary*, Canon Law Studies, No. 296, Washington, DC: Catholic University of America, 1950, pp. 14-17. Also see A. Borras, *Les communautés paroissiales: droit canonique pastorales*, Paris, Les Editions du Cerf, 1996, pp. 15-16. G. Lobina, "Parrocchia e parroco nei nuovi orientamenti giuridici postconciliari," in *Apollinaris*, 49 (1976), pp. 418-449, here at pp. 418-419.

[11] Societas Goerresiana (ed.), *Concilium Tridentinum: diariorum, actorum, epistularum, tractatuum nova collectio*, t. 8, *Actorum pars quinta, complectens acta ad preparandum concilium, et sessiones anni 1562 a prima (XVII) ad sextam (XXII)*, collegit, edidit, illustravit S. Ehses, Friburgi Brisgoviae: B. Herder, 1919, Session XXI, "Decretum de reformatione...," Canon quartus, p. 702. English translation in N.P. Tanner (ed.), *Decrees of the Ecumenical Councils*, vol. 2, *Trent to Vatican II*, Washington, DC: Sheed & Ward and Georgetown University Press, 1990, pp. 729-730.

[12] *Codex iuris canonici, Pii X Pontificis Maximi iussu digestus, Benedicti Papae XV auctoritate promulgatus, praefatione, fontibus annotatione et indice analyticio-alphabetico ab Emo Petro Card. Gasparri auctus*, Romae, Typis polyglottis Vaticanis, 1933: Canon 216 §1. "Territorium cuiuslibet diocesis dividatur in distinctas partes territoriales; unicuique autem parti sua peculiaris ecclesia cum populo determinato est assignanda, suusque peculiaris rector, tamquam proprius eiusdem pastor, est praeficiendus pro necessaria animarum cura." "The territory of each diocese shall be divided into distinct territorial parts; and to each part there shall be assigned its own church with a specific group of people in the district, and its own rector is to be placed in charge as its proper pastor for the necessary care of souls." English translations not otherwise attributed are by the author.

but if such parishes already had been constituted, their status was not to be changed without prior consultation with the Apostolic See.

In its turn, the Second Vatican Council was far more comprehensive, as it considered parishes and pastors from a purposefully pastoral perspective.[13] The Council did not, however, express its important insights in one specific document dealing with parishes; nor did the Council provide a precise definition of *a parish.*

In its documents too, the Council did not make a clear distinction in its use of the Latin terms *pastores* and *pastores animarum.* Both terms appear sometimes to be used of bishops, sometimes of priests who hold the ecclesiastical office of pastor and sometimes of all priests who minister in parishes. For purposes of this initial survey of Second Vatican Council teachings there is little practical difference, because pastors of parishes and all priests engaged in pastoral ministry have a general responsibility to cooperate with and assist their bishops in the bishops' tasks of serving the needs of the people — historically the very reason why parishes came into existence.

1.1.2 — The basic elements of a parish

The most comprehensive single statement of the Second Vatican Council about the makeup of a parish is found in the Constitution on the Sacred Liturgy, *Sacrosanctum concilium,* n. 42, and is a serviceable foundation for a study of more than half of the elements of "parish" identified in conciliar teaching:

> But as it is impossible for the bishop always and everywhere to preside over the whole flock in his church, he

---

[13] See supra footnote 9. In the paragraph cited, Cardinal Felici, who had served as secretary of the Second Vatican Council, acknowledges and comments on its pastoral character. Also see supra footnote 6, in which the *CLSA Commentary* alludes to the same pastoral orientation.

must of necessity establish groupings of the faithful; and, among these, parishes, set up locally under a pastor who takes the place of the bishop [*sub pastore vices gerente episcopi*], are the most important, for in some way they represent the visible Church constituted throughout the world.

Therefore the liturgical life of the parish and its relation to the bishop must be fostered in the spirit and practice of the laity and clergy. Efforts must also be made to encourage a sense of community within the parish above all in the common celebration of the Sunday Mass.[14]

Among the elements of a parish present in these two paragraphs, three may be considered necessary for the establishment of a parish as they are also mentioned even more pointedly in another conciliar document, *Christus Dominus*, nn. 20 and 32.[15] These *basic elements* have to do with canonically establishing a parish at its very beginning.[16] A fourth basic element is also present. Canonists have debated its exact importance over the years and the 1983 Code, in c. 518, identifies it as a "general rule" for the establishment of a parish.

The *First Basic Element* of a parish is the existence of a *group of the faithful* who are in need of spiritual help, but to whom the

---

[14] SECOND VATICAN COUNCIL, Constitution on the Sacred Liturgy *Sacrosanctum concilium* (=SC), December 4, 1963, in *AAS*, 56 (1964), pp. 97-133, here at n. 42, pp. 111-112. English translation in A. FLANNERY (gen. ed.), *Vatican Council II*, 2 vols.: vol. 1, *The Conciliar and Post Conciliar Documents*, New Revised Edition, Dublin, Ireland, Dominican Publications, 1992, p. 15.

[15] SECOND VATICAN COUNCIL, Decree on the Pastoral Office of Bishops in the Church *Christus Dominus* (=CD), October 28, 1965, in *AAS*, 58 (1966), pp. 673-696, here at nn. 20 and 32, pp. 683, 688-689. English translation in FLANNERY, *Conciliar and Post Conciliar Documents*, pp. 575 and 583.

[16] Over the years various canonists have written about the "constitutive" elements of a parish. They have disagreed with one another. Brief reviews of these disagreements may be found in MICKELLS, *The Constitutive Elements of Parishes*, pp. 4-12, and M.A. HACK, *Stability of the Office of Parish Priest*, pp. 106-114. These disputes are not within the purview of this work; the term "basic" is used here to identify those significant elements of a parish which are treated.

diocesan bishop is not personally able to minister to because of the great number of faithful in his diocese, also called the *particular church*, for which he is responsible.[17]

Parishes are established in order to meet the needs of the faithful. As *Christus Dominus*, n. 31, plainly taught: "Moreover, the whole reason for the parochial office is the good of souls."[18] The same document in n. 32 also set down:

> Finally, the same concern for the salvation of souls should be the motive for the determining or reconsidering the erection or suppression of parishes and other changes of this kind. The bishop may act in these matters on his own authority.[19]

---

[17] F. COCCOPALMERIO, "Il concetto di parrocchia nel Vaticano II," in *La scuola cattolica*, 106 (1978), pp. 123-142, here at pp. 124-130. COCCOPALMERIO draws together conciliar teachings about the effects of relationships of the *"fidelium coetus"* or "grouping of the faithful" with their pastor and their bishop. Because the pastor is appointed by the bishop to care for the group of the faithful, the group becomes a parish and together they are an image of the Church. Because the pastor is appointed by the bishop to serve the parish in the bishop's place, through that legitimate appointment and the presence of the pastor the parish is in essential relation to the diocesan community; as part of the diocesan community the parish represents and makes present Christ and his Universal Church. It should be noted that the establishment of each of the interrelationships mentioned by COCCOPALMERIO depends on a juridic act regulated by canon law. Also see *SC*, n. 42, and SECOND VATICAN COUNCIL, Dogmatic Constitution on the Church *Lumen gentium* (=*LG*), November 21, 1964, in *AAS*, 57 (1965), pp. 5-67, here at, n. 26, pp. 31-32 and n. 28, pp. 33-36, English translation in FLANNERY, *Conciliar and Post Conciliar Documents*, pp. 384-387.

[18] *CD* n. 31, p. 689: "Praeterea cum muneris paroecialis tota ratio sit bonum animarum...." English translation in FLANNERY, *Conciliar and Post Conciliar Documents*, pp. 582-583. See: *LG*, n. 37, English translation in FLANNERY, *Conciliar and Post Conciliar Documents*, p. 394; SECOND VATICAN COUNCIL, Decree on the Catholic Eastern Churches *Orientalium ecclesiarum* (=*OE*), November 21, 1964, in *AAS*, 57 (1965), pp. 76-85, here at n. 4, pp. 77-78, English translation in FLANNERY, *Conciliar and Post Conciliar Documents*, pp. 442-443; *CD*, n. 23 (3), n. 32, English translation in FLANNERY, *Conciliar and Post Conciliar Documents*, pp. 576-577 and 583; SECOND VATICAN COUNCIL, Decree on the Ministry and Life of Priests *Presbyterorum ordinis* (=*PO*), December 7, 1965, in *AAS*, 58 (1966), pp. 991-1024, here at n. 3, pp. 993-995, English translation in FLANNERY, *Conciliar and Post Conciliar Documents*, pp. 866-868; *PO*, n. 9, English translation in FLANNERY, *Conciliar and Post Conciliar Documents*, pp. 880-881.

[19] *CD*, n. 32.

Not only did Vatican Council II highlight the community aspect of a parish but also of a diocese and of various other stably organized groups of Christ's faithful. The general tenor of the documents of Vatican Council II indicates that the purpose of such emphasis was clearly (a) to identify and acknowledge the interactions of divine gifts and precepts with human needs and efforts within the Church and (b) then, in light of those interactions, to point out how the Christian faithful as individuals and as members of recognized groups should live their lives in accord with God's revelation to promote the salvation of all.[20]

The *Second Basic Element* of a parish is that the group of the faithful whose needs are to be met must be *within the boundaries of the diocese* whose bishop is seeking to provide for the members of the group. The observance of diocesan boundaries is important for the reasons taught by Vatican II in *Christus Dominus*, n. 22:

> For a diocese to fulfill its purpose it is necessary that the nature of the Church be clearly manifested in the People of God belonging to the diocese. Bishops must be able to carry out their pastoral function effectively among their people, and finally the spiritual welfare of the People of God must be catered for as perfectly as possible. This requires not only a proper determination of the territorial limits of the diocese but also a reasonable distribution of clergy and resources in accordance with the needs of the apostolate. All these things contribute to the good, not only of the clergy and the faithful who are directly involved, but also the whole Church.[21]

The admixture of prayer, confidence in divine guidance and the use of human organizational and administrative ele-

---

[20] *LG*, nn. 1-4.
[21] *CD*, n. 22.

ments within the Church should not come as a surprise. The Church sees itself as a complex reality with a human and a divine element. The social structure of the Church is perceived as serving the Spirit of Christ who gives life to the Church, in somewhat the same manner as the way in which the human nature assumed by God the Son became inseparably united to him and served in the work of our salvation.[22]

Although recognizing the theological importance and the administrative need of specific diocesan boundaries, the Second Vatican Council often encouraged bishops and sometimes requires them to cooperate on matters which may best be treated by several dioceses working together. Recalling the spirit of fraternal charity and zeal for the universal mission entrusted to the apostles which, from the earliest ages of the Church, has led individual churches to work together for the common good, *Christus Dominus*, n. 36 issued particular directives concerning the purpose, membership and authority of episcopal conferences. The same conciliar document in n. 40 urged that all dioceses and their territorial legal equivalents be incorporated into ecclesiastical provinces as a general rule; n. 42 encouraged the establishment of various offices to serve several dioceses in a particular area.[23]

The *Third Basic Element* of a parish is that the diocesan bishop must appoint a *priest as pastor* of the group of the faithful

---

[22] *LG*, n. 8. Also see *CD*, n. 23 on the matters to be taken into account when the revision of diocesan boundaries is under consideration.

[23] See canons 237 interdiocesan seminaries; 271 §§1-2 bishops and better inter-diocesan distribution of clergy; 382 §2 bishop to provide for needs of persons of other rites (*sui iuris* churches) residing in his diocese; 385 bishop to foster missionary vocations; 431- 434 Ecclesiastical Provinces and Regions; 775 §§1-3; 838 §3 translations of liturgical books into vernacular languages; 1274 §§2-4, 1275 combined financial efforts of several dioceses; 1316 in establishing penal laws, bishops are to strive for uniformity within the same city or area; 1423 §1 and 1439 §§1-3 bishops setting up first and second instance interdiocesan tribunals. In addition there are many matters in which the Code calls for superdiocesan action by various conferences of bishops.

to minister to them in the diocesan bishop's place.[24] *Christus Dominus*, n. 30 indicated:

> Parish priests are in a special sense collaborators with the bishop. They are given, in a specific section of the diocese, and under the authority of the bishop, the care of souls as their particular shepherd.[25]

Even where the first two basic elements of a parish exist simultaneously, only the bishop can bring a parish into existence. Canonically, the diocesan bishop establishes a parish after required consultation with the presbyteral council, by a juridic act.[26] For a parish to come alive both theologically and humanly as well, a pastor must be appointed to serve the parishioners in

---

[24] Although the appointment of a priest as pastor is a basic element of a parish in a usual situation, the salvation of souls is the supreme law of the Church (c. 1752). The Church recognizes that in special circumstances, particularly where there is a shortage of priests, it may not be possible to provide a pastor for each parish. Canons 517 §1 and §2, 520 §1, 526 §1 and 542-544 authorize and regulate various special approaches to providing the exercise of pastoral care for parishioners of parishes in such circumstances. Applications of those canons are treated in Chapter Five.

[25] *CD*, nn. 30-31. See also *LG*, n. 28: "...In each local assembly of the faithful, they [priests] represent in a certain way the bishop with whom they are associated.... Those who, under the authority of the bishop, sanctify and govern that portion of the Lord's flock assigned to them render the universal Church visible in their locality...." English translation from FLANNERY, *Conciliar and Post Conciliar Documents*, pp. 384-387.

[26] Here two canonical considerations need to be recalled. Canon 515 §2 stipulates: "The diocesan bishop alone is competent to erect, suppress or alter parishes; he is not to erect, suppress or to notably alter them without hearing the presbyteral council." If that required consultation has not taken place, then, in accord with c. 127 §2, 2°, the bishop is stopped from validly erecting the parish. After having heard the presbyteral council, the diocesan bishop must also complete the juridic act of specifically establishing the parish (c. 124) before anyone can be appointed to the ecclesiastical office of pastor of such a parish. Canonically a diocesan bishop may establish a parish and within the text of the same document appoint its pastor, but two separate decrees, one establishing the parish and another appointing the pastor would be a clearer way to proceed, since the parish is not being erected for the pastor, but the pastor is being appointed to serve the parish community. In addition, the diocesan bishop may establish a parish without immediately appointing a pastor, but c. 151 directs that unless there is a serious reason, the bishop should not put off the provision of the office of pastor because that office entails the care of souls.

the bishop's stead.[27] The new parish community begins to grow into a community with the arrival of the pastor, a priest or a team of priests,[28] who, sent by the diocesan bishop minister to the community under the authority of the bishop and in a personal relationship with the bishop, the juridic aspects of which are treated in the Code of Canon Law.[29]

Commenting on one consequence of the pastor serving the parish in the stead of the diocesan bishop (*sub pastore vices gerente episcopi*), Coccopalmerio points out that because the pastor ministers acting in place of the bishop: "The parochial community is therefore in essential relationship with the diocesan community."[30] That essential relationship with the diocesan community

---

[27] LOBINA, "Parrocchia e parroco nei nuovi orientamenti," pp. 420-421. Lobina finds such an interwoven theology of parish and pastor in conciliar and postconciliar documents that he asserts they give the impression that one can no longer talk abstractly about the concept of parish without almost identifying it with the concept of pastor, the pastor and the faithful entrusted to him become inseparable.

[28] As noted above in footnote 24, other possibilities than a single pastor are treated in cc. 517 §1 and §2, 520 §1, 526 §1 and 542-544. In his 1976 article, "Parrocchia e parroco nei nuovi orientamenti," pp. 422-427 and 436-438, LOBINA treats a number of possibilities, which he calls "Teams," other than the pastor being one priest: 1. Union of a number of two or three parishes entrusted to the care of only one pastor; 2. A deacon, religious or lay person caring for a parish in accord with their position in the Church, with a priest supervising their activity; 3. A *Coetus sacerdotum*, a group of priests, ministering *in solidum*, one of whom directs and is responsible for their activity.

[29] Prior to the reforms of the Second Vatican Council, the establishment or suppression of parishes was complicated by the fact that many parishes were benefices. Although established for the good of souls, parish/benefices involved financial considerations, distractions and complications for bishops, pastors and parishioners. *PO*, n. 20 called for the system of benefices to be abandoned or reformed. The 1983 Code addressed the reform of benefices in c. 1272, and in c. 515 §2 set forth the diocesan bishop's sole authority in establishing parishes after consulting the presbyteral council of his diocese.

[30] Coccopalmerio argues that precisely because the priest serves "in place of the Bishop" ("vices gerente Episcopi"), the parish community exists in an essential relationship with the diocesan community. See COCCOPALMERIO, "Il concetto di parrocchia," p. 125. Coccopalmerio also takes the position that a pastor "is the bishop's vicar" ("...è vicario del vescovo"). Indeed, the pastor is appointed by the diocesan bishop and in a broad sense the pastor fills in for the bishop by serving the spiritual needs of the parishioners; there is an essential relationship within the diocesan community. Nevertheless, it is not at all clear how the descriptive expression of *SC*, n. 42: "vices gerente Episcopi," which does not appear in the

would appear logically also to place the parish community in essential relationship with the Holy Father with whom the diocesan bishop is in apostolic communion. Perhaps it is just such an essential relationship that provided the foundation for *Sacrosanctum concilium*, n. 42 which teaches about parishes "in some way representing the visible Church constituted throughout the world."

The *general rule* for establishing a parish is that the group of the faithful to be served, in addition to living within the boundaries of the diocese, should be set up *locally* within the diocese. On this point there has been some debate about the teaching of Vatican II. Is the designation of a precise, geographically limited area for a parish an element necessary in order to bring a parish into existence, or is such a designation simply a reasonable administrative action to individuate various communities of the faithful within a diocese?

This debate is alluded to by Coccopalmerio.[31] The point at

CIC with respect to the pastors of parishes, could alter the ecclesiastical office of pastor of a parish, so that a pastor would be a canonical vicar of the diocesan bishop. Canon Law has established that the bishop's vicars have specific ecclesiastical offices: Vicar General, Episcopal Vicar or Judicial Vicar. In accord with c. 524 the bishop confers the office of pastor of a parish, which has been established by the Church, and confers ordinary, personal power on the pastor together with the other obligations and rights which the Church has attached to that office. In addition, precisely because the pastor holds the ecclesiastical office of pastor of a parish he must, in virtue of c. 532, represent the parish in all juridic affairs. As a result it could happen that a pastor might have rights and/or obligations to enter into a canonically adversarial position with the bishop in respect to the rights of the parish as a juridic person or his personal rights as pastor. Finally, c. 519 refers to the pastor of a parish as the "proper pastor of the parish" ("proprius pastor paroeciae"), not as the "bishop's vicar in the parish" ("vicarius eposcopi in paroecia").

[31] COCCOPALMERIO, "Il concetto di parrocchia," on p. 137, provides an insight into a very *Catholic* aspect of *individuating* a parish community by means of territorial boundaries. Coccopalmerio holds that such individuation is based on the principle that calling everyone living within specific territorial boundaries to take part in forming their parish community presupposes the affirmation of the equality of all the faithful in the eyes of the Church and the commitment of each of the faithful to overcome any differences with one another within the ambit of the parish.

issue appears to have been whether a parish could exist if it did not have local boundaries. Whichever meaning the Council may have intended, c. 518 explicitly establishes that as a *general rule* a parish is to be territorial, but that personal parishes *are to be established* where they are judged to be useful. In addition, c. 813 explicitly calls for personal parishes for ministry to university students. It is clear that now territoriality is to be the general rule in constituting a parish, but if serving the pastoral needs of a group of the faithful requires greater flexibility, the diocesan bishop may establish personal parishes.[32]

1.1.3 — The characteristics of a parish

In addition to the three basic elements of a parish, the Second Vatican Council also described ten characteristics of a parish community.[33] Some of those characteristics express principally intra-parish relationships and activities, while others signify an openness on the part of members of a parish community to interests and concerns that lie beyond the boundaries of

---

[32] In the 1917 Code, c. 216 §1 required territorial divisions for parishes. Nevertheless, in the same Code, indeed in the same canon, c. 216 §4, it was recognized that non-territorial parishes could exist. Canon 216 §4 restricted the establishing of any new personal parishes on the basis of different languages or nationalities residing in the same city or territory, or merely family or personal parishes without an indult from the Apostolic See; nor were any changes to be made in those such parishes which did already exist without consulting with the Apostolic See. Such regulations would seem to lead to the conclusion that even in the 1917 Code territoriality could not have been constitutive in the sense of being essential for the establishment of a parish. Also see supra footnote 16.

[33] It would be no less accurate to describe these "characteristics" of a parish as "obligations" of a parish; either terminology describes what the Second Vatican Council teaches a parish ought to be. The purpose of this analysis of the Council's teaching is informational rather than exhortatory.

their parish community itself, that is, to those of the diocese and of the universal Church.[34]

The *First Characteristic of a parish*, is that a parish is a *Eucharistic community*. Most forcefully and most frequently of all, Vatican II teaches that any Christian community within the Church, and especially a parish, is to be a Eucharistic community. Specific teaching relative to a parish as a Eucharistic community is found in *Christus Dominus*, n. 30:

> ...parish priests should assure that the celebration of the Eucharistic sacrifice is the center and culmination of the entire life of the Christian community.[35]

Presbyterorum ordinis teaches that the center of the assembly of the faithful is the Eucharistic celebration and that for a Christian community to grow it must be rooted in and hinge upon the celebration of the Eucharist.[36] *Ad gentes divinitus*, considering Christian communities developing in mission areas, taught that such communities have regular access to the Father by means of the Eucharistic sacrifice.[37] In addition conciliar docu-

---

[34] COCCOPALMERIO, "Il concetto di parrocchia," pp. 135-140, deduced characteristics of a parish from two points of view. From a *static-structural view* a parish consists of: (a) a number of the faithful, (b) living in a particular section of a diocese with specific territorial boundaries, (c) a priest in the capacity of pastor, (d) who acts in the bishop's place and renders the bishop present in some way, (e) and whose ecclesiastical status as representing the bishop causes the parish community to be in essential relationship with the diocesan community. From a *dynamic-goal oriented view* parish activity is not that of single individuals but of the parish community precisely as a community; the fundamental characteristic of a parish is that it is, somehow, the Church, it renders the Church present and visible in a particular place. Parish activities are focused in either of two directions. *Inwardly*, actions by which the parish builds itself up in the spiritual life, liturgical actions especially the celebration of the Eucharist; in addition, charitable activity and the general living of the Christian life following the Lord's commands. Parish activities directed *outwardly* include the apostolate toward non-believers and Christian testimony which makes the saving presence of God and Christ present in the world.

[35] *CD*, n. 30 (2).

[36] *PO*, nn. 5-6.

[37] SECOND VATICAN COUNCIL, Decree on the Church's Missionary Activity *Ad gentes* (=*AG*), December 7, 1965, in *AAS*, 58 (1966), pp. 947-990, here at n. 15, pp. 963-967. English translation in FLANNERY, *Conciliar and Post Conciliar Documents*, pp. 829-831.

ments contain eighteen general references to communities of the faithful as Eucharistic communities.[38]

With respect to the Eucharistic community aspect of the parish it is important to note that the teachings of the Second Vatican Council are clearly focused on Eucharist as the complete Eucharistic Sacrifice and shared sacred meal celebrated by the priest and the people of the parish together.

Priestless parishes may in fact exist in the sense that priests are simply not available to serve in previously established parishes. The distribution of Holy Communion consecrated elsewhere and transported to such a parish and/or a prayer service, perhaps with Benediction of the Most Blessed Sacrament, may be the best that can be accomplished in straitened circumstances. Those services may, under God, enable a community to survive for some time (and are even recommended where a Eucharistic celebration is impossible — see c. 1248 §2), but they are far less than the Eucharistic community called for by the Council.

The *Second Characteristic of a parish* is its *representative* note. This has its foundation in the Second Vatican Council's teaching that, among various groups of the faithful established by the diocesan bishop, parishes "are the most important" for in some way they represent the visible Church constituted throughout the world.[39]

Reflecting on the significance of the words "in some way they represent the visible Church constituted throughout the

---

[38] *SC*, nn. 2, 6, 10, 41, 106; *LG*, nn. 3, 7, 10, 23, 42, 50; SECOND VATICAN COUNCIL, Decree on Ecumenism *Unitatis redintegratio* (=*UR*), November 21, 1964, in *AAS*, 57 (1965), pp. 90-107, here at nn. 2, 4, 15, pp. 91-92, 94-96, 101-102, English translation in FLANNERY, *Conciliar and Post Conciliar Documents*, pp. 453, 456-459, 465-466; *CD*, n. 15; SECOND VATICAN COUNCIL, Decree on the Up-To-Date Renewal of Religious Life *Perfectae caritatis* (=*PC*), October 28, 1965, in *AAS*, 58 (1966), pp. 702-712, here at n. 15, pp. 709-710, English translation in FLANNERY, *Conciliar and Post Conciliar Documents*, p. 620; SECOND VATICAN COUNCIL, Decree on the Apostolate of Lay People *Apostolicam actuositatem* (=*AA*), November 18, 1965, in *AAS*, 58 (1966), pp. 837-864, here at n. 8, pp. 844-846, English translation in FLANNERY, *Conciliar and Post Conciliar Documents*, pp. 775-776; *PO* n. 8.

[39] *SC*, n. 42.

world," Coccopalmerio opined that the words "they [parishes] represent" can be understood not only in the sense of the parishes being a representation or a sign of another reality, but also in the sense of the parishes indeed making that other reality (the visible Church constituted throughout the world) present so that it becomes perceptible.[40] Parishes are, in some way, images of the Church. The same author also carefully notes that the Council uses the words "in some way" in order to remind us that the diocese, not the parish, is the "perfect" image of the Church.[41]

Lumen gentium, the Second Vatican Council's Dogmatic Constitution on the Church, in n. 26, not only made very much the same point, but also taught that in the community united with its bishop, Christ himself is present:

> In each altar community, under the ministry of the bishop, a manifest symbol is to be seen of that charity and "unity of the mystical body, without which there can be no salvation." In these communities, though they may often be small and poor, or existing in the diaspora, Christ is present through whose power and influence the One, Holy, Catholic and Apostolic Church is constituted.[42]

This statement does not appear to be referring principally or directly to the presence of Christ in the Eucharist, or Christ among the worshipers because two or three are gathered in his name. It seems rather to mean that Christ, active in the community and in its few poor members, influences and motivates them to spread the faith by word and example. In that way, life as a community will accomplish, where they live, the work that Christ sent his apostles to begin.

The *Third Characteristic of a parish* is that the liturgical life

---

[40] COCCOPALMERIO, "Il concetto di parrocchia," p. 125.

[41] *Ibid.*

[42] *LG*, n. 26.

of the parish *and* the relation of the parish's liturgical life to the bishop *are to be fostered, in the spirit and practice of the laity and clergy* precisely because a parish united through its pastor with the bishop does in some way represent (or even make present) the visible Church constituted throughout the world. The Council has amplified both points in its teachings.

Presbyterorum ordinis, n. 5, recalling a teaching which extended back to St. Ignatius of Antioch, taught:

> But in the celebration of all the sacraments — as St. Ignatius Martyr already attested in the early Church — priests are hierarchically united with the bishop in various ways and so make him present in a certain sense in individual assemblies of the faithful.[43]

With specific reference to the relationship between parish communities and the bishop, *Christus Dominus*, n. 15 taught:

> It is the bishops who enjoy the fullness of the sacrament of orders, and both priests and deacons are dependent on them in the exercise of their power. The former in order that they may be prudent cooperators with the episcopal order…; the latter… serve the people of God in union with the bishop and his presbyterate. It is therefore bishops who are the principal dispensers of the mysteries of God, and it is their function to control, promote and protect the entire liturgical life of the Church entrusted to them.[44]

In general *Presbyterorum ordinis*, n. 6, pointed out that the pastor's task goes beyond dealing with individual parishioners and even the parish community alone. The pastor must lead the

---

[43] *PO*, n. 5.

[44] *CD*, n. 15, English translation in Flannery, *Conciliar and Post Conciliar Documents*, pp. 571-572, with the exception that the Latin word "presbyterio" rendered "clergy" in the Flannery translation has here been translated by us as "presbyterate." Also see *CD*, n. 30 (1), *LG*, n. 28.

parish community to embrace both the local church and the universal Church.[45]

Within parish liturgical celebrations there are a number of elements which, if adverted to, point out the very close relationship of the diocesan bishop to the liturgical life of a parish. Each time Baptism, Confirmation or the Anointing of the Sick is publicly or privately celebrated, holy oils are used, which were blessed during Holy Week by the bishop at the cathedral church of the diocese and carried back by a member of the parish to the parish church. At every celebration of the sacraments of Eucharist, Reconciliation, Confirmation, or Anointing of the Sick the priest exercises powers he has received from the sacrament of Holy Orders conferred by the bishop and/or has been authorized to exercise through delegation from the bishop. Translations of Sacred Scripture and liturgical texts have been approved by conferences of bishops. Celebrations of Holy Thursday, Ascension Thursday, feasts of the apostles throughout the year, all direct attention to the unity and work of the apostles, the predecessors of today's bishops. Also, the celebration of the feast of the patron saint of the diocese and the reading of various pastoral letters from the bishop provide reminders of the connection of parishes with the diocese.

However, it also needs to be borne in mind that, although an awareness of the vital relationship between the parish liturgy and the diocesan bishop is a characteristic of a parish, liturgy itself has a much wider role in the Church. The liturgy is not some public demonstration which the clergy perform to edify the laity. All of Christ's faithful, the clergy and the laity, need to come to the liturgy motivated by the proper dispositions and eager for God's graces. The laity have a proper part in the celebration of the liturgy, of which they should be fully aware and in which they should fully participate.[46] Nor is the liturgy sim-

---

[45] *PO*, n. 6.
[46] *CD*, n. 30 (2).

ply a series of beautiful ceremonies in which all of the faithful take part. The liturgy is the source of spiritual nourishment for all; it is the means by which the work of redemption is carried out and all of the faithful "...are enabled to express in their lives and manifest to others the mystery of Christ and the real nature of the true Church...."[47]

The *Fourth Characteristic of a parish* is that efforts are also to be made to encourage a *sense of community* within the parish. This topic was frequently mentioned in the Second Vatican Council's teachings. Perhaps the best summary is found in *Christus Dominus*, n. 30 (2), which directed the attention of pastors to:

> ...all the faithful so that they... may grow in Christ, and the Christian community may give that witness to charity which the Lord commanded... In carrying out their duties as pastors parish priests should make it their special concern to know their parishioners. Since they are the shepherds of all the individual sheep they should endeavor to stimulate a growth of the Christian life in each one of the faithful, in families, in associations, especially those dedicated to the apostolate, and finally, in the parish as a whole. They should, therefore, visit the homes and the schools as their pastoral function requires of them. They should manifest a special interest in adolescents and young people; they should exercise a paternal charity towards the poor and the sick. Finally, they should have a special care for the workers, and should urge the faithful to give their support to apostolic activities.[48]

Vatican Council II in *Lumen gentium* also reminded everyone that pastors themselves know very well that they are not sent by God to carry out the entire salvific mission of the Church by themselves alone. The same document further pointed out that

---

[47] *SC*, n. 2. Also see *CD*, n. 30 (1).
[48] *CD*, n. 30 (2). Also see *CD*, n. 30 (3); *LG*, n. 37; *PO*, n. 9; *AA*, n. 30.

pastors recognize the "contributions and charisms" by which all of the faithful, clergy and laity, cooperate to work for the salvation of all.[49] *Apostolicam actuositatem*, n. 10, identified the parish as "...an outstanding example of community apostolate...." Cited as reasons for that statement are the necessity of the cooperation of the laity in order that the pastor's efforts can bear fruit, the fact that the human diversity among the people of the parish can fit within the universal Church. The faithful of the parish, clergy and laity, are encouraged to work together as a community to face and hopefully to ameliorate common problems.[50]

The Code appears to have many canons which can serve to promote a spirit of community and cooperation, among them: cc. 204-231 concerning the obligations and rights of all Christ's faithful and of the lay faithful, cc. 273-289 about the obligations and rights of clerics, c. 529 §2 about the pastor recognizing the role of laity, c. 536 §§1-2 concerning parish pastoral councils, and c. 537 which requires parish finance councils.

The *Fifth Characteristic of a parish* is that its *greatest efforts* are made to encourage a sense of parish community within the *common celebration of the Sunday Mass*. This is very similar to the general idea of a Eucharistic Community, but it is more focused on the particular day for the Christian community to gather.

Teachings bearing on encouraging a sense of community in the common celebration of the Sunday Mass are found in *Sacrosanctum concilium*, n. 49. The Council indicated that the Eucharistic liturgy was to be revised "...so that the sacrifice of the Mass, even the ritual forms (of its celebration) may have full pastoral efficacy"; in n. 52 the importance of the Sunday homily was stressed; in n. 53 the restoration of the Prayer of the Faithful was announced; even the teaching in n. 110 that "During Lent, penance should be not only internal and individual but also

---

[49] *LG*, n. 30.
[50] *AA*, nn. 10, 30.

external and social," could be an appropriate topic for more than one homily.[51]

A thorough integration of the laity of a parish into the celebration of the Sunday liturgy would in practice be very likely to encourage community spirit by generating groups or teams of parish members who would grow closer to one another as they sing together in a choir, or serve as extraordinary ministers of the Eucharist, lectors, ushers or greeters, leaders of song and activities of that kind. In that way, parish community members could not only experience being together with their particular team or group, but could also realize that their liturgical praise of God arises from the cooperative activity of the whole parish.

The *Sixth Characteristic of a parish* is that the *word of God is effectively preached* to all. *Christus Dominus,* n. 30 (2) directed that as part of the care of souls the word of God is to be taught by parish priests to all the faithful, who should become firmly rooted in faith, hope and charity.[52] *Presbyterorum ordinis,* n. 4 went into more detail on the same subject:

> The People of God is formed into one in the first place by the Word of the living God, which is quite rightly sought from the mouth of priests. For since nobody can be saved who has not first believed, it is the first task of the priests as co-workers of the bishops to preach the Gospel of God to all men. In this way they carry out the Lord's command "Go into all the world and preach the Gospel to every creature" (Mk 16:15) and thus they set up and increase the People of God.... Priests then owe it to everybody to share with them the truth of the Gospel in which they rejoice in the Lord.... Moreover, the priest's preaching, often very difficult in present day conditions, if it is to be effective in moving the minds

---

[51] *SC,* n. 49. Also see *SC,* nn. 52-53, 110.

[52] *CD,* n. 30 (2).

of his hearers, must expound the Word of God not merely in a general way but by an application of the eternal truth of the Gospel to the concrete circumstances of life.[53]

Realizing that these thoughts and others very much like them come from the deliberations of a Spirit-guided Ecumenical Council, all bishops, priests and deacons (and, *mutatis mutandis*, other teachers in the Church) must recognize that they face a great challenge, opportunity, command and obligation.

The *Seventh Characteristic of a parish* is that *parish priests must promote effective catechetical instruction for all of the faithful. Christus Dominus* set a definite goal:

They [parish priests] should likewise by means of catechetical instruction lead all the faithful according to their capacity, to a full knowledge of the mystery of salvation. In providing this instruction, they should invoke the help not only of religious, but of the laity by establishing the Confraternity of Christian Doctrine.[54]

Earlier in the same decree, *Christus Dominus*, n. 14 taught directly of the bishop's obligations with regard to catechetics, but made no specific reference to parishes in the text. Mention is made, however, of the cross section of faithful who are to be catechized. It is easy to see, therefore, that thorough parish involvement is implied. Several other points are made in the same section of *Christus Dominus*. The function of catechetical formation is to see to it that Catholics of all ages develop an informed, active, faith-filled way of life. Catechetical instruction should be presented fully and accurately, employing professional teaching skills and

---

[53] *PO*, n. 4. Also see *LG*, n. 26; SECOND VATICAN COUNCIL, Dogmatic Constitution on Divine Revelation *Dei Verbum* (=*DV*), November 18, 1965, in *AAS*, 58 (1966), pp. 817-830, here at n. 24, pp. 828-829, English translation in FLANNERY, *Conciliar and Post Conciliar Documents*, pp. 763-764.

[54] *CD*, n. 30 (2).

methodologies suited to the age and situation of the students. Basics to be presented in catechetical instruction include a thorough grounding in holy scripture, tradition, liturgy and the teaching authority and life of the Church.[55]

Just short of fourteen years after the close of Vatican Council II, Pope John Paul II taught:

> Accordingly, the definitive aim of catechesis is to put people not only in touch, but in communion, in intimacy, with Jesus Christ: only he can lead us to the love of the Father in the Spirit and make us share in the life of the Holy Trinity.[56]

The *Eighth Characteristic of a parish* is that within each parish *fervor for missionary activity and evangelization is fostered*. A very straightforward and challenging teaching of the Second Vatican Council from the decree *Ad gentes divinitus*, n. 30, stated:

> In their pastoral work priests will stimulate and maintain among the faithful a zeal for the evangelization of the world by teaching them through preaching and religious instruction of the Church's duty to proclaim Christ to the nations; by impressing on Christian families the honor and the need for fostering missionary vocations among their own sons and daughters; by promoting missionary fervor among young people from Catholic schools and associations so that future preachers of the Gospel might spring from them. They should not be ashamed to ask them for alms, being made beggars for Christ and the salvation of souls.[57]

---

[55] *CD*, n. 14.

[56] JOHN PAUL II, Apostolic exhortation "Catechesis in Our Time," *Catechesi tradendae*, October 16, 1979, in *AAS*, 71 (1979), pp. 1277-1340, here at n. 5, pp. 1280-1281. English translation in A. FLANNERY (gen. ed.), *Vatican Council II*, 2 vols.: vol. 2, *More Postconciliar Documents*, Collegeville, MN: The Liturgical Press, 1982, pp. 764-765.

[57] *AG*, n. 39. Also see *PO*, n. 6.

No matter how venerable the history of one parish may be, or how cohesive and locally active the congregation of another, the Church by its very nature is missionary. The Son and Holy Spirit were sent, came "on mission," to the whole human race in accord with God's plan, and the apostles were sent out, were made "missionaries" to baptize and to teach the message of Jesus.[58] Indeed the task of the missions, sharing with others the wonderful things God has given us, flows from the "fountain-like love" of God the Father.[59] All of the faithful, clergy and laity, might become more intensely interested in missionary activity if they prayerfully pondered the likelihood that they are able to live their faith today because of missionaries who led their ancestors to the Church centuries ago.

The *Ninth Characteristic of a parish* is that the Christian community which is a parish makes *a great contribution to the fostering of vocations to the priesthood and the religious life*. Such is the teaching of *Optatam totius*, n. 2:

> The duty of fostering vocations falls on the whole Christian community, and they should discharge it principally by living full Christian lives. The greatest contribution [in fostering vocations to the priesthood] is made by families which are animated by a spirit of faith, charity and piety and which provide, as it were, a first seminary, and by parishes in whose abundant life the young people themselves take an active part.... All priests should show their apostolic zeal by fostering vocations as much as possible, and should draw the hearts of young men to the priesthood by the example of their humble, hardworking and happy lives, as well as by their mutual charity and fraternal cooperation.[60]

---

[58] Mt 28:14.

[59] *AG*, n. 2. Also see *LG*, n. 23; *AG*, n. 35.

[60] SECOND VATICAN COUNCIL, "Decree on the Training of Priests" *Optatam totius* (=*OT*), October 28, 1965, in *AAS*, 58 (1966), pp. 713-727, here at n. 2, pp. 714-715. English translation in FLANNERY, *Conciliar and Post Conciliar Documents*, pp. 708-710.

The decree *Perfectae caritatis*, n. 24, also addressed the promotion of vocations by all of the faithful; not surprisingly, its principal focus was on vocations to the religious life. Priests and Christian educators were urged to set about meeting the Church's need for new vocations; more frequent preaching was recommended about the evangelical counsels and religious vocations. Parents were urged to nurture and protect religious vocations in their children.[61]

Prayer and other activity on behalf of priestly and religious vocations would seem to be important projects for which associations of the Catholic faithful might be formed. In various dioceses, parishes and religious institutes both private and public associations have been founded for this purpose. Such activity would certainly be in keeping with the Council's call for fostering vocations.

The *Tenth Characteristic of a parish* is that the parish community takes part in *outreach to those with special needs or problems not ordinarily met by general parish ministries*. Writing directly to bishops, but outlining needs and problems which ultimately are most likely to be discovered and addressed in a parish community, the Second Vatican Council indicated the need for the cooperation of all of the faithful in certain situations. *Christus Dominus*, n. 18 began with these words:

> Special consideration should be shown for those members of the faithful who, on account of their way of life are not adequately catered for by the ordinary pastoral ministry of the parochial clergy or are entirely deprived of it. These include many migrants, exiles and refugees, sailors and airmen, itinerants and others of this kind.[62]

Perhaps for some people, or a group, who are in circumstances which make it impossible that their spiritual needs could

---

[61] *PC*, n. 24.
[62] *CD*, n. 18.

be cared for by a territorial parish, the bishop might appoint a chaplain to be with them as they move about within the diocese as provided in cc. 564-572, or establish for them a quasi parish as provided in c. 516 §2, or even a personal parish as noted in c. 518. In *Presbyterorum ordinis*, n. 9, priests are reminded:

> Those who have abandoned the practice of the sacraments, or even perhaps the faith, are entrusted to priests as special objects of their care. They will not neglect to approach these as good shepherds.[63]

Caring for the souls of people who are harder to contact has a missionary quality to it wherever they may be. If the apostolate requires contact with individuals or groups whom the pastor cannot contact personally, the lay members of the parish should be called upon to help so that the message and the ministry of the gospel may be extended to all.[64]

There is another important apostolate to which many parish communities devote a great deal of time, effort and financial support, but which Vatican Council II did not identify as a characteristic to be expected in all parishes. That apostolate is the operation of a Catholic parish school. It seems reasonable to judge that the Council was well aware that in many areas throughout the world parishes were financially unable to establish and support parish schools, while in other areas the practice simply has never developed, because private or public schools provide time for religious education, or for other reasons specific to different localities.[65]

---

[63] *PC*, n. 9.

[64] *CD*, n. 30 (1).

[65] The Council supported and praised the idea of Catholic schools at all levels of education, and called on pastors and laity to make sacrifices to develop Catholic schools more completely. The Council, however, did not expect that most parishes would have built, or could regularly operate, a Catholic school. Without question, the support of a well ordered Catholic parish school is indeed a very apostolic component of a parish, but not a universally attainable one. Conciliar teaching is that all pastors are expected to support and lead others to support

In concluding this section on characteristics of a parish as presented by Vatican Council II, it seems worthwhile to project ahead a bit to indicate which canons of the Code translate into law the conciliar teachings about the basic elements and the characteristics of a parish.

The Code reflects the Second Vatican Council's teachings on the parish in many canons. The three basic elements of a parish are found in cc. 515 and 519. The importance of a specific locale or "territory" is c. 518's general rule, although when judged useful, personal parishes are to be established.[66]

With respect to the ten characteristics of a parish, basic canonical references are:

1. Eucharistic community — c. 528 §2.
2. Parish represents the visible Church constituted throughout the world — some vague traces may be seen in cc. 839 §1 and 204 §§1-2. This appears to have developed more as a theological conclusion about an element of ecclesiology rather than as matter which could be the subject of legislation.
3. Relationship of liturgical life of a parish to the bishop being fostered in the spirit and practice of clergy and laity — a vague and tangential reference in cc. 528 §2, 592 §2.
4. Encouraging a sense of community within the parish — c. 529 §1.
5. Greatest effort at establishing community spirit to be made in common Sunday celebration — traces in cc. 1247, 1248.

Catholic education and Catholic schools. See SECOND VATICAN COUNCIL, "Declaration on Christian Education" *Gravissimum educationis* (=GE), October 28, 1965, in *AAS*, 58 (1966), pp. 728-739, here at nn. 8-9, pp. 734-736, English translation in FLANNERY, *Conciliar and Post Conciliar Documents*, pp. 732-735. Also see COCCOPALMERIO, "Il concetto di parrocchia," p. 141, where he concludes that the Council's documents establish a real, supernatural obligation proper to each parish community to have the attributes which the Council has indicated a parish should have.

[66] Also see c. 813.

6. Word of God to be preached to all — cc. 528 §1, 767.
7. Catechetical instruction for all ages as their needs may require — cc. 528 §1, 773-780.
8. Spirit of missionary activity and evangelization — cc. 791 §§1, 3, 4, 225 §1 and 275 §2.
9. Fostering religious vocations — cc. 233 §§1-2, 385 and 791, 1°.
10. Parish outreach to persons in special circumstances — cc. 528 §1 and 592 §1.

1.2 — VATICAN COUNCIL II ON THE PASTOR

1.2.1 — The nature of the pastor's ministry

The Second Vatican Council taught about many facets of what it means to be a pastor. All of those passages which describe the pastor's goal, role and service make it clear, implicitly or explicitly, that the care of souls, the spiritual good of the members of the parish community, is the basic reason for the existence of a parish and for most of the activities of the pastor and parochial vicars. *Christus Dominus*, n. 31, stated concisely: "Moreover, the whole reason for the parochial office is the good of souls."[67]

Christus Dominus, n. 30 (1) and (2) provided the Council's single most complete presentation, although not a taxative one, of the duties of a pastor of a parish. The Council's directives with respect to parish pastors are more thoroughly presented in cc. 528-530 and are concisely summarized in c. 519.

---

[67] *CD*, n. 31, pp. 689-690: "Praeterea cum muneris paroecialis tota ratio sit bonum animarum...." Also see the emphasis on caring for the good of the people and the good of souls in: *CD*, nn. 22, 23 (3), 30 (1), 32; *LG*, nn. 27, 37; *OE*, n. 4; *PO*, nn. 3, 9.

In a word, the service of the pastor is *Leadership.*[68]

The Council also presented a general rule about how a pastor should understand and carry out his office, his service of leadership. Writing about all priests, and certainly including pastors, the Second Vatican Council stated succinctly in *Lumen gentium*, n. 28:

> Exercising, within the limits of the authority which is theirs, the office of Christ, the Shepherd and Head, they [priests] assemble the family of God as a brotherhood fired with a single ideal, and through Christ in the Spirit they lead it to God the Father. In the midst of the flock they adore him in spirit and in truth (cf. Jn. 4:24).[69]

Presbyterorum ordinis, n. 9 provided further details. Even though priests have a special work, they are members of the faithful and brothers among brothers and sisters. Priests are to seek the things that are Christ's, in partnership with all the faithful, following Jesus' example of serving rather than being served. Priests should grasp the reality of the special role and dignity of laity in the Church's mission and should promote it. It is also necessary for priests to respect the just liberty of others in civil matters.[70] A pastor then, is to have as his basic goal the good of souls and as his role, his fundamental attitude, that he is a brother Christian among and serving his Christian sisters and brothers.[71]

---

[68] *PO*, n. 9.

[69] *LG*, n. 28.

[70] *PO*, n. 9. Also see *LG*, n. 27; *CD*, nn. 16, 30 (2); *PO*, nn. 3, 17; Mk 10:45; Lk 22:26-27; Jn 10:11; Jn 13:12-17; 1 Cor 9:18-19.

[71] The Apostles and early Christian communities give examples of living in communities with consultative leadership. A few examples can be seen in the selection of a community member to fill the apostolic post left empty by Judas, Ac 1:15-26; holding and administering goods in common, Ac 4:32-35; solving an administrative problem within the community by the selection and ordination of deacons, Ac 6:1-6 (also reminiscent of Nb 11:16-30); the two crucial meetings held in Jerusalem, Ac 11:1-18 and 21:17-25; Paul's being sent on his first missionary journey, Ac 13:1-3.

The pastor's leadership service is multidirectional, and with respect to dispensing the mysteries of God, it is unique and supernatural. The goal of this leadership is always to be the good of souls. The different spheres of leadership required of a pastor in many ways mirror the ministry of Jesus as priest, prophet and king.[72]

1.2.2 — The pastor's sharing in Jesus' priestly ministry

The Second Vatican Council placed a proper emphasis on the pastor's need to develop the parish into a Eucharistic community. That should not, however, detract from an appreciation of wider aspects of the pastor's sharing in Jesus' priestly ministry by exercising leadership in the parish liturgies. The whole liturgy of the Church includes the celebration of the sacraments along with other ceremonies and prayers authoritatively designated as liturgy, and the proper pastoral *preparation* of members of the parish community to participate in those liturgies actively and intelligently.[73] As *Sacrosanctum concilium*, n. 19 taught:

---

[72] The expression that *pastors share in the kingly ministry of Jesus* is theologically accurate, but could be confusing because of the many different shades of meaning conveyed by the English word *king* and by the associated notion that *kings rule*. This study of the teachings of the Second Ecumenical Council of the Vatican and the Code of Canon Law concludes that for a pastor, *sharing in the kingly ministry of Jesus* means living as a servant-leader, not having absolute power over the people of a parish, but, under the authority of the diocesan bishop, governing the members of the parish community by providing leadership in a consultative, cooperative way, recognizing and helping to develop the spiritual gifts and charisms of the parishioners as well as his own. Also see c. 519.

[73] *SC*, n. 11 instructed pastors to realize the importance of developing among the people proper dispositions for participating in the liturgy. *SC*, n. 14 taught about the need to utilize proper pedagogy to enable the members of the parish community to achieve full participation in the liturgy, and the need for the pastors themselves to fully accept and appreciate the value of the liturgy before they can successfully teach others about liturgy. *SC*, n. 100 directed that various hours of the Church's Liturgy of the Hours, especially Vespers, be celebrated "…in common in church on Sunday and on the more solemn feasts." Also see *CD*, n. 30 (2) and *PO*, n. 13 in which pastors are instructed to be readily available to hear confessions when reasonably asked to do so and to provide for those who speak other languages to be able to approach that sacrament.

With zeal and patience pastors of souls must promote the liturgical instruction of the faithful and also their active participation, both internal and external, taking into account their age, condition, way of life and standard of religious culture. By so doing pastors will be fulfilling one of the chief duties of a faithful dispenser of the mysteries of God, and in this matter they must lead their flock not only by word but also by example.[74]

It does not appear that "liturgical instruction" and/or "active participation" simply mean standing in the right place at the right time, or leading song correctly at Mass. Liturgical instruction should be more concerned with why certain symbols are used or why one should pray in a community, or what a solemn, day by day, responsibility catechumens, parents of children and sponsors accept by seeking baptism themselves or having their children baptized, or the total gift of one's self and total acceptance of another person's total gift of himself or herself which is the substance of marriage.[75]

In addition to promoting full understanding of, and participation in, the liturgy, another priestly task of the pastor is to foster religious vocations. That holy work also has elements which share in the prophetic ministry of Jesus. However, fostering religious vocations will be treated here as a sharing in Jesus' priestly ministry because, when faithfully followed, such vocations lead to lives consecrated to God and/or the reception of the sacrament of Holy Orders. *Perfectae caritatis* addressing all priests wrote of the necessity seriously to address the Church's need for religious vocations.[76] *Optatam totius,* broadly implying

---

[74] *SC,* n. 19.

[75] Concerning the sacraments' functions in the liturgy, cf. *SC,* nn. 19, 59; *LG,* n. 11. For preparation for the liturgy of Baptism, cf. *SC,* nn. 64, 67; *LG,* n. 14; *AG,* n. 14; c. 851 §2. For preparation of the liturgy of Marriage, cf. *SC,* nn. 77-78; c. 1063, 1°, 2° and 3°.

[76] *PC,* n. 24. Also see c. 233 §§1-2 with respect to the duty of the entire Christian community to foster vocations to the sacred ministry.

the importance of the pastor's leadership, called to mind the contribution made by the life of an active parish community toward vocations to the priesthood.[77]

The most personal appeal to promote priestly vocations is also found in the words of *Optatam totius*, and is addressed to priests themselves: "All priests... should draw the hearts of young men to the priesthood by the example of their humble, hardworking and happy lives, as well as by their mutual charity and fraternal cooperation."[78]

1.2.3 — The pastor's sharing in Jesus' prophetic ministry

The Second Vatican Council specified five teaching duties, not unlike the prophetic ministry of Jesus, for the pastor. First of all, the word of God is to be preached to the People of God. *Dei Verbum*, the Second Vatican Council's Dogmatic Constitution on Divine Revelation, pointed out:

> The ministry of the Word, too — pastoral preaching, catechetics and all forms of Christian instruction, among which the liturgical homily should hold pride of place — is healthily nourished and thrives in holiness through the Word of Scripture.[79]

Of itself that passage did not treat of an obligation to preach, but it indicated the importance and pastoral nature of the ministry of the Word. The ministry of the Word itself is to be nourished and kept thriving by personal dedication to Sacred Scripture on the part of those who preach and teach. The Council alluded to different ways in which the ministry of the Word

---

[77] *OT*, n. 2.
[78] *OT*, n. 2. Also see *CD*, n. 30 (1).
[79] *DV*, n. 24.

can be exercised, most of which would be expected — and found — in most parishes.

Christus Dominus, n. 30 (2) stated that preaching is part of the priest's role as a teacher, and went on to supply more details.[80] *Presbyterorum ordinis*, n. 4, taught "…it is the first task of the priests as co-workers of the bishops to preach the Gospel of God to all men."[81]

Preaching is a specialized manner of teaching and generally takes place within the liturgy. Catechetical programs, which present Catholic teaching in a more school and class-like atmosphere, are also to be instituted and carried on according the teachings of Vatican Council II. The conciliar teaching about the pastor's leadership role in catechetical instruction is correlative with the obligation of the bishop, but is also very much the pastor's personal responsibility.[82]

Here, however, note should be taken of a point in *Christus Dominus*, n. 30 (2). There it is stated that in his effort to make catechetical instruction available, the pastor is to call upon both the religious and the laity. Such a call is in keeping with the Second Vatican Council's directive that the pastor should not only recognize, work with and help to develop the abilities and talents of God's People, but also to acknowledge their right to spread the faith.[83] In addition, invoking assistance from the laity of the parish community, in this case specifically for the purpose of catechetical instruction, appears similar to one way in which Jesus shared his prophetic role by sending his disciples out, from time to time, to announce the good news.

Another way in which the good news is spread and integrated into the lives of the faithful is through Catholic schools.

---

[80] *CD*, n. 30 (2).

[81] *PO*, n. 4. Also see *LG*, n. 26; *DV*, n. 24. The Council gave a directive about the special training of future priests with respect to ecumenical matters in *UR*, n. 10.

[82] *CD*, n. 30 (2). Also see *CD*, n. 14.

[83] *AA*, n. 10. Also see *LG*, nn. 32-33; *CD*, n. 30 (2); *AA*, n. 3.

The Council called upon pastors to lead members of the parish community in support of Christian education and Catholic schools at all levels.[84] Indeed, conciliar documents declared that pastors have a grave obligation to promote Christian education. *Gravissimum educationis*, n. 2 taught:

> Accordingly the sacred Synod directs the attention of pastors of souls to their very grave obligation to do all in their power to ensure that this Christian education is enjoyed by all the faithful and especially by the young who are the hope of the Church.[85]

With respect to Catholic schools, the same conciliar document declared in n. 9:

> The sacred Synod earnestly exhorts the pastors of the Church and all the faithful to spare no sacrifice in helping Catholic schools to become increasingly effective, especially in caring for the poor, for those who are without the help and affection of family, and those who do not have the Faith.[86]

Note is also taken in *Gravissimum educationis* of the special importance and needs of students at the university level.[87]

Catholic schools are undeniably faith-oriented, but it is often in the area of conducting a Catholic school that the pastor of the parish may become most deeply involved with civil govern-

---

[84] X. Ochoa, *Index verborum cum documentis Concilii Vaticani Secundi (Index Verborum Concilii Vaticani Secundi* (=Ochoa, *Index verborum Concilii Vaticani Secundi*), Roma, Commentarium pro Religiosis, 1967, pp. 174-175. The term "Catholic education" does not appear in the documents of the Second Vatican Council, yet the term "Christian education" is used seven times. Whatever prompted that particular choice of words, the context suggests that the subject identified by the term "Christian education" is "the Catholic understanding of Christian education."

[85] *GE*, n. 2.

[86] *GE*, n. 9.

[87] *GE*, n. 10. Also see *AA*, n. 30.

ment regulation and law. In many countries the operation of any school is subject to certain standards and syllabuses for all subjects taught and services provided except strictly religious ones. There are also obligations to employees of the school which arise not only from the practice of justice but *in specie* from the *canonization* of particular civil laws.[88]

Accompanying the several approaches to *teaching* within the parish community, the pastor has a broader vision to share: the spirit of missionary activity and evangelization is to be instilled in the People of God. *Ad gentes divinitus* taught straightforwardly that pastors are required to stimulate interest in missionary work, encourage families to foster vocations to the missions among their children, promote missionary fervor among young people, and willingly beg for alms to support missionary activity.[89]

The pastor of a parish is not left exclusively to his own devices in the matter of missionary zeal. *Ecclesiae sanctae*, a motu proprio of Paul VI on the implementation of several conciliar documents, gave instructions about daily sacrifices for the missions, an annual celebration of mission day, and the appointment of a priest "…in each diocese to effectively promote the work of the missions…."[90]

In addition to diocesan programs, some parishes work with parishioners who are relatives of missionaries to personalize mission day in various ways. Parishes may also have priests from the missions who come to work among them as summer help,

---

[88] Canons 231 §§1-2, 1286, 1° and 2°, 1290. Also see c. 532.

[89] *AG*, n. 39. Also see *PO*, n. 6.

[90] PAUL VI, Apostolic letter, *motu proprio*, Presenting Norms Established for Carrying Out Certain Decrees of the Most Holy Second Vatican Council *Ecclesiae sanctae*, August 6, 1966, in *AAS*, 58 (1966), pp. 757-787, here at section III: Norms for the Carrying out of the Decree *Ad gentes divinitus*, nn. 3-4, p. 783, English translation in FLANNERY, *Conciliar and Post Conciliar Documents*, p. 858. Also see c. 791 for the canonical statement of instructions cited above. Also see c. 385 which states the bishop's special duty in regards to vocations and the missions.

or who are studying nearby. These priests can, in appropriate ways, foster the mission apostolate in such parishes.

The final specific teaching task which the Second Vatican Council assigns to pastors is that they are to provide information to the faithful about the proper use of the means of social communication, often called *the media*. In the Decree *Inter mirifica*, n. 3, the Council taught: "Pastors of souls have the task of instructing and directing the faithful how to use these media in a way that will ensure their own salvation and perfection and that of all mankind."[91] Not only advice is envisioned, but even personal involvement seems broadly implied in *Inter mirifica*, n. 13: "Pastors of souls should be particularly zealous in this field [means of social communication], since it is closely linked with their task of preaching the Gospel."[92]

Aware that pastors would need information and assistance in their efforts to give proper instruction about the means of social communication, Vatican II called for the establishment of a special office in the Holy See on the media and called for the publication of a pastoral instruction on the means of social communication.[93] In response to the Council's directives an already existing office of the Holy See was expanded and given a new name, The Pontifical Council for the Instruments of Social Communication. That office published the mandated Pastoral Instruction in 1971 under the title *Communio et progressio*.[94] The general

---

[91] SECOND VATICAN COUNCIL, Decree on the Means of Social Communication *Inter mirifica* (=IM), December 4, 1963, in *AAS*, 56 (1964), pp. 145-153, here at n. 3, p. 146. English translation in FLANNERY, *Conciliar and Post Conciliar Documents*, pp. 284-285.

[92] *IM*, n. 13.

[93] *IM*, nn. 19 and 23.

[94] PONTIFICIUM CONSILIUM INSTRUMENTIS COMMUNICATIONIS SOCIALIS, Pastoral Instruction for the Proper Implementation of the Decree of the Second Ecumenical Council of the Vatican Concerning the Means of Social Communication *Communio et progressio* (=CP), May 23, 1971, in *AAS*, 63 (1971), pp. 593-656. English translation in FLANNERY, *Conciliar and Post Conciliar Documents*, pp. 293-349. The Flannery translation gives a date of January 29, 1971 for this document, p. vii; *AAS* provides a date of May 23, 1971, pp. 656, 981.

approach of that document concerning the means of social communication is fundamentally positive, and ample theological content and practical applications are provided to enable a pastor to offer thoughtful sermons and prudent counsel to members of the parish community.

Long before the *Internet* or the *Web* had either of those names or had become easily accessible worldwide, *Communio et progressio* predicted in its concluding paragraphs: "Suddenly, and in proportion with these changes [the latest technological developments in communication], the responsibilities of the People of God will enormously increase. Never before will they have been offered such opportunities...."[95] Now, at the beginning of the twenty-first century, it appears that the pastor will need to know more and more about — and perhaps personally make more and more use of — the still constantly expanding means of social communication.

1.2.4 — The pastor's sharing in Jesus' kingly ministry

The Second Vatican Council also saw that the pastor would need to imitate the kingly ministry of Jesus governing the parish community by calling on its members, clergy, religious and laity to grow, and to recognize the rights, charisms and duties which are their own as variously gifted members of the People of God.

The *governing* tasks of the pastor are very broad precisely because various members of the faithful, whether lay, religious or clergy, have distinct personal gifts, interests, and graces, which can be developed by the different opportunities or challenges that are placed before them and by the manner in which Church authority invites them to respond. Sometimes in particu-

---

[95] *CP* n. 182. English translation in FLANNERY, *Conciliar and Post Conciliar Documents*, pp. 348.

lar circumstances Church law requires that a pastor present opportunities or challenges, but most often the pastor does so by recognizing and encouraging the development of, and working cooperatively with, the abilities and indeed the charisms of his fellow members of the parish community in order to help the work of various apostolates to flourish.

A parochial vicar is a co-worker with the pastor. The vicar's daily exercise of his ministry is to be carried out under the authority of the pastor, with whom he is to have a fraternal, charitable and respectful relationship within which they assist each other with advice and practical help, as they work together for the needs of the parish.[96] Deacons serving the parish community are also to cooperate with the pastor.[97] It is clear that the pastor should not be autocratic or non-consultative; it is equally clear that the Council envisioned the pastor as having general authority to direct and supervise the parochial ministry of his vicar and of parish deacons.[98]

Presbyterorum ordinis and *Apostolicam actuositatem* both call upon priests to acknowledge and properly value the proper role which the laity have in the Church's mission; priests are also reminded of the dignity of the laity together with the laity's right and duty of exercising the apostolate.[99]

Conciliar documents also encouraged the laity to work together with their priests. *Apostolicam actuositatem* taught that the

---

[96] *CD*, n. 30 (3).

[97] Canon 519. For conciliar teaching concerning deacons, also see *AG*, n. 16; *LG*, nn. 29, 41.

[98] Among the canons implementing the conciliar teachings are c. 519 — the vicar assists the pastor; c. 548, 1°, 2°, 3° — the vicar is given his mandate by the pastor, assists the pastor with the whole parochial mission, is regularly to consult with the pastor on planned or existing programs. Also certain obligations of the pastor involve supervising activities of the vicar and others. Canon 767 §4 imposes a specific obligation on the pastor to see to the regulation of homilies in his parish and canon 528 §2 imposes a specific obligation that the pastor be vigilant against liturgical abuses creeping into parish liturgical celebrations.

[99] *PO*, n. 9; *AA*, n. 25.

cooperation of the lay parishioners was so necessary that without it their pastors can scarcely be fully effective and calls for lay people to "...follow in the footsteps of the men and women who assisted Paul in the proclamation of the Gospel." The laity are urged to develop a habit of close cooperation and consultation with their priests and the whole parish community.[100]

There also exists a less directly spiritual sphere of governance and cooperative action for the pastors and laity. It is concerned with both justice and charity and it can consume a great deal of time and energy. It is the management of the temporal goods of the parish community. *Presbyterorum ordinis*, n. 17 directed: "Priests are to manage ecclesiastical property, properly so called, according to the nature of the case and the norm of ecclesiastical laws and with the help, as far as possible, of skilled laymen."[101]

1.2.5 — Other important issues related to the pastor's ministry

There are also some other issues about interrelationships of pastor and parishioners which the Council judged to be sufficiently important to require specific comment. The following are those issues:

1. All should understand that the pastor cannot do his job alone.[102]
2. The faithful, clergy, religious and lay members of the parish community, have an obligation to cooperate with the pastor's leadership.[103]

---

[100] *AA*, n. 10.

[101] *PO*, n. 17. Also see c. 532.

[102] *LG*, n. 30. The direct reference is to bishops, but *mutatis mutandis*, it applies to pastors.

[103] *AA*, n. 10. Also see *PO*, n. 9.

3. The pastor is not expected to have a *firm answer* to every question — not even every important question.[104]

4. The parish is to support the pastor financially — even to paying for his proper holiday each year. The bishop is to see to it that priests are able to have this proper holiday.[105]

5. The pastor should have that security of tenure in his parish as the good of souls requires.[106]

6. The pastor who cannot serve fully and fruitfully because of age or for other grave reasons is urged to submit his resignation.[107]

7. Learning is not the only important quality for a pastor to bring to his work, but also his piety, his zeal for the apostolate, and those other gifts and qualities which are necessary for the proper care of souls.[108]

A complete review of the conciliar texts that touch upon the interrelations between the pastor-brother-servant-leader and the lay members of the parish community is well beyond the

---

[104] SECOND VATICAN COUNCIL, Pastoral Constitution on the Church in the Modern World *Gaudium et spes* (=*GS*), December 7, 1965, in *AAS*, 58 (1966), pp. 1025-1115, here at n. 43, pp. 1061-1064. English translation in FLANNERY, *Conciliar and Post Conciliar Documents*, pp. 943-946 (that translation, however, renders "quaestione" as "problem" and "solutionem concretam" as "a ready answer"). With regard to the need for answers, it is worth noting that the Church itself "does not always have a ready answer to every question," *GS*, n. 33. English translation in FLANNERY, *Conciliar and Post Conciliar Documents*, p. 933.

[105] *PO*, n. 20.

[106] *CD*, n. 31. The point is that the good of the parishioners' souls is the criterion by which the security of a pastor's tenure is to be determined. Cf. cc. 1740-1752.

[107] Ibid. For requirement of resignation not later than age 75, see *CD*, n. 20 (3) and *Ecclesiae sanctae*, in *AAS*, 58 (1966), here at section I: Norms for the Carrying out of the Decrees *Christus Dominus* and *Presbyterorum ordinis*, n. 20 (3), pp. 768-769. English translation in FLANNERY, *Conciliar and Post Conciliar Documents*, p. 603.

[108] Ibid. Also see LOBINA, "Parrocchia e parroco nei nuovi orientamenti," in *Apollinaris*, 49 (1976), pp. 418-449, here at pp. 438-439. Here LOBINA indicated that he would like to see "a missionary spirit and a practical sensibility for touching and communicating with people" added to the prerequisites for appointment as a pastor. The qualifications, however, remain substantially the same in c. 453 §2 of the 1917 Code and its 1983 counterpart c. 521 §2.

scope of this research.[109] The point made here is that the Council saw in each parish a relationship for apostolic action with the pastor as one who serves by leading, assisted and counselled by the laity according to the skills of each working to achieve the mission of the Church.

CONCLUSION

The teachings of the Second Vatican Council about parishes and pastors provide *five* conclusions pertinent to appreciating the obligations and rights of the pastor of a parish. Two of the conclusions provide descriptive definitions of *parish* and *pastor*. A third presents several facts about all of the baptized. Those conclusions provide perspective for understanding the canons that explicitly or implicitly affect the pastor. A fourth and fifth conclusion are drawn from the information contained in the preceding conclusions and provide an approach and a caution for the study of the Code.

The descriptive definition of a parish which arises from the documents of Vatican Council II is that:

> A parish is a Eucharist-centered community of the faithful, both clergy and laity, under a priest-pastor, who ministers in place of, and under the authority of, the diocesan bishop; thus it is through the diocesan bishop that the parish liturgical life is made possible. Because of the interrelationships among the parish community, pastor and bishop, the parish in some way represents the visible Church constituted throughout the world. All members of a parish, whether clergy or laity, share a community spirit, participate fully in the liturgy, understand that they are members of a diocese and of the Universal Church, are well informed about the details

---

[109] For pertinent material in other conciliar teachings, see *LG*, nn. 30, 37; *CD*, n. 30 (1); *AA*, nn. 3, 24, 30; *GS*, n. 43 and n. 92.

and practice of their faith, show true Christian love and concern for one another, foster religious vocations and are also alert to and spend effort on extra-parochial relationships, apostolates and concerns, especially missionary work and evangelization.

The descriptive definition of a pastor drawn from the documents of the Second Vatican Council is that:

A pastor, aware of the responsibilities and dignity conferred on him by the reception of the sacrament of Holy Orders, should see himself as a brother Christian among and serving his Christian brothers and sisters in the parish. The pastor has as his basic goal the good of souls. Under the authority of the diocesan bishop, assisted by and in cooperation and mutual respect with his sisters and brothers, the pastor serves the parishioners by carrying out different specific leadership tasks which reflect the ministry of Jesus as priest, prophet and king. Through these tasks the pastor leads his brothers and sisters to keep their parish community vibrant. Depending on the size of the parish, the pastor may also be assisted by a parochial vicar and/or a deacon, who minister in the parish under the authority of the bishop who has assigned them and under the authority of the pastor who leads them.

With respect to all members of the Catholic Church, Vatican Council II taught in part:

The members of the Church have a common dignity which derives from their reception of Baptism, they have a common grace as God's children, a common vocation to perfection, one salvation, one hope and undivided charity.[110] All of the baptized are incorporated

---

[110] *LG*, n. 32.

into Christ, are members of the People of God and have some kind of share in the priestly, prophetic and kingly office of Christ.[111] There is an essential difference between the ministerial priesthood and the common priesthood shared by all the faithful.[112]

The first conclusion to be drawn from the preceding conclusions is that since the content of the concepts of *parish* and *pastor* have been infused with substantially more, and to some extent different, detail than previously, it will be necessary carefully to interpret the canons of the 1917 and 1983 Codes because the proper theological content and context of those terms will be different. This will also be true of other key words employed by both Codes which may have been graced with new meanings by the intervening Council.

Finally it may be concluded that since both the pastor and the members of the parish community share in the priestly, prophetical and kingly ministry of Jesus, that threefold classification of activity can provide a basis for classifying and understanding the obligations and rights of a pastor of a parish which in large part involve the pastor together with the parishioners. It will be an especially useful approach because the Code of Canon law concentrates Book 3 on the Teaching (or prophetic) Office of the Church and Book 4 on the Office of Sanctifying (or priestly functions) in the Church. The canons about sharing the kingly (or governing) ministry of Christ are found in various places among the other canons of the Code.

---

[111] *LG*, n. 31.
[112] *LG*, n. 10.

CHAPTER TWO

Ministry of the Divine Word

INTRODUCTION

Combining a renewed proclamation of the universal call to holiness with a powerful emphasis on the missionary and pastoral characteristics of the Church, the Second Vatican Council focused the attention of Christ's faithful on two essential aspects of faith: the accurate and complete *knowledge* of the content of faith and the *experience* of living the faith explicitly and productively. In various ways ministry of the Divine Word strives to provide those essentials.

In this chapter, consideration will be given first to some general concerns about the extent, expression and bases of various obligations and rights which are found in the Code. Next to be treated will be how, in providing his leadership in this ministry, the pastor has basic, general obligations and rights, and specific ones with respect to preaching and the homily. Then the pastor's obligations and rights vis-à-vis catechesis will be considered: in general, in the parish, as an element of liturgy, and in Catholic education. After that, a pastor's obligations and rights with respect to the missionary activity of the Church and instruments of social communication will be reviewed. Finally the question of the extent to which a pastor may, and sometimes should, share with others the fulfillment of his obligations and the exercise of his rights relative to the ministry of the Divine Word will be considered.

Before directly addressing the ministry of the Divine Word, however, certain general concerns will be treated at the beginning of this chapter because they affect the interpretation of all of the canons studied in this book.

2.1 — GENERAL CONCERNS

General preliminary concerns important to this study are (a) the extent of the application of c. 223 §§1-2, (b) *explicit* and *implicit* expression in the texts of laws and (c) certain different kinds of obligations and rights.

2.1.1 — Extent of the application of c. 223 §§1-2

The extent of the application of both paragraphs of c. 223 is important to a study of the obligations and rights of the pastor of a parish because it addresses a very practical question: What happens when the obligations or rights of the faithful, clerics or lay, conflict with the obligations or rights of others of the faithful, clerics or lay, or with others who are not of the faith at all? Although the focus of this book is on the existence of obligations and rights rather than on the exercise of rights, or the fulfillment of obligations, the answer to this question is significant because it could be of assistance in deciding when and how the rights of one party constitute an obligation for another party and thereby affect the rights of the obligated party.

The text of c. 223 is:

§1 — In exercising their rights the Christian faithful, both as individuals and when gathered in associations, must take account of the common good of the Church and of the rights of others as well as their own duties toward others.

§2 — In the interest of the common good, ecclesiastical

authority has competence to regulate the exercise of the rights which belong to the Christian faithful.

A possible difficulty arises because c. 223 is not located in Book I of the Code, *General Norms*, but rather is situated as the last canon in Book II, Part I, Title I, *The Obligations and Rights of All of the Christian Faithful*. Is the application of c. 223, therefore, restricted to only those rights enumerated in cc. 208 through 222, or is c. 223 in fact a norm which applies generally to all rights of all of the Christian faithful governed by the Latin Code?

The expression "the rights which belong to the Christian faithful" used in c. 223 §2 could be construed to restrict application of that canon to the rights identified in cc. 208 through 222. In context, however, canon 223 §1 states that the principle for judging the exercise of rights is "the common good of the Church," and c. 223 §2 identifies the goal of moderating the exercise of rights as "in the interest of the common good." It would defy logic, moral theology, and the Church's social teaching to maintain that c. 223 regulates only the rights mentioned in cc. 208 through 222, as if only those rights were subject to the common good of the Church, or the common good in general, while other rights could be exercised without such basic canonical constraints even in cases of conflict of rights.[1]

It is also to be noted that c. 223 §1 is practically a quotation of the second paragraph of *Dignitatis humanae*, n. 7,[2] which taught about "moral law... and the common good..." as elements

---

[1] Not every conflict which might arise among Christian faithful exercising their rights would directly endanger the common good of the Church or even the common good in general. Canons 1713-1716 and 1733 suggest various ways of resolving some disputes.

[2] SECOND VATICAN COUNCIL, Declaration on the Right of the Person and Communities to Social and Civil Liberty in Religious Matters *Dignitatis humanae* (=DH), December 7, 1965, in *AAS*, 58 (1966), pp. 929-941, here at n. 7, p. 934. English translation in FLANNERY, *Conciliar and Post Conciliar Documents*, pp. 804-805.

prompting the need for justice in exercising one's rights.[3] In addition, the basic text of c. 223 §§1-2 was first proposed in legal form as part of the *Lex Ecclesiae fundamentalis*. The specific purpose of the *Lex Ecclesiae fundamentalis* was to express the *constitutive law of the Church*, principles even more basic and all inclusive than the Code's General Norms. Canon 26 of the CCEO is substantially the same as c. 223 of the CIC and there is no commentary suggesting that c. 26 of the CCEO is limited in its application.[4]

For the sake of completeness, it may also be noted that in their treatments of c. 223 §§1-2 three standard commentaries do

---

[3] A clear unbroken, but developing, textual trail leads from *DH*, n. 7 through the *Lex Ecclesiae fundamentalis* to c. 223 §§1-2. The text of *DH*, n. 7 is the result of four textual revisions during the Vatican Council's deliberations: First revision, see, SECOND VATICAN COUNCIL, *Acta synodalia sacrosancti Concilii Oecumenici Vaticani II* (=*Acta synodalia*), vol. 3, period 3, part 3, Typis polyglottis Vaticanis, 1976, pp. 432-433. Second revision, *Acta synodalia*, 1976, vol. 4, period 4, part 1, pp. 150-151. Third revision, *Acta synodalia*, 1978, vol. 4, period 4, part 5, pp. 84-85. Fourth revision, *Acta synodalia*, 1978, vol. 4, period 4, part 6, p. 707. After Pope Paul VI raised the question of whether it would be a good idea to establish one common and fundamental Code containing the constitutive law of the Church, a schema titled *Prima quaedam adumbrata propositio Codicis Ecclesiae fundamentalis* was produced. The schema known as the *Lex Ecclesiae fundamentalis* (=*LEF*) eventually developed from that basic document by means of consultations, see *Communicationes*, 1 (1969), pp. 114-115. The content and text of *LEF* c. 19, which had a footnote reference to *DH*, n. 7, are substantially the same as c. 223 §§1-2; later that canon's number was changed from *LEF* c. 19 to *LEF* c. 24, see PONTIFICIA COMMISSIO CODICI IURIS CANONICI RECOGNOSCENDO, Schema *Legis Ecclesiae fundamentalis, textus emendatus cum relatione de ipso schemate deque emendationibus receptis*, Typis polyglottis Vaticanis, 1971, p. 18, and PONTIFICIA COMMISSIO CODICI IURIS CANONICI RECOGNOSCENDO, *Relatio complectens synthesim animadversionum ab em.mis atque exc.mis patribus commissionis ad novissimum schema Codicis iuris canonici exhibitarum, cum responsionibus a secretaria et consultoribus datis*, Typis polyglottis Vaticanis, 1981, pp. 352-353.

[4] No *fontes* are listed for c. 223 §§1 or 2 in PONTIFICIA COMMISSIO CODICI IURIS CANONICI AUTHENTICE INTERPRETANDO, *Codex iuris canonici, auctoritate Ioannis Pauli PP. II promulgatus, fontium annotatione et indice analytico-alphabetico auctus*, Libreria editrice Vaticana, 1989, p. 59, nor are any *fontes* indicated for c. 26 of the *CCEO*, PONTIFICIUM CONSILIUM DE LEGUM TEXTIBUS INTERPRETANDIS, *Codex canonum Ecclesiarum orientalium, auctoritate Ioannis Pauli PP. II promulgatus, fontium annotatione auctus*, Libreria editrice Vaticana, 1995, p. 8. Both canons, however, are clearly related to *DH*, n. 7.

not even allude to any possibility that c. 223 might only apply to rights mentioned in cc. 208 through 222.[5] Such commentaries certainly would have elucidated a restriction of that sort if their authors had judged that it existed.

From a practical, conflict-resolution point of view, it appears that a just resolution for almost any case of conflicting rights which involves either the good of the Church and/or the common good, would need to be preceded by sincere dialogue and information gathering and sharing among all of the parties whose rights are encompassed in the matter. Those charged with seeking to resolve such situations also need to keep in mind that, by definition, each party in the conflict does have real rights which need to be respected, otherwise c. 223 §§1-2 would not apply at all.

2.1.2 — Explicit and implicit expression in the texts of laws

The text of the Code of Canon Law is no stranger to the reality and canonical importance of the *implicit* expression of

---

[5] A. McGRATH, "Christ's Faithful," Commentary on cc. 204-367, in G. SHEEHY et al. (eds.), *The Canon Law Letter & Spirit: A Practical Guide to the Code of Canon Law* (=*Letter & Spirit*), prepared by the Canon Law Society of Great Britain and Ireland in association with The Canadian Canon Law Society, Collegeville, MN: The Liturgical Press, 1995, nn. 470-471, p. 126; J. HERVADA, "The Obligations and Rights of all Christ's Faithful," Commentary on cc. 208-223, in E. CAPARROS, M. THÉRIAULT and J. THORN (eds.), *Code of Canon Law Annotated* (=*Code Annotated*), Latin-English edition of the Code of Canon Law and English-language translation of the 5th Spanish-language edition of the commentary prepared under the responsibility of the Instituto Martín de Azpilcueta, Montréal: Wilson & Lafleur Limitée, 1993, pp. 196-197; J.H. PROVOST, "The Christian Faithful," Commentary on cc. 204-329, in *CLSA Commentary*, pp. 158-159. Also see G. NEDUNGATT, *A Companion to the Eastern Code for a New Translation of Codex canonum Ecclesiarum orientalium*, vol. 5 of *Kanonica*, Roma, Pontificio Instituto Orientale, 1994, p. 19. This work is not a standard commentary, but rather a translation with some explanatory notes. Those notes make no mention of any delimitation of the application of *CCEO* c. 26 §1 or §2.

meaning. Some canons make specific mention of implicit communication.[6]

Texts of various canons require that some conditions must be explicit for them to have an effect on the law.[7] Those canons demonstrate the legislator's awareness that if, in a given canon the legislator finds it necessary to rule out any implicit interpretation of words or actions, such an exclusion must itself be very clearly and explicitly expressed.

Canonists in general also acknowledge both explicit and implicit expression in laws. One canonist commenting on the canonical reality, meaning and acceptability of *explicit* and *implicit* expression in legal texts wrote:

> Indeed there are two ways in which the will of the legislator can be contained in his words..., namely explicitly or implicitly. Something is *explicitly* contained or manifested in a law, when... [it] appears distinctly and by name.... [Something] is *implicitly* contained when it... is out of sight..., enfolded in the words, so that it is not actually obvious or apparent.[8]

An important element of systematically analyzing canons, therefore, will be to give clear and precise expression to obligations and/or rights which are implied in the texts of the canons studied. Several logical, general factors will assist in these analyses: (a) A canon which explicitly or implicitly imposes an obli-

---

[6] Canons 33 §2 and 34 §3 treat of the cessation of the force of certain documents through implicit revocation by competent authority. Canon 85 indicates that the law itself and/or lawful delegation can implicitly give someone the power to dispense from merely ecclesiastical laws. Canon 1006 legislates that an implicit request made by a sick person when in control of his or her faculties is grounds for administering the sacrament of Anointing of the Sick.

[7] This is often the case with *nisi* clauses, e.g., cc. 135 §2 and 157. Other canons show the legislator specifically requiring an explicit expression where it is the mind of the legislator that an implicit expression is not acceptable, e.g., cc. 206 §1, 697, 2°.

[8] G. MICHIELS, *Normae generales iuris canonici commentarium libri I Codicis iuris canonici*, second edition, Paris: Typis Societatis S. Joannis Evangelistae Desclée et Socii, 1949, vol. 1, p. 132.

gation is also legislating that the person thus obliged has not only a duty but also a right to fulfill that obligation. (b) The pastor has a canonical obligation to obey the laws which set down how he is to interrelate with others. (c) The pastor has a canonical right to require of others that they obey the laws which set down how they are to relate to the pastor.

2.1.3 — Different kinds of *obligations* and *rights*

Specifically with respect to ecclesiastical offices, c. 145 §2 states:

> The obligations and the rights proper to individual ecclesiastical offices are defined either in the law by which the office is constituted or in the decree of a competent authority by which it is at the same time constituted and conferred.

However, there are other canons which do not constitute the office of pastor, but do empower a pastor to exercise the executive power of governance in special ways under particular circumstances. In such particular circumstances then, the pastor also becomes endowed with additional, special obligations and/or rights. Still other canons may implicitly involve a pastor, imposing obligations and/or rights in the process.

In general, various canons of the Code have different sources, have different degrees of authority behind them and may even be seeking to achieve different levels of compliance. As a result those canons may express different kinds of obligations and rights. Some canons state divine positive or natural law, or present a divinely revealed truth, or state simply ecclesiastical law, or even endow local civil laws with canonical force.[9]

---

[9] For types of law, see L. Örsy, "The Interpreter and His Art," in *The Jurist*, 40 (1980), pp. 27-56; J.H. Provost, "The Participation of the Laity in the Governance of the Church," in *Studia canonica*, 17 (1983), pp. 417-448. For types of expression, Latin

Still other canons are exhortatory, pointing to a goal which is to be sincerely and earnestly sought rather than absolutely and immediately achieved. One canonist holds that the Code recognizes six different kinds of rights:

> Just as human rights originate with human nature and civil rights derive from citizenship, so ecclesial rights occur with baptism. Religious rights derive from final profession; ecclesiastical rights are attached to office and contractual rights come from contract. In ascertaining any hierarchy of rights, the canonist must consider the correlative responsibilities involved....[10]

Because of those quite significant specific and general differences and in order to approach the subject of obligations and rights in a complete rather than a restrictive manner, in this book the term "obligation" will be used to encompass whatever the Code acknowledges, restates or institutes as something that is to be done or strived for; the term "right" will be used to describe whatever entitlement or beneficial involvement the Code acknowledges, restates or institutes in relation to the office of a pastor of a parish.

Some obligations or rights may be absolute, but many will be relative; the interpretation and enforcement of relative obligations or rights can in practice be affected by various circumstances. As a result, a person's canonical obligations or rights, expressed explicitly or implicitly in the Code, although they have a *real basis* and are *real*, may not always be fully enforceable in practice.

---

usage and practical application, see P. ERDÖ, "Expressiones obligationis et exhortationis in Codice iuris canonici," in *Periodica*, 76 (1987), pp. 3-27. For a specific study of the expression and interpretation of the Christian faithful's obligations and rights, see J.P. MC INTYRE, "Lineamenta for a Christian Anthropology: Canons 208-223," in *Periodica*, 85 (1996), pp. 249-276.

[10] MCINTYRE, "Lineamenta for a Christian Anthropology," p. 264. It may also be noted that c. 197 uses the term "subjective right" (*"iuris subiectivi"*).

2.2 — PASTOR'S GENERAL OBLIGATIONS AND RIGHTS CONCERNING MINISTRY OF THE DIVINE WORD

Canons 204 through 231 directly treat *The Christian Faithful*, *The Obligations and Rights of All The Christian Faithful* and *The Obligations and Rights of The Lay Christian Faithful*; another section of the Code, cc 273 through 289 presents *The Obligations and Rights of Clerics*. Some of the basic obligations and rights of a pastor of a parish with respect to the ministry of God's word are based on responses to obligations and rights shared by all of Christ's faithful, bishops, priests, deacons and lay people. A close relationship of that sort really ought to be expected because pastors of parishes are so completely involved in providing the service of leadership within their parish communities.

Among cc. 204-232 the rights considered often implicitly express obligations on the part of the pastors. Pastors are to lead conscientiously, to teach accurately, to listen to the faithful and work to fulfill their spiritual needs, to bring the faithful to know and live the mystery of salvation, to work with the faithful to enable all to receive a *Christian education*, so that they can spread the message of divine salvation.

Canons 212 and 213 which deal with basic obligations and rights of all of the faithful and of the lay faithful are directed toward bishops and the pastors of parishes.[11] Canon 212 §1 explicitly and with some detail reminds Christ's faithful that they are bound to follow what sacred pastors declare as teachers of the faith or determine as leaders of the Church. Since this canon binds the faithful to follow their diocesan bishops and parish pastors, it also implicitly: (a) obliges pastors to lead conscientiously and in communion with the Holy Father and the College of Bishops and (b) conveys to such pastors not only the duty to lead the faithful but also the right to have the faithful follow them

---

[11] "...their pastors. These latter are primarily the Bishops (can. 375 §1) and parish priests under their authority (see Can. 515 §1)," MᴄGʀᴀᴛʜ, "Christ's Faithful," in *Letter & Spirit*, n. 443, p. 120.

when they lead in communion with the Church.

Christ's faithful, however, are not simply to follow their pastors, they also have an explicit right expressed in c. 212 §2 "to make known their needs, especially spiritual ones, and their desires to the pastors of the Church." Among Christ's faithful the right to "make known" clearly implies a precisely focused obligation on the part of the pastors of the Church, to whom needs and desires are to be made known, that they listen attentively and sincerely and respond in some appropriate manner. That is not to say that all perceived needs, desires and wants must be fulfilled. In fact, in particular cases some individuals may need to be warned against fulfilling what they experience as needs or desires. The same observations would also apply to that part of c. 212 §3 which speaks of competent opinions being made known to sacred pastors.

Canon 213 declares a right of all of the faithful "to receive assistance from the sacred pastors" out of the Church's spiritual goods, especially God's word and the sacraments. The assistance due is spiritual and may be supplied in various ways, but there is also specific reference to ministry of God's word and the sacraments. Such an explicit right of the faithful implies a general obligation and right of the sacred pastors to do all that is possible to assist Christ's faithful through their ministry of preaching, teaching and sanctifying.

Canon 217 clearly and explicitly states that the baptized have a right to a Christian education to help them mature properly and "at the same time come to know and to live the mystery of salvation." Given the general context of Church organization and the role of the pastor of a parish in providing practical ways in which Christian education can, in fact, be obtained, it appears that most of the faithful must depend on the assistance of the pastor of a parish in order to exercise the right to Christian education.[12] To the extent that the Christian faithful cannot

---

[12] HERVADA, "The Obligations and Rights of all Christ's Faithful," in *Code Annotated*, p. 194 notes with respect to c. 217 that "parallel to the right of the faithful ex-

receive Christian education without the action of a parish pastor, c. 217 implies a conditional and very generally expressed obligation on the part of parish pastors to work with Christ's faithful so that all may achieve a Christian education.[13]

Among the canons concerning the obligations and rights of the clergy, c. 279 §2 requires that they are to attend pastoral lectures as determined by particular law, and also other lectures and theological meetings or pastoral conferences in order to acquire fuller knowledge. Even if there are no particular laws, the requirement to attend other lectures and theological meetings or pastoral conferences would still bind. Canon 279 §2, considered in conjunction with c. 519, would appear to place some obligation on the pastor of a parish to make just and reasonable efforts to schedule the duties of priests assigned to the parish in such a way that they would have opportunities to satisfy their obligation under c. 279 §2. If no way can be found to do so because of conflicts of rights, canon 223 §§1-2 should be prudently applied.

2.2.1 — Pastor's obligations and rights with respect to ministry of the Divine Word in cc. 519 and 528 §§1-2

Two canons from Book II, Title III, Chapter VI, *Parishes, Pastors and Parochial Vicars*, establish the pastor's general obligation to teach the word of God to everyone in the parish

---

pressed here is the obligation of the hierarchy and of Catholic teaching institutions to provide the means by which each member of the faithful might obtain the best formation possible."

[13] Canon 519 declares that the pastor has the duty of teaching within his community; c. 528 §1 points out the pastor's obligation to make sure that the entire word of God is announced to all who live in the parish; c. 773 sets down that the pastor has "a proper and serious duty... to provide for the catechesis of the Christian faithful"; c. 776 specifies that the pastor must "provide for the catechetical formation of adults, young people and children"; c. 794 §2 determines the pastor's "duty to arrange all things so that all the faithful may enjoy a Catholic education."

through homilies, catechetical instruction and the liturgy. These are cc. 519 and 528 §§1-2.

Canon 519 relates to the pastor's obligation of teaching, but is far more inclusive and sets out in juridic terms some of the theological and dynamic interrelationships among the diocesan bishop, the pastor, other priests, deacons, religious and lay people of a parish as individuals and as a parish community. An awareness of these relationships needs to be kept in mind and thoughtfully applied throughout as the pastor's services of leadership in sharing Jesus' teaching, sanctifying and governing ministries are investigated.

Canon 519 establishes that: (a) the pastor is *proper* to a particular parish, that is, he belongs among the people of God in a particular parish ministering to them; (b) the pastoral care of the community has been entrusted to the pastor under the authority of the diocesan bishop; (c) the pastor has been called to share in the diocesan bishop's ministry of Christ[14]; (d) for his community the pastor carries out the duties of teaching, sanctifying and governing; (e) the pastor is to carry out those duties in accordance with the law and in cooperation with other presbyters or deacons and the assistance of lay members of the Christian faithful.

From the perspective of obligations and rights, c. 519 explicitly and with some details spells out the obligation of the pastor to carry out for his community the duties of teaching (and sanctifying and governing). The same canon, equally explicitly, expresses the obligation of other presbyters, deacons and lay faithful of the parish to cooperate with the pastor in his work. In addition, c. 519 implicitly expresses a right of the pastor that the other presbyters, deacons and lay persons who are members of the parish community cooperate with him in his work of teaching (and sanctifying and governing).[15]

---

[14] "The bishops as vicars and legates of Christ, govern the Particular Churches assigned to them." *LG*, n. 27. English translation in FLANNERY, *Conciliar and Post Conciliar Documents*, pp. 382-384.

[15] With respect to teaching the word of God, c. 519 is echoed in c. 774 §1 and filled out with considerably more details in c. 776.

2.2.2 — Pastor's obligations and rights with respect to ministry of the Divine Word in Book III of the Code

In the canons of Book III, *The Teaching Office of the Church*, obligations and rights of the pastor are set forth with respect to proclaiming the gospel. The pastor is to enforce certain regulations concerning preaching in general and the *homily* in particular. Canon 771 §§1-2 require a special outreach needed to contact and teach the word of God to groups of people in various circumstances. Canons 773-780 reinforce and specify in various ways the pastor's obligations to provide catechetical instruction and his rights to be assisted in that task of instruction by the clergy and laity of the parish. Additional canons treat other obligations and rights of the pastor of a parish with respect to missionary activity — cc. 781-792, Catholic education and Catholic schools — cc. 793-806, and instruments of social communication — cc. 822-832.

2.3 — PREACHING IN GENERAL

Many if not all of the *principal* duties of the pastor of a parish are found in cc. 528, 529 and 530, which, in English translation, express themselves in 52 lines of print.[16] The very first obligation of the pastor of a parish enumerated in those canons is explicit and stated with precise detail in c. 528 §1: the pastor is to take care that the word of God is made known to everyone in the parish. In addition to making God's word known, c. 528 §1 requires that the pastor "...is to foster works by which the spirit of the gospel, including issues involving social justice, is promoted."

The pastor is further explicitly obliged to use the first of the special ways for this to be accomplished, which is through homi-

---

[16] See these canons in *Code of Canon Law, Latin-English Edition*.

lies preached on Sundays and holy days of obligation. Although homilies are preached, there is a difference between preaching or proclamation in general and delivering a homily.

The concepts of *preaching*, or *proclaiming* and *homily* are important with respect to the obligations and rights of pastors of parishes. Nevertheless, the words "homily" (and "homiletics") appear in only four canons of which only two pertain to pastors of parishes.[17] Preaching is the broader topic and is considered here first. In practice, however, much of the preaching done by bishops, priests and deacons is comprised of homilies.

Three other canons stress the general obligation of the pastor to preach. Canon 213 is very general and concise: "The Christian faithful have the right to receive assistance from the sacred pastors out of the spiritual goods of the Church, especially the word of God and the sacraments."[18] The canon explicitly expresses a general right of the faithful, but in so doing, it implicitly expresses a general obligation of pastors to preach the word of God (and provide a sacramental ministry). Canon 757 explicitly treats of the obligation of pastors and others who have been entrusted with the care of souls to carry out the task of proclaiming the Gospel of God to those entrusted to their care. Canon 762 is very much like, but less general than c. 213; it explicitly focuses on the obligation of bishops, priests and deacons "to value greatly the task of preaching." The canon even supplies a reason for the obligation "…since among their principal duties is the proclaiming of the gospel of God to all."[19]

---

[17] Canon 256 §1 concerns seminary training; c. 386 §1 concerns a bishop's obligations.

[18] In c. 213 the term "sacred pastors," "sacris Pastoribus" would principally identify the bishops of the Church, but pastors of parishes and probably parochial vicars would have some obligation under this canon, because of the broadness of the right expressed and the basic nature of the priesthood.

[19] Canon 762 also implies that there is a right to require that the people accept the word of God from the mouth of priests, but the canon does not indicate whose right this would be. It could be a general right that "The Church" has, or a right that the ecclesiastical superiors of the sacred ministers, or the preachers themselves have, or a right that the faithful have as a community, or even as individuals.

Preaching is not defined, or even especially described in the Code, but the word is used to indicate the most general and inclusive, spoken-word presentation of the Gospel message to instruct and motivate. The Second Vatican Council used the word "homily" only five times, while there are more than a hundred references to "preaching," and "preacher(s)."[20] Canon 770 mentions "...types of preaching which are called spiritual exercises or sacred missions or for other types of preaching." What other types of preaching? There is *catechetical preaching*, as might be done in conducting classes which follow an academic curriculum rather than being directly drawn from the liturgy; there is *ordinary pastoral preaching*, for instance, taking part in a public debate regarding the Church's teaching on abortion, addressing a Parent Teacher gathering on Catholic schools or vocations, or exhorting people at one or another ecumenical or even civil meeting to acknowledge publicly and pray to God, presenting the Church's teaching as related to a news event covered by the media, e.g., moral questions raised by the possibility of cloning human beings.[21]

Canon 766 gave expression to a remarkable change in Church discipline with the words "lay persons can be admitted to preach in a church or oratory...." The 1917 Code of Canon Law, in c. 1342 §1, established that only priests or deacons have the faculty to preach; c. 1342 §2 specifically provided that the laity, even members of religious institutes, were forbidden to preach in church.[22] Previous to the 1917 Code the same disciplin-

---

[20] OCHOA, *Index verborum Concilii Vaticani Secundi*, "homilia," p. 235, col. 1, "praeco, praeconium, praedicans, praedicatio, praedicator, praedicatus, praedico," pp. 390, cols. 1-2, 391, col. 1.

[21] *AG*, n. 16, English translation in FLANNERY, *Conciliar and Post Conciliar Documents*, pp. 831-833; *PC*, n. 24, English translation in FLANNERY, *Conciliar and Post Conciliar Documents*, pp. 622-623; *DV*, n. 24, English translation in FLANNERY, *Conciliar and Post Conciliar Documents*, pp. 763-764.

[22] Both cc. 766 of the 1983 Code and 1342 §2 of the Code of 1917 deal with lay persons preaching or not preaching in "a church" and c. 776 adds "or oratory." What about lay persons preaching outside of a church as defined in c. 1214 or an oratory as defined in c. 1223? Canon 229 §1 affirms the right of the lay faithful "to

ary practice can be traced back in the general law of the Church to Pope St. Leo I (440-461).[23]

Canon 766 further specifies conditions under which lay persons may be allowed to preach, those conditions are: "…if it is necessary, in certain circumstances or if it is useful in particular cases… according to the prescriptions of the conference of bishops and with due regard for can. 767 §1." If a particular conference of bishops has not provided any guidelines, however, can lay people be allowed to preach within the territory of such a conference?[24]

An American canonist has argued that if the conference of bishops does not act and there are no diocesan laws on the mat-

---

announce [the faith]," while c. 519 mandates that, subject to the bishop and in accord with the norm of law, the pastor of a parish "carries out for his community the duties of teaching, sanctifying and governing…." Therefore, since both a lay person and a pastor have rights which could affect preaching by a lay person outside of a church or oratory, it would be prudent for the member of the lay faithful to discuss preaching plans with the pastor of the parish community within which the preaching is planned to take place. If a disagreement arose from such a discussion, c. 223 §§1-2 would present an avenue for resolution of the matter.

[23] A.L. RICHTER and A. FRIEDBERG, (eds.), *Corpus Iuris canonici*, Graz, Akademische durck - u. verlagsanstalt, 1959, pars prior, *Decretum Gratiani*, c. 19, C. XVI, q. 1, columns 765-766; pars secunda, *Decretales Gregorii P. IX, De haereticis*, c. 12, X, liber V, titulus VII, columns 784-787.

[24] Various conferences of bishops have acted in different ways: neither the conferences of bishops of the United States nor Mexico, have issued prescriptions in response to c. 766; the Canadian Conference of Bishops has done so, see *Code Annotated*, Appendix III, "Complementary Norms to the Code Promulgated by English-Language Conferences of Bishops," p. 1322; also see p. 1336 for England and Wales, p. 1347 for Gambia, Liberia, Sierra Leone, p. 1359 for Ireland, p. 1377 for Nigeria, p. 1397 for the Philippines. Also see J.A. FUNETES, "Predicación de los laicos," Commentary on c. 766, in Instituto Martin de Azpilcueta Facultad de Derecho Canónico Universidad De Navarra, *Comentario exegético al Código de derecho canónico* (=*Comentario exegético*), coordinated and directed by A. Marzoa, J. Miras and R. Rodríguez-Ocaña, second edition, Pamplona: EUNSA Editiones Universidad de Navarra, S.A., 1997, vol. III/1, pp. 110-111, note the requirements of some Episcopal Conferences in this regard: that of Spain requires that the person receive a canonical mission, that of Italy requires a mandate together with permission of the ordinary, and those of Spain, France and others require permission of the ordinary, while those of Chile, the Philippines, Ireland, Peru and others require permission of the diocesan bishop.

ter, "…the code may be followed by pastors."[25] The same author presents seven examples of such action in lieu of decisions by conferences of bishops. He concludes: "Hence, particular churches can permit lay preaching in churches and oratories in accordance with common law, diocesan legislation and prudent decisions of pastors even though the conference has established no norms.…"[26]

In summary, the argument presented here implies that a parish pastor, who knows c. 766, is aware that neither the conference of bishops nor his own diocese has any regulations which address the situation, has his own obligations and rights under c. 528 §1 "to see to it that the word of God in its entirety is announced to those living in the parish"; therefore, a pastor in such circumstances may fulfill his duty and exercise the right correlative to that duty by deciding that the preaching by a competent

---

[25] B.F. GRIFFIN, "Canon 766, Lay Preaching," in CLSA *Advisory Opinions 1984-1993*, P.J. Cogan (ed.), Washington, DC, Canon Law Society of America, 1995, pp. 217-220. Also see Congregatio pro Clericis, Pontificium Concilium pro Laicis, Congregationes de Doctrina Fidei, de Cultu Divino et Disciplina Sacramentorum, pro Episcopis, pro Gentium Evangelizatione, pro Institutis Vitae Consecratae et Societatibus Vitae Apostolicae and Pontificium Concilium de Legum Textibus Interpretandis, Instruction, *On Certain Questions Regarding the Collaboration of the Non-Ordained Faithful in the Sacred Ministry of Priest Ecclesiae de mysterio*, August 15, 1997, in AAS, 89 (1997), pp. 852-877, here at art. 2, nn. 3° and 4°, pp. 863-864. English Translation, *On Certain Questions Regarding the Collaboration of the Non-Ordained Faithful in the Sacred Ministry of Priest* (=*Certain Questions Regarding Collaboration*), Vatican City, Liberia editrice Vaticana, 1997, p. 12. Article 2, n. 3° reaffirms the law while pointing out that the expression "admitti possunt" of c. 766 clearly establishes that no right or faculty to preach is conferred on the non-ordained person who might be admitted to preach and in n. 4° teaches that preaching in church by the non-ordained faithful "…cannot, however, be regarded as an ordinary occurrence nor as an authentic promotion of the laity." It may also be noted that the text of the English title: "*On Certain Questions Regarding the Collaboration of the Non-Ordained Faithful in the Sacred Ministry of Priest*" inserts the word "Sacred," which is not in the original Latin and uses "Priest," although the Latin is in the plural and should be translated "Priests."

[26] GRIFFIN, "Canon 766, Lay Preaching," p. 218.

lay person is necessary or useful and may permit such a person to preach.[27]

In any case the pastor would need to be personally convinced of the competence and orthodoxy of the lay person admitted to preach in the church. By analogy with c. 767 §4 the pastor would have an implicit obligation to see to it that any lay preachers stick to their subjects and present the teachings of the Church.

Canon 768 §§1-2 is concerned about the content of preaching or proclaiming the word of God. A simple reading of the canon establishes that its listing of the subject matter for preaching is not taxative, but it is directive. That is, many other topics should be preached about in order to fulfill the explicitly stated obligation to present the whole of God's word, but there is also an explicitly expressed obligation to preach on the subjects mentioned in this canon, which have a special importance in our day and age, along with other topics as well.[28]

Canon 769 directs that "Christian doctrine is to be proposed in a manner accommodated to the condition of its listeners and adapted to the needs of the times." This canon explicitly sets down the obligation to exercise good pedagogy in preaching and teaching. Also, together with cc. 519 and 528 §1 (in part), which call to mind the ultimate responsibility of the pastor for what is, in fact, preached and taught, c. 769 implicitly obliges the pastor

---

[27] Since the pastor exercises his office under the authority of the diocesan bishop and c. 766 explicitly calls for episcopal involvement when the law operates exactly as written, it would appear to be prudent for a pastor to discuss a decision he has made about allowing lay preaching with the diocesan bishop before announcing or acting on that decision. Also see a more recent document, *Ecclesiae de mysterio*, Art. 2, no 3, the text of which appears to lead to the conclusion that no judgment can be made to allow a lay person to preach unless the prescriptions indicated in c. 766 have been established by the conference of bishops and have received the required *recognitio* of the Apostolic See; those prescriptions now appear to be a *sine qua non* foundation for reaching a reasonable decision in the matter. English translation *Certain Questions Regarding Collaboration*, p. 12.

[28] See J.A. CORIDEN, "Book III: The Teaching Office of the Church," Commentary on cc: 747-833, in *CLSA Commentary*, p. 554. Coriden identifies the source of this canon as *CD*, n. 12, opining "that full paragraph is a very valuable source.... The terseness of the canon may be admirable, but the original text is a much more direct and helpful guide."

to know and to supervise the thoroughness with which Christian doctrine is being provided and the manner in which this is being done in the parish which he leads.

Two canons concentrate on the explicit obligations of pastors to provide, in accord with diocesan prescriptions, preaching on special matters. Canon 770 calls for providing "spiritual exercises," "sacred missions," or "other types of preaching..."; canon 1063, 1° obliges the pastor to provide several types of marriage preparation, one of which is "preaching, catechesis adapted to minors, youths and adults...."

Canon 771 §§1-2 explicitly notes the obligations of the pastor with respect to preaching to those who do not receive sufficient (or any) common pastoral care because of their life conditions, and to unbelievers who have not even heard the word of God. Canons 528 §1 (the last three lines) and 529 §1 (toward the end), refer to the pastor's broader obligations than preaching alone in respect to people with such problems and difficulties.[29]

Two of the canons about preaching, cc. 764 and 765, have to do with consent to preach. Unlike bishops who enjoy the *right* to preach everywhere,[30] priests and deacons, in accord with c.

---

[29] The diocesan bishop's obligations toward people in the same circumstances are found in c. 383. A pastor trying to assist people whose conditions of life interfere with their hearing the gospel or receiving common pastoral care might wish to consider asking the bishop to appoint a chaplain to assist the people in such straits, in accord with cc. 564 through 572.

[30] Canon 763 directs: "It is the right of bishops to preach the word of God everywhere, including the churches and oratories of religious institutes of pontifical rite, unless the local bishop has expressly refused this in particular cases." The "local bishop," "Episcopus loci" is terminology found only in the text of c. 763. In two other canons, 271 §1 and 1469 §2, which have to do with priests being active in a different diocese than their own, the "diocesan bishop of the place," "Episcopo diocesano loci, Episcopi diocesani loci" is used. CORIDEN, "Teaching Office," in *CLSA Commentary*, p. 551, col. 2, and F.G. MORRISEY, "The Ministry of the Divine Word," Commentary on cc. 756-772, in *Letter & Spirit*, n. 1525, p. 423 are in agreement that c. 763 is referring to a diocesan bishop of the place. It is important for the pastor of a parish to know of c. 763, but it would be incorrect to conclude that c. 763 implicitly imposes an obligation on the pastor to give a bishop permission to preach in the pastor's parish church; a bishop has a canonical right in this matter and simply does not need the pastor's permission.

764 have "the *faculty* to preach everywhere *to be exercised with at least the presumed consent of the rector of the church.*" The Code understands rectors of churches "...to be priests to whom is given the care of some church which is neither parochial nor capitular nor connected with a house of a religious community" (c. 556).[31] By analogy, if the consent of the rector of a church is required to preach in such a church, *a fortiori* the consent of the pastor of a parish is required to preach in a parish church and the consent of the appropriate religious superior to preach to religious in their churches or oratories.[32]

Canon 764 places an explicit obligation on the priest or deacon who wishes to preach either to obtain the pastor's consent or consider whether he has proper grounds to presume the requisite consent. Such a presumption would need to be reasonable, based on the priest's or deacon's orthodoxy in teaching, on not having had his diocesan or religious institute faculties revoked by his own bishop or religious superior, or by the law itself, and other similar considerations. The wording of this canon also suggests that it would be prudent of parishioners and/or parish groups, who are planning to invite a priest or deacon to address them, to ask for the pastor's consent before extending an invitation. Canon 764 implicitly points out the right of a pastor to refuse consent for a priest or deacon to preach within the boundaries of the parish. Nothing in the text of c. 764 suggests that consent is required only if the preaching is to be done in a church and c. 519 establishes that, subject to the diocesan bishop, the pastor's proper role includes exercising pastoral care and

---

[31] The term "the rector of the church" is used in both c. 764, which concerns permission to preach, and c. 903, which concerns permission to celebrate Mass. In both canons its meaning is obviously much wider than the particular definition found in c. 556. Such usage may be seen as an example of the law's economy of expression, using "rector of the church" as a least common denominator in view of the matter being treated to express implicitly the person in charge, i.e., "the pastor of the parish, the competent religious superior or the rector of a church as the case may be."

[32] As per c. 765.

carrying out the duties of teaching, sanctifying and governing for the community entrusted to him. Acting in that capacity, therefore, if the pastor has legitimate reason to refuse his consent for another priest or deacon to preach to his flock, that lack of consent would be coextensive with the pastor's jurisdiction.

Refusing consent is a right which the pastor would have to use with great discretion, prudence, and for serious reasons of faith or other common good concerns. The pastor should have objective reasons for refusing to give his consent. It must be understood that another's good name (c. 220) and conflicts of rights (c. 223 §§1-2) would be very much involved in a decision to refuse consent to preach.

2.3.1 — The homily

Although the term "homily" was not defined by the Second Vatican Council, an understanding of various elements of the concept of "homily" was advanced by the Sacred Congregation of Rites in the Instruction for the Proper Implementation of the Constitution on the Sacred Liturgy *Inter oecumenici*, n. 54:

> By a homily derived from the sacred text is understood an explanation either of some aspect of the readings from holy scripture or of another text from the Ordinary or Proper of the Mass of the day, taking into account the mystery which is being celebrated and the particular needs of the hearers.[33]

Many additional details, descriptive elements and insights into a *homily* have been presented in various official documents. An analysis and amalgamation of those insights suggest at least a descriptive definition of a homily.

---

[33] Sacra Congregatio Rituum, *Inter oecumenici*, September 26, 1964, in *AAS*, 56 (1964), pp. 877-900, here at n. 54, p. 890. English translation in *The Canon Law Digest* (=*CLD*), vol. 6 (1963-1967), p. 88.

The homily is an integral part of the liturgy,[34] but not reserved only to the liturgical celebration of the sacraments[35]; when
presented during the Mass, the homily is part of the liturgy of
the word, which liturgy of the word together with the eucharistic liturgy "are so closely connected with each other that they
form but one single act of worship."[36] The homily's purposes are:

---

[34] *SC*, n. 52. English translation in FLANNERY, *Conciliar and Post Conciliar Documents*,
pp. 17-18. SACRED CONGREGATION FOR DIVINE WORSHIP (=*SCDW*), General Instruction on the Roman Missal, *Cenam paschalem*, March 26, 1970, in *Missale Romanum
ex decreto Sacrosancti Oecumenici Concilii Vaticani II instauratum, auctoritate Pauli
PP. VI promulgatum, Ordo Missae* (=*Missale Romanum*), 1969, Typis polyglottis
Vaticanis nn. 9 and n. 41. English translation in FLANNERY, *Conciliar and Post Conciliar Documents*, pp. 164 and 172-173.

[35] Two separate interpretations of c. 767 §1 are to be found in *Ecclesiae de mysterio*,
art. 3, nn. °1 and °4. The first declares: "All previous norms which may have admitted the non-ordained faithful to preaching the homily during the Holy Eucharist are to be considered abrogated by canon 767 §1." English translation *Certain Questions Regarding Collaboration*, p. 13. The second clarifies: "Homilies in non-
eucharistic liturgies may be preached by the non-ordained faithful only when
expressly permitted by law and when its prescriptions for doing so are observed."
English translation *Certain Questions Regarding Collaboration*, p. 14. Also see POPE
JOHN PAUL II, Apostolic Exhortation, Catechesis in Our Time *Catechesi tradendae*
(=*CT*), October 16, 1979, in *AAS*, 71 (1979), pp. 1277-1340, here at n. 48, p. 1316.
English translation in FLANNERY, *More Postconciliar Documents*, p. 791. SACRA
CONGREGATIO PRO CULTU DIVINO, *Ordo professionis religiosae ex decreto sacrosancti
oecumenici Concilii Vaticani II instauratus, auctoritate Pauli PP. VI promulgatus*, editio
typica, Typis polyglottis Vaticanis, 1975, 6, p. 8. English translation in FLANNERY,
More Postconciliar Documents, p. 191. SACRA CONGREGATIO PRO CULTU DIVINO, *Rituale
Romanum ex decreto sacrosancti oecumenici Concilii Vaticani II instauratum, auctoritate
Pauli PP. VI promulgatum, Ordo paenitentiae*, editio typica, Typis polyglottis
Vaticanis, 1974, n. 26, p. 20, and n. 36, p. 23. English translation in FLANNERY, *More
Postconciliar Documents*, pp. 45 and 48. SACRA CONGREGATIO PRO CULTU DIVINO, *Rituale
Romanum ex decreto sacrosancti oecumenici Concilii Vaticani II instauratum, auctoritate
Pauli PP. VI promulgatum, De benedictionibus*, editio typica, Typis polyglottis
Vaticanis, 1985, n. 21, p. 15. English translation in *The Book of Blessings*, approved
for use in the dioceses of the United States of America by the National Conference of Catholic Bishops and confirmed by the Apostolic See, prepared by the
INTERNATIONAL COMMISSION ON ENGLISH IN THE LITURGY, Collegeville, MN: The Liturgical Press, 1989, pp. xxviii-xxix. Also see POPE PAUL VI, Apostolic Exhortation, Evangelization in the Modern World *Evangelii nuntiandi* (=*EN*), December
8, 1975, in *AAS*, 68 (1976), pp. 5-76, here at n. 43, pp. 33-34. English translation in
FLANNERY, *More Postconciliar Documents*, pp. 728-729, in which there is also reference to homilies having a place during para-liturgies (*in caeremoniis liturgiae
adsimillioribus*).

[36] *SC*, n. 56. English translation in FLANNERY, *Conciliar and Post Conciliar Documents*,
p. 19.

(a) to explain the scripture readings or some other text carefully selected from the ordinary or the proper of the Mass for the day during the course of the liturgical year, expounding the mysteries of faith and the guiding principles of the Christian life,[37] with regard for the mystery being celebrated or the special needs of those who hear it,[38] in a way relevant to the present day[39]; (b) to show points of convergence between revealed divine wisdom and noble human thought seeking truth by various paths[40]; (c) to note at a celebration with a particular group, that group's link with the local and universal Church.[41] The homily should be imbued with love, inspired by apostolic zeal, express the intimate faith of the minister and foster peace and unity; its style should be simple, clear, straightforward, well adapted to the hearers, firmly rooted in the teachings of the gospel, faithful to the magisterium, and filled with salutary hope.[42]

Also, the homily is the preeminent form of preaching and

---

[37] *SC*, n. 52. English translation in FLANNERY, *Conciliar and Post Conciliar Documents*, pp. 17-18.

[38] *Missale Romanum*, n. 41, p. 37. English translation in FLANNERY, *Conciliar and Post Conciliar Documents*, pp. 172-173.

[39] *SCDW*, Third Instruction on the Correct Implementation of the Constitution on the Sacred Liturgy *Liturgiae instaurationes* (= *Third Instruction on Correct Implementation*), September 5, 1970, in *AAS*, 62 (1970), pp. 692-704, here at n. 2, pp. 695-696. English translation in FLANNERY, *Conciliar and Post Conciliar Documents*, pp. 212-213.

[40] POPE JOHN PAUL II, Letter to all Bishops of the Church, "On the Mystery and Worship of the Eucharist" *Dominicae cenae*, February 24, 1980, in *AAS*, 72 (1980), pp. 113-148, here at n. 10, pp. 134-137. English translation in FLANNERY, *More Postconciliar Documents*, pp. 77-79.

[41] *SCDW*, Instruction on Masses for Special Groups *Actio pastoralis Ecclesiae*, May 15, 1969, in *AAS*, 61 (1969), pp. 806-811, here at n. 6 (g), p. 809. English translation in FLANNERY, *Conciliar and Post Conciliar Documents*, p. 145.

[42] *EN*, n. 43. English translation in FLANNERY, *More Postconciliar Documents*, pp. 728-729.

is reserved to priests and deacons.[43] In addition, the liturgical homily holds pride of place among all forms of pastoral preaching and catechetical instruction,[44] and it would be a serious error to deny that the homily is a powerful and most suitable instrument of evangelization.[45]

In 1987 the Pontifical Commission for the Authentic Interpretation of the Code of Canon Law declared that a diocesan bishop was not able to dispense from the canon requiring reservation of the preaching of a homily to a priest or deacon; the Commission's decision was published at the direction of Pope John Paul II.[46] As is the practice, no arguments were presented on the basis of which the negative decision had been reached.[47]

---

[43] *Third Instruction on Correct Implementation* n. 2. English translation in FLANNERY, *Conciliar and Post Conciliar Documents*, pp. 212-213. *SCDW*, Instruction on Certain Norms Concerning the Worship of the Eucharistic Mystery *Inaestimabile donum*, April 3, 1980, in *AAS*, 72 (1980), pp. 331-343, here p. 332. English translation in FLANNERY, *More Postconciliar Documents*, p. 93. Also see c. 767 §1. The *CCEO*, mindful of the various theological, spiritual, liturgical and disciplinary patrimonies of the number of *sui iuris* Churches within its ambit, is even somewhat more precise in c. 614 §4: "The homily is reserved to a priest or, according to norm of particular law, also to a deacon." English translation, *Code of Canons of the Eastern Churches, Latin-English Edition*, translation prepared under the auspices of the Canon Law Society of America, Washington, DC: Canon Law Society of America, 1992. Unless otherwise attributed, English translations of the canons of the *CCEO* will be derived from this source.

[44] *DV*, n. 24. English translation in FLANNERY, *Conciliar and Post Conciliar Documents*, pp. 763-764.

[45] *EN*, n. 43. English translation in FLANNERY, *More Postconciliar Documents*, pp. 728-729.

[46] PONTIFICIA COMMISSIO CODICI IURIS CANONICI AUTHENTICE INTERPRETANDO, *Acta Commissionum*, in *AAS*, 79 (1987), p. 1249. For a discussion of this decision, see L.G. WRENN, *Authentic Interpretations on the 1983 Code*, Washington, DC: Canon Law Society of America, 1993, pp. 41-43.

[47] See R.J. CASTILLO LARA, "De iuris canonici authentica interpretatione in actuositate pontificiae commissionis adimplenda," in *Communicationes*, 20 (1988), pp. 265-287, here at p. 285. The author indicates that no arguments are presented, because an authentic interpretation does not derive its power to oblige from reasons on which it is based, but from the mandate which the Commission [Pontificia Commissio Codici Iuris Canonici Authentice Interpretando] has received from the legislator. Put another way, the responses of the Commission for Interpretation have the power to oblige not because they are supported by weighty arguments, but because the power of the legislator makes them obligatory. Castillo

A 1997 *Instruction on Certain Questions Regarding the Collaboration of the Non-Ordained Faithful in the Sacred Ministry of Priest* included a general treatment of various theological principles behind the distinction of roles of laity and clergy together with some material specific to the restriction of the homily at the Eucharist to priests and deacons.[48]

The four paragraphs of c. 767 provide basic regulations concerning the homily. Taken together, c. 767 §1 with c. 767 §4 express an explicit obligation of the pastor to see to it that only a priest or a deacon does preach a homily.[49] The same canonical combination explicitly expresses the pastor's obligation to provide that homilies treating mysteries of faith and norms of Christian living are presented regularly throughout the liturgical year. The pastor may fulfill this obligation to some extent through others, provided they are priests or deacons.[50]

In addition, since the pastor is obliged to be sure that c. 767 §1 is conscientiously followed, he is implicitly required to achieve a degree of certainty that his own and the homilies delivered by other priests or deacons present at least in a general way the subjects called for by c. 767 §§1-4, based on the appropriate liturgical texts for at least the Sundays and holy days

---

Lara's comment calls to mind the ancient adage: "Quod principi placuit, legis habet vigorem" - What pleases the ruler has the force of law. Also see F.J. URRUTIA, "Responsa pontificiae commissionis Codici iuris canonici authentice interpretando," in *Perodica*, 77 (1988), pp. 613-628, here at pp. 613-624, J. Fox, "The Homily and the Authentic Interpretation of Canon 767 §1," in *Apollinaris*, 62 (1989), pp. 123-169, L. ROBITAILLE, "An Examination of Various Forms of Preaching: Toward an Understanding of the Homily and Canons 766-767," in *CLSA Proceedings*, 58 (1996), pp. 308-325.

[48] *Ecclesiae de mysterio*, Theological Principles; art. 3. English translation *Certain Questions Regarding Collaboration*, pp. 5-9, 13-14. Also see J. HUELS, "Interpreting an Instruction Approved *in forma specifica*," in *Studia canonica*, 32 (1998), pp. 5-46.

[49] See footnote 34.

[50] Canons 528 §1 and 757 both indicate a personal obligation of pastors — along with other priests — to proclaim the Gospel.

throughout the year.[51] Other priests and deacons, aware of the pastor's implicit obligation in this matter, should understand his proper pastoral interest and concern about the content and quality of their homilies.

Canon 767 §2 explicitly sets down particular times and circumstances at which a homily is to be given. Of itself this is a serious obligation for any priest who celebrates a Mass in the circumstances indicated. The obligation is a serious one, since the canon specifies that a serious reason would be necessary to omit the homily. Canon 767 §4 not only makes clear the pastor's personal obligation of vigilance in seeing that c. 767 §2 is carried out but also confers on him the serious obligation of seeing that other priests and deacons conscientiously preach homilies as required by c. 767 §1.

Canon 767 §3 would be very much the same as c. 767 §2 for any priest offering Mass in the circumstances described and for collateral obligation of the pastor under c. 767 §4, except that the text of c. 767 §3 utilizes *persuasion* — "it is strongly recommended" — in its expression. Does such an expression impose an obligation? In view of the text of a canon "strongly recommending" a particular course of action, prudence would appear to dictate that the recommendation should be followed unless an individual has a really strong reason, i.e., objective, logical and capable of consistent application, for doing something else. In using a persuasive expression the law maker presumably judged that persuasion would more easily achieve the Church's goal detailed in c. 767 §3 because of the willing cooperation of the celebrant.[52]

---

[51] FUENTES, "Predicación de la homilia," Commentary on c. 767, in *Comentario exegético*, vol. III/I, p. 115 expresses the opinion that since pastors have a responsibility for all matters touching the general pastoral care of the faithful and a concrete responsibility for places of worship, an especially important obligation is imposed when a canon specifically points out an element which is already part of the pastor's general obligations.

[52] Early in 1967 consultors of the Pontifical Commission for the Revision of the Code of Canon Law developed a number of principles to guide the work of revising the Code of Canon Law. The Synod of Bishops, meeting in 1967 for the first time

Canon 767 §4 expresses an explicit obligation of the pastor of a parish to see to it that the prescriptions of c. 767 §§1-3 are "conscientiously observed."

Canon 767 §§2 and 4 with c. 548 §2, which require that parochial vicars are "to assist the pastor in fulfilling the total parochial ministry," and c. 757, which requires that "deacons also are to serve the people of God in the ministry of the word in communion with the bishop and his presbyterate," coalesce to focus implicitly on a right of the pastor to assign parochial vicars and deacons serving a parish community to assist him in the preaching of homilies on a regular schedule in a reasonable way.

2.4 — CATECHESIS IN GENERAL

The term "catechesis" has a technical meaning which is quite complex. As was the case with the term "homily," many Church documents comment on different aspects of catechesis, but none fully define it. In addition, official Church documents use, with regularity and apparent inter-changeability, several different words or expressions to identify the same subject: *catechetical*

---

since the conclusion of the Second Vatican Council, reviewed and approved the principles. The third of these principles stated in part: "In establishing the law, the Code is to cultivate not only justice but also a wise equity, which is the fruit of kindness and true love; in order to assure the thorough practice of those virtues the Code is to fulfill its duty to stir up the discretion and the knowledge of Pastors and judges. Therefore, canonical norms are not to impose duties *where instructions, exhortations, persuasions and other helps*, by which communion among the faithful is warmly promoted, *seem sufficient to achieve the Church's goal more easily.*" See *Communicationes*, 1 (1969), pp. 79-80 (emphases added). In those cases in which "instruction, exhortation, persuasion or other help," are found in the texts of canons, therefore, it would appear accurate to conclude that such forms of expression have been chosen *precisely because* the law giver has reached a judgment that such a manner of expression "seems sufficient to achieve the Church's goal...." It would appear that, although the legislator may have judged that one or another manner of expression would be better suited to achieving the Church's goal, nevertheless the legislator's unwavering intention is that persons subject to the canons are to act according to the canons in order to achieve the Church's goal, the *salus animarum*, the *suprema lex*.

formation, catechetical instruction, catechetics and *instruction in Christian doctrine.* If a catholic usage may be spoken of in regard to these words, it seems that *catechesis,* a noun, refers to the overarching concept of a progressive communication of a broad body of religious truths and interpersonal relations to a particular group of persons. *Catechetics,* a noun, refers to different elements or methods or courses which are related to the progressive communication involved in *catechesis.* Anything described by the adjective *catechetical* is somehow related to *catechesis* and / or *catechetics.*[53]

An effort to gather all of the elements found in various documents has produced the following descriptive definition:

> Catechesis is a cooperative activity of all members of the Church community[54] focused on communicating, in an accurate, systematic and complete manner, the whole of God's revelation, adapted to the capacities of the listeners,[55] to all who already have some belief in Christ[56]; while at the same time leading them by individual and

---

[53] The term "religious education," which is quite often colloquially used in the United States as equivalent to "catechetical instruction," appears only in c. 799. That canon principally addresses parents' rights with respect to the religious and moral education their children might receive in public schools.

[54] *CT,* n. 24. English translation in Flannery, *More Postconciliar Documents,* pp. 776-777.

[55] *CD,* n. 14. English translation in Flannery, *Conciliar and Post Conciliar Documents,* pp. 571. *EN,* n. 44. English translation in Flannery, *More Postconciliar Documents,* pp. 729-730. *CT,* nn. 19, 21-22, 29-30. English translation in Flannery, *More Postconciliar Documents,* pp. 773, 775-776, 779-781. For an extensive listing of the more outstanding elements of the Christian Message, see: Sacra Congregatio pro Cleris, General Catechetical Directory *Ad normam decreti* (=*AN*), April 11, 1971, in *AAS,* 64 (1972), pp. 97-176, here at nn. 37, 47-69, 77-97, pp. 120, 125-141, 145-156. English translation in Flannery, *More Postconciliar Documents,* pp. 550, 555-570, 574-85. Also see Congregatio pro Cleris, General Directory for Catechesis, *Directorium Catechisticum Generale,* Città del Vaticano, Libreria editrice Vaticana, 1997, pp. 175-205. English translation in United States Catholic Conference, *General Directory for Catechesis,* Washington, DC, 1998, pp. 157-180.

[56] *CT,* nn. 18-19. English translation in Flannery, *More Postconciliar Documents,* p. 772-774.

community example, shared prayer and love,[57] to develop their own intense personal love of Jesus,[58] moved by their deepening knowledge of his life and teachings,[59] and their experience of sharing his followers' faith-filled lives.[60]

2.4.1 — Catechesis in the parish

There are a number of canons throughout the code which call attention to the responsibility of the pastor to provide catechetical formation for parishioners. As a brief prelude to reviewing several such canons, it may be worthwhile at this point to list, altogether, at least the numbers of canons which in one way or another acknowledge that a pastor's obligation to "give" catechetical instruction is not a task which the pastor is expected to carry out alone; these are cc. 211, 215, 216, 222 §1, 225 §1, 226 §2, 229 §1, 519, 528 §1, 548 §2, 757, 774, 776, 780, 785 §§1-2.

Canon 519 indicates that the pastor is to carry out his duty of teaching God's word subject to the diocesan bishop's author-

---

[57] *AG*, n. 14. English translation in FLANNERY, *Conciliar and Post Conciliar Documents*, pp. 828-829. *AN*, n. 53. English translation in FLANNERY, *More Postconciliar Documents*, p. 558-559. *EN*, n. 79. English translation in FLANNERY, *More Postconciliar Documents*, pp. 754-755. *CT*, nn. 24-25. English translation in FLANNERY, *More Postconciliar Documents*, pp. 776-777.

[58] *AN*, nn. 12, 15, 64. English translation in FLANNERY, *More Postconciliar Documents*, pp. 538-539, 541, 566. *EN*, n. 45. English translation in FLANNERY, *More Postconciliar Documents*, p. 730. *CT*, n. 5. English translation in FLANNERY, *More Postconciliar Documents*, pp. 764-765. See *Catechism of the Catholic Church* (=*Catholic Catechism*), New York: Catholic Book Publishing Co., 1994, nn. 426-429, pp. 107-108.

[59] *AN*, n. 53. English translation in FLANNERY, *More Postconciliar Documents*, pp. 558-599. *CT*, n. 19. English translation in FLANNERY, *More Postconciliar Documents*, pp. 773-774.

[60] *SC*, n. 64. English translation in FLANNERY, *Conciliar and Post Conciliar Documents*, p. 21. *AG*, n. 14. English translation in FLANNERY, *Conciliar and Post Conciliar Documents*, pp. 828-829.

ity and "in accord with the norm of law." The center section of c. 528 §1 directs that the faithful are to be instructed through homilies "and through the catechetical formation which he [the pastor] is to give." Canon 773, certainly addresses both bishops and pastors of parishes (and quite possibly all priests serving in parish communities). Canon 773, however, does not widen the obligation itself, but explicitly and precisely establishes: (a) that the general obligation "is a proper and serious duty... to provide the catechesis of the Christian people..." and (b) that two means are to be used, both "formation in doctrine," and "the experience of Christian living."[61] Canon 773 also indicates what the results of effective catechetical formation should be. The pastor of a parish is not canonically obliged by c. 773 to achieve fully such results; the pastor is, however, implicitly obliged to provide a catechesis which a prudent person would expect to produce such effects.[62]

The phrase "under the supervision of legitimate ecclesiastical superiors" which begins c. 774 §1 touches the pastor of a parish in two ways. First, as a member of the church he is explicitly obliged in a general way in his role as pastor to cooperate with superior ecclesiastical authority in forming and carrying out parochial, interparochial and/or diocesan programs of catechetical formation. Second, as pastor and a legitimate ecclesi-

---

[61] Other canons explicitly and with more precise detail oblige the pastor of a parish to provide instructions in preparation for the reception of sacraments: Baptism, c. 851, 2°, Confirmation, c. 890, Holy Eucharist, c. 914, Marriage, c. 1063, 1°.

[62] The Latin of the clause is: "...ut fidelium fides, per doctrinae institutionem et vitae christianae experientiam, viva fiat explicita atque operosa." The "ut" plus the subjunctive mood of the verb can denote a necessity, but also may indicate something happening, peculiar, supposed, appearing, imagined, or granted; cf. *Cassell's Latin Dictionary*, J.R.V. MARCHANT and J. F. CHARLES [revisers], New York: Funk & Wagnalls Company, n.d., p. 601, col 2. A strict obligation cannot be based on such an indefinite foundation. Also see *Harper's Latin Dictionary: A New Latin Dictionary founded on the Translation of Freund's Latin-German Lexicon*, edited by E.A. ANDREWS, revised, enlarged and in great part rewritten by C.T. LEWIS and C. SHORT (= LEWIS and SHORT, *Latin Dictionary*), Franklin Square, New York: Harper & Brothers, Publishers, 1891, pp. 1939-1944.

astical authority in his own parish, the pastor has a right and a duty to supervise all catechesis in his own parish. Canon 774 §§1-2 implicitly establishes that the pastor has the right to anticipate: (a) that all members of the parish, all parents and all godparents will fulfill their own particular responsibilities with regard to catechetical instruction, and (b) will cooperate with the pastor's leadership in providing catechetical formation for all concerned.

Canon 776 explicitly reiterates the obligation of the pastor to provide all parishioners with catechetical formation, and explicitly requires him to "promote and foster the role of parents in the family catechesis…"[63] At the same time c. 776 also explicitly declares the obligation and the right of the pastor to call upon various individuals and groups to assist him in the work of catechesis, and explicitly imposes upon those who are asked for assistance by a pastor an obligation "not to refuse to furnish their services willingly unless they are legitimately impeded."[64]

The provision of several specific types or circumstances of catechetical formation are set down as the pastor's obligations in c. 777.[65] The pastor is to provide suitable catechesis for the reception of the sacraments, which, in the case of Penance, Eu-

---

[63] A measure of the pastor's catechetical obligation can be seen by comparing c. 776 with c. 774 §2. Parents are specifically obliged to provide Christian formation for their children; the pastor, however, is obliged to provide Christian formation for everyone even as they grow from childhood through youth into and during adult life.

[64] In Book II, Title II, *The Obligations and Rights of the Lay Christian Faithful*, c. 225 §1 explicitly notes that the lay faithful are bound "…to work as individuals or in associations so that the divine message of salvation becomes known and accepted by all persons.… [T]his obligation has a greater impelling force in those circumstances in which people can hear the gospel and know Christ only through lay persons." Of itself, c. 225 §1 does not oblige the lay faithful to relate to the pastor in a particular way as c. 776 does. A pastor, however, might well make appeal to c. 225 §1 in conjunction with exercising the canonical duty and right, which he has from c. 776, to call on lay members of the Christian faithful for their help in providing catechetical formation.

[65] Also see c. 843 §2.

charist and Confirmation is to be given over a period of time.[66] Following the reception of First Communion, children are to be more profoundly instructed.[67] In accord with c. 777, 4° and 5° the mentally or physically handicapped are to be catechized to the extent possible, and the faith of young people and adults is to be "fortified, enlightened and developed through various means and endeavors." In each instance the pastor's obligation is expressed explicitly, but in a rather general way.

Among the canons devoted to Catechetical Formation, the final one which affects the pastor is a direction about utilizing all up-to-date means of communication appropriate to the varying talents, ages and conditions of those who are being taught. Although c. 779 is not addressed specifically to pastors, its subject is the means by which catechetical instruction should be communicated, and it is clear from other canons that the pastor is responsible for the presentation of catechetical formation in the parish. It can be concluded, therefore, that c. 779 expresses by implication a general obligation of the pastor of a parish, similar to that of the diocesan bishop, about the means of communicating catechetical formation to the residents of the diocese.

2.4.2 — Catechesis as an element of liturgy

Liturgy is a many faceted reality, which will be treated in considerably more detail in Chapter Three. Chief among the concepts of liturgy which come readily to mind is that liturgy is

---

[66] With respect to the sacrament of Confirmation being received by children, c. 777, 2° is slightly more specific than c. 890, which regards the obligation of all of the faithful to receive that sacrament. *Ecclesiae de mysterio*, art. 2, n. 5° requires: "Above all in the preparation for the sacraments, catechists take care to instruct those being catechized on the role and the figure of the priest as the sole dispenser of the mysteries for which they are preparing." English translation *Certain Questions Regarding Collaboration*, p. 12

[67] Canon 777, 3°. One kind of such instruction might be drawn from c. 1252: "...pastors and parents are to see to it that minors who are not bound by the law of fast and abstinence are educated in an authentic sense of penance."

the official public worship of the Church. Liturgy certainly is that.[68] Some elements of liturgy, especially the homily,[69] and the readings and prayers of the liturgy drawn from Sacred Scripture, are recognized also to be elements of Catechetical Instruction:

> And the visible signs which the sacred liturgy uses to signify invisible divine things have been chosen by Christ or by the Church. Thus not only when things are read "which were written for our instruction" (Rm 15:4), but also when the Church prays or sings or acts, the faith of those taking part is nourished, and their minds are raised to God so that they may offer him their spiritual homage and receive his grace more abundantly.[70]

Those elements of the liturgy which are mentioned in canons dealing with the obligations and rights of the pastor of a parish in relation to preaching, catechetical instruction in general, or the instructional component of sacramental preparation will be treated in this Chapter; aspects of liturgy related to the obligations and rights of the pastor with respect to sacramental ministry in general, or the spiritual component of sacramental preparation, will be reviewed in the following pages.

In addition to the canons which specifically treat Catechetical Formation,[71] several canons from Book IV address an instructional component of sacramental preparation. Canon 851, 1° has to do with the Catechumenate for adults who intend

---

[68] *SC*, n. 2. English translation in FLANNERY, *Conciliar and Post Conciliar Documents*, p. 1. *Catholic Catechism*, nn. 1067-1069, pp. 277-278.

[69] *DV*, n. 24. English translation in FLANNERY, *Conciliar and Post Conciliar Documents*, pp. 763-764. Also see *Ecclesiae de mysterio*, art. 3. English translation *Certain Questions Regarding Collaboration*, pp. 13-14, especially art. 3, n.° 4, p. 14: "Homilies in non-eucharistic liturgies may be preached by the non-ordained faithful only when expressly permitted by law and when its prescriptions for doing so are observed."

[70] *SC*, nn. 24, 33. English translation in FLANNERY, *Conciliar and Post Conciliar Documents*, pp. 10, 11-12.

[71] Canons 773-780.

to receive Baptism; it does not explicitly impose an obligation on the pastor of a parish. It does, however, have to do with proper preparation for reception of the sacrament of Baptism. The Catechumenate involves not only an instructional component, but also liturgical and social ones as well. Taken in the context of the pastor's obligations expressed explicitly in c. 528 §1 "...see to it that the word of God in its entirety is announced... through the catechetical formation which he is to give..." and c. 528 §2 "...participation in the sacred liturgy, which the pastor must supervise in his parish...," c. 851, 1° implies an obligation and right of the pastor of the parish with focus on his being sure that the Catechumenate experience is available as described and employed "...to the extent possible."

Canon 851, 2°, concerning the parents and sponsors of infants, is divided into two clauses. The first clause, without indicating who is to provide it, requires proper instruction "...about the meaning of this sacrament [Baptism] and the obligations which are attached to it..." for parents and sponsors. Just as c. 851, 1°, and for the same reasons, the first clause of c. 851, 2° implies an obligation of the pastor to see to it that the people involved receive the instructions specified. The second clause of c. 851, 2° is concerned with the spiritual preparation and formation of parents of infants who are to be baptized, as such it is treated in the following pages.

With respect to any of the requirements of c. 851, many members of the parish community, or other persons from outside of it, may assist the pastor in fulfilling his implicit and explicit obligations, and the pastor has a right to call upon those within the parish to do so.[72]

Canon 890 states the obligation of each of the faithful them-

---

[72] D. KELLY, "Baptism," Commentary on cc. 849-878, in *Letter & Spirit* n. 1676, p. 470, points out: "In addition to assistant priests and religious working in the parish, other members of the community may be entrusted with this task: indeed this would be an obvious opportunity for the laity to exercise the functions mentioned in Cann. 225 §1 and 529 §2."

selves, their parents, shepherds of souls and especially the pastor, to see to it that all are properly prepared and receive the sacrament of Confirmation. The canon expresses an explicit obligation of the pastor to provide proper preparation.

Canon 914 is concerned with reception of the Holy Eucharist by children as soon as they have reached the use of reason and have been properly prepared. The canon expresses the obligations and rights of the pastor in this regard: "...to see that children who have reached the use of reason are correctly prepared and are nourished by the divine food as early as possible..." and "...to be vigilant lest any children come to the Holy Banquet who have not reached the use of reason or whom the pastor judges not to be sufficiently disposed."

It is worth noting that whether admitting children to Holy Communion or requiring them to wait until they become more properly disposed, the pastor may not be arbitrary in his decision and should have objective reasons for such judgments. Respect for the Holy Eucharist does require that at least the minimum knowledge, faith and devotion necessary for reception be adhered to.[73] On the other hand, young as the child in question may be, he or she, if minimally prepared and acting with knowledge, faith and devotion, has a right to receive[74]; in addition, the girl or boy is a member of the Christian faithful and has rights both to a good reputation and to privacy, either or both of which could be violated by an individual being excluded from participating in a public ceremony.[75]

Canon 914 raises questions about preparation for and the reception of the sacrament of Penance itself, and the specific role which that preparation has in the complete preparation required for the reception of First Communion. The only other canon which mentions preparation for the sacrament of Penance is c.

---

[73] Canon 913 §1.
[74] Canons 912 and 914.
[75] Canon 220.

777, 2°, which, after declaring that the pastor is to make "...particular provision..." adds, among other concerns, "...that children are properly prepared for the first reception of the sacraments of penance and Most Holy Eucharist." Canon 914, however, states that properly prepared children who have the use of reason: "...are [to be] nourished by the divine food as early as possible, preceded by sacramental confession...."

What then, are the pastor's obligations? Must preparation for and reception of the sacrament of Penance precede or be an integral part of preparation for the reception of Holy Communion? Can a child who has not received the sacrament of Penance be admitted to receive Holy Communion?

Commenting on the questions of preparation and the order of reception of First Penance and First Eucharist, one writer states:

> The canon [914] requires that children be properly prepared. This preparation will take place within the family and in school, and in special cases — e.g., lack of a catholic school, where there are learning difficulties etc. — it will be done by individual catechesis. In addition to this preparation the canon requires that the children have made their first confession.... During the 1960's and 1970's the practice grew up of postponing first confession until some years after first communion. However there was a strong official reaction against this practice, and the phrase 'having made their sacramental confession' was added to the final draft of this Code. This restores and makes obligatory the practice which had become traditional.[76]

Shortly after the Code became effective another position was presented, and appears to have still been held in 1995 when

---

[76] J. McAreavey, "The Blessed Sacrament," Commentary on cc. 897-958, in *Letter & Spirit*, n. 1799, p. 502.

it was republished.[77] According to that position, requiring the reception of the sacrament of Penance before the reception of First Communion is at variance with the Church's prior tradition that no one is required to seek the sacrament of Penance unless he or she is conscious of being guilty of serious sin. The position also holds that c. 213 conveys a right to the Eucharist which pertains to all of the faithful.

In addition to offering a more detailed, but still concise, review of the documents which relate to the First Penance before First Communion question, another canonist provides a practical manner in which to comply with c. 914 while respecting individual rights. He writes:

> Pastoral practice should respect this norm that has been incorporated into the Code and take fully into account the freedom of the child receiving first communion. Certainly the child should be effectively free to receive the sacrament of penance or not. This freedom is not respected if the child is told that confession is absolutely necessary. On the other hand, if the child is not prepared, taught how to receive the sacrament of penance, and given a real opportunity to go to confession, the child is not in fact free to make a choice.
>
> In practice the child should be prepared for the sacrament and given the opportunity to receive it before making first communion. The child's freedom is properly respected, if all this is done and it is told that there is no obligation to go to confession if a mortal sin has not been committed. Needless to say the persons preparing the child for confession could restrict the child's freedom by conveying during the instruction a negative attitude toward the child's receiving the sacrament. A person acting in this way would not only violate this

---

[77] J.H. Provost, "Diocesan Guidelines for First Eucharist and Penance," in *CLSA Advisory Opinions 1984-1993*, pp. 281-283. Also see J.H. Provost, "The Reception of First Penance," in *The Jurist*, 47 (1987), pp. 294-340.

canon, but would be in fact restricting the child's freedom.[78]

Simply put, the pastor is explicitly required to provide for children a preparation for First Communion which includes a true and complete preparation for and opportunity to receive First Penance, about which the child may make an informed and free choice.

Canon 1063 presents a number of general pastoral obligations with regard to marriage preparation (and helping marriages to succeed). The catechetical elements of marriage preparation are basically contained in 1063, 1°, which needs to be interpreted with the declaration from c. 773 in mind: "There is a proper and serious duty, especially on the part of pastors of souls, to provide for the catechesis of the Christian people...." Not only is the canonical duty of c. 1063, 1° serious, but the number of divorces and failed marriages throughout the world demonstrate sociologically the serious need for practical programs to teach people about marriage, prepare them in physical, emotional and spiritual ways for marriage and help them to develop, mature and sustain their marriage relationship throughout life.

Item 1° of c. 1063 stipulates that the pastors' obligation is:

> ...to see to it that their own ecclesial community furnishes the Christian faithful assistance so that the matrimonial state is maintained in a Christian spirit and makes progress toward perfection.

The pastor has an explicit obligation to lead and supervise his ecclesial community in this activity; the pastor therefore has an implied right that the members of the ecclesial community will cooperate with his service of leadership with regard to marriage preparation and preservation.

---

[78] W.H. WOESTMAN, *Sacraments: Initiation, Penance, Anointing of the Sick*, Ottawa: Faculty of Canon Law, Saint Paul University, 1992, pp. 129-131 for the historical context, and pp. 130-131 for a solution in practice.

Canon 1063, 1°-4° also presents general types of activities or services through which assistance is to be given to help parishioners prepare for and live successfully in marriage. The first of these calls for "instructing minors, youths and adults about the meaning of Christian marriage and the duty of Christian spouses and parents." The pastor therefore, has an obligation to be sure that instructions concerning these subjects are provided in parish schools, catechetics classes, RCIA programs and, where liturgically appropriate, in general preaching and homilies. Canon 1063, 1° adds some specificity in the area of marriage preparation to all of the other canons which stress the pastor's obligation to "...see to it that the word of God in its entirety is announced to those living in the parish."[79]

2.4.3 — Catechesis in Catholic education and Catholic schools

Because of its very nature *catechesis* must be found in various elements of Catholic education in general and in particular in the formation offered by Catholic schools.[80] What is *Catholic*

---

[79] Canon 528 §1.

[80] In addition to the term "Catholic education," which is found in cc. 528 §1, 793 §§1-2, 794 §2, 798, 801, 804 §1 and once in the general title of cc. 793 through 821, the Code also employs the term "Christian education" in cc. 217, 226 §2 and 835 §4. See X. Ochoa, *Index verborum ac locutionum Codicis iuris canonici*, second and complete edition, Città del Vaticano, Libreria editrice Lateranense, 1984, p. 162. Canon 217's use of "Christian education" can be interpreted broadly: "...deepening any Christian's communion and commitment to Christ...," J.H. Provost, "People of God," Commentary on cc. 204-264, in *CLSA Commentary*, p. 151; "...a much broader concept than the education of children or even than catholic education as legislated for in Cann. 793-821. The goal of this education is twofold: the maturity of the human person, and the knowledge and living of the mystery of salvation. Neither can be separated from the other," McGrath, "Christ's Faithful," in *Letter & Spirit*, n. 456, p. 123. Other commentators see c. 217 as referring to a right "...to receive Christian formation within the Church, i.e. regarding ecclesiastical hierarchy and Church teaching institutions," Hervada, "The Obligations and Rights of all Christ's Faithful," in *Code Annotated*, p. 194. Canon 226 §2 specifically refers to the teachings of the Church and so it appears to use "Christian education" and "Catholic education" as synonyms. The same seems to be true of c. 835 §4, because of the references there to "...active participation in celebrations of liturgy especially in the Eucharist."

education with respect to which parish pastors have both obligations and rights? Clear ideas can be found in the teachings of the Second Vatican Council even though that Council did not use the term Catholic education in any of its documents. The Council did indicate the differences among *education in general*, the *content and means of Christian education* and the *special function of Catholic schools*,[81] which provide a carefully thought out matrix of concepts against which to study the canons which specify the obligations and rights of the pastor of a parish in the area of formal Catholic education.

While the entire teaching of the Second Vatican Council on these points cannot be quoted here, the following highlights indicate important distinctions and also underline the call *not only* for intellectual content *but also* for dynamic personal integration *and* practice as elements of *Catholic education*. With respect to education in general, *Gravissimum educationis* taught:

> True education is directed toward the formation of the human person in view of his final end and the good of that society to which he belongs... children and young people should be helped to develop harmoniously their physical, moral and intellectual qualities.... trained to acquire gradually a more perfect sense of responsibility in the proper development of their own lives.... As they grow older they should receive a positive and prudent education in matters relating to sex. Moreover, they should be prepared to take their part in the life of society.... They should be open to dialogue with others and

---

[81] Catholic education is not synonymous with Catholic schools. Nevertheless, the Catholic education actively provided at home within the family together with the systematic and time intensive presentation possible in a Catholic school appears more complete than Catholic education provided by other approaches. Also see cc. 798, 802 §1; Sacra Congregatio pro Institutione Catholica, *L'école catholique*, March 19, 1977, in *La documentation catholique*, 74 (1977), pp. 705-716, here at nn. 73-76, pp. 713-714, nn. 81-82, pp. 714-715, n. 89, p. 715. English translation in Flannery, *More Postconciliar Documents*, pp. 606-629; H.A. Buetow, *The Catholic School: Its Roots, Identity and Future*, New York: Crossroad, 1988, pp. 74-94.

should willingly devote themselves to the promotion of the common good.... children and young people have the right to be stimulated to make sound moral judgments based on a well-formed conscience and to put them into practice with a sense of personal commitment, and to know and love God more perfectly.[82]

Christian education adds very significant elements to the general picture.

[Christian education] is especially directed toward ensuring that those who have been baptized, as they are gradually introduced to a knowledge of the mystery of salvation, become daily more appreciative of the gift of faith which they have received. They should learn to adore God the Father in spirit and in truth..., especially through the liturgy... be trained to live their own lives in the new self, justified and sanctified through the truth.... Thus come to true [adulthood]..., and make their contribution to the growth of the Mystical Body... conscious of their vocation they should learn to give witness to the hope that is in them... to promote the Christian concept of the world whereby the natural values, assimilated into the full understanding of man redeemed by Christ may contribute to the good of society as a whole... an education by virtue of which their whole lives may be inspired by the spirit of Christ.[83]

In addition to every regular means of imparting education, Christian education relies on a special method of its own:

Catechetical Instruction, which illumines and strengthens the faith, develops a life in harmony with the spirit

---

[82] *GE*, n. 1, pp. 729-730. English translation in FLANNERY, *Conciliar and Post Conciliar Documents*, pp. 726-727.

[83] *GE*, n. 2-3. English translation in FLANNERY, *Conciliar and Post Conciliar Documents*, pp. 727-730.

of Christ, stimulates a conscious and fervent participation in the liturgical mystery, and encourages [all] to take an active part in the apostolate.[84]

With respect to *Catholic schools, Gravissimum educationis* taught:

It is, however, the special function of the Catholic school to develop in the school community an atmosphere animated by a spirit of liberty and charity based on the Gospel. It enables young people, while developing their own personality, to grow at the same time in that new life which has been given them in baptism. Finally it so orients the whole of human culture to the message of salvation that the knowledge which the pupils acquire of the world, of life and of men is illuminated by faith.[85]

Canon 794 §2 is largely a case of cc. 519 and 528 §1 revisited. It does impose an explicit obligation, but not a new one. Read in the light of *Gravissimum educationis'* descriptions of education in general and Christian education in particular, the obligation is precisely focused. However, c. 794 §2 does not impose an obligation to operate a Catholic school, nor would its obligation be fulfilled by operating a Catholic school while providing poor (or no) catechetical programs for students who do not attend Catholic schools. Nor would the obligation be met even if both a Catholic school and good catechetical programs were in place, but parish liturgies were celebrated poorly, or homilies were few and/or ill delivered. The obligation of c. 794 §2 is "...to arrange *all* things so that *all* the faithful may enjoy a Catholic education" (emphasis added).

As a member of the faithful, the pastor is called upon by c.

---

[84] *GE*, n. 4. English translation in FLANNERY, *Conciliar and Post Conciliar Documents*, p. 730.

[85] *GE*, n. 8. English translation in FLANNERY, *Conciliar and Post Conciliar Documents*, pp. 732-734. Also see BUETOW, *The Catholic School*, pp. 74-94.

796 §1 "...to greatly value schools." This is an explicit obligation, but very generally stated. In context the schools in question need not even be Catholic schools, but they would have to be schools providing a good general education as described in *Gravissimum educationis*, and not inimical to Christian education.

Canon 798 explicitly requires that: (a) parents entrust their children to schools which provide Catholic education, or (b) parents provide for their suitable Catholic education outside of the schools. In many, if not most, circumstances this canon would also be implying an obligation of parents to cooperate with the leadership of their pastor in order to render organized Catholic education attainable. In such circumstances, the pastor would have a right arising from this canon to require in a reasonable way and to expect to receive the cooperation of the parents involved.

Canon 800 §2 is addressed to the faithful in general and states their obligation "...to foster Catholic schools by supporting their establishment and their maintenance in proportion to their resources." As a member of the faithful, the pastor would share the same personal obligation as the other faithful. In addition, as pastor of a parish, he is responsible for the Catholic education of all in the parish, c. 800 §2 establishes the pastor's implicit right to call for and to receive from the parishioners the resources described. Presumably such resources would involve, but not be limited to, volunteered services and financial support.

Including ministry of the word, but also comprising a broader context, c. 813, which is one possible application of c. 518, calls on the diocesan bishop "...to have serious pastoral concern for students" of Catholic universities and institutes of higher studies "...by erecting a parish for them or by assigning priests for this purpose on a stable basis." Where the diocesan bishop does establish that kind of a parish, the regular canonical obligations and rights of pastors would become the responsibilities and prerogatives of the pastor of such a parish.

2.5 — MISSIONARY ACTIVITY OF THE CHURCH

No canon describes any special duties for missionaries precisely as pastors of parishes, although some special tasks of missionaries in general are mentioned in cc. 781-792, which deal with the *Missionary Action of the Church*.

Canons 385 and 791, however, place obligations on the diocesan bishop to promote missionary vocations and to have an annual missions' day observance. If a diocesan bishop calls for a special annual mission observance or promotion of missionary vocations, c. 791 would express an implicit obligation (and correlative right) on the part of the pastor of a parish to carry out the bishop's program.

Canon 781 enjoins on all the Christian faithful, which certainly includes pastors, that they be conscious of their own responsibility for the work of evangelization and assume their own role in missionary work. Although c. 781 expresses an explicit obligation for each Christian, beyond that the canon is extremely general, if not to say vague.

Do pastors of parishes have their *own role* in missionary work? In seeking the meaning of words used in the text of a canon "...recourse is to be taken to parallel passages... to the purpose and circumstances of the law."[86] The *fontes*, which often indicate the purpose and/or circumstances of a canon, specify that c. 781 is to some extent based on *Ad gentes*, n. 39, in which the Second Vatican Council directed that priests will "...so organize their pastoral care that it will contribute to the spread of the Gospel among non-Christians." In addition, specific directions are provided.[87] It would seem, therefore, that c. 781 im-

---

[86] Canon 17.

[87] *AG*, n. 39. English translation in FLANNERY, *Conciliar and Post Conciliar Documents*, p. 853. These means suggested include: stimulating and maintaining the faithful's zeal for evangelization by preaching and religious instruction about the Church's duty to proclaim Christ to the world, by impressing on Christian families the honor and the need that they foster missionary vocations among their own children, by encouraging missionary fervor among young persons in Catholic schools and missionary associations, teaching people to pray for the missions, and beg-

poses on the pastor of a parish that, in view of his leadership position, he be mission-minded and provide more instruction and encouragement about missionary work than would be found in sermons during annual Mission Sunday celebrations, annual collection for the missions, and occasional petitions within the Prayers of the Faithful.

2.6 — USE OF INSTRUMENTS OF SOCIAL COMMUNICATION

This title in the Code is comprised of cc. 822 through 832.[88] In these canons the term "pastors" is used only three times: cc. 822 §§ 1-2 and 823 §1. In c. 822 §§1-2 there is some lack of clarity about whether the pastors of parishes are included in the use of the term "pastors."[89] Among the *fontes* for Canon 823, *Inter mirifica*,

---

ging alms to assist missionaries. Also see *PO*, n. 6. English translation in FLANNERY, *Conciliar and Post Conciliar Documents*, pp. 872-875. *AG*, n. 39 together with *PO*, n. 6, are the conciliar teachings which form the basis for the assertion in Chapter 1 that the *Eighth Characteristic of a parish* is that within each parish fervor for missionary activity and evangelization is being fostered.

[88] Seven other canons also use the term "instruments," or "means," or "media" of social communication," OCHOA, *Index verborum ac locutionum*, "communicatio socialis," p. 88, "instrumentum communicationis socialis," p. 232, "medium communicationis socialis," p. 274. Canon 747 §1 declares the Church's innate duty and right to use means of social communication to preach. (Canons 761, 779, 804 §1, and 1063, 1°) direct that means of social communication are to be used in spreading the gospel in general, in catechetics, in Catholic formation, religious education, and sacramental preparation. Canon 666 requires those who have consecrated their lives to God to be prudent in using media of communication and to avoid it if it threatens their vocation or chastity. Canon 1369 calls for a just penalty for those guilty of using the means of social communication for immoral, irreligious and anti-Church purposes.

[89] CORIDEN, "Teaching Office" in *CLSA Commentary*, specifically interprets the pastors to be bishops, pp. 579-580. J.M. GONZÁLEZ DEL VALLE, "The Means of Social Communication and Books in Particular," Commentary on cc. 822-832, in *Code Annotated* does not directly comment on who the pastors are, but the treatment suggests that the commentators assume them to be bishops, pp. 532-533. BORRAS, *Les communautes paroissiales*, pp. 89-162 treats the duties of pastors of parishes, but make no mention of cc. 822-832. MORRISEY, "The Ministry of the Divine Word," in *Letter & Spirit* does not comment explicitly or implicitly on the status of the pastors addressed, n. 1608, p. 447.

nn. 1-3 are listed and in n. 3 of *Inter mirifica* the Second Vatican Council taught that the obligation encompassed "…instructing and directing the faithful how to use the media in a way that will ensure their own salvation and perfection and that of all mankind."[90] Such a broad responsibility laid upon the bishops seems to imply that subordinate pastors of souls are also to share in the work under the bishop's authority. It appears reasonable, therefore, to conclude that pastors of parishes are implicitly expected, under the bishop's direction, to share in the task of fulfilling c. 822 §§1-2.

Because the bishops' obligations and rights with respect to speaking for the Church are primary, pastors of parishes would need to follow diocesan directives in such matters and might prudently confer with their diocesan bishop about making use of instruments of social communication before doing so.

Canons 826 §3 and 827 §§2 and 4 do not place obligations upon pastors of parishes directly. Nevertheless, the pastor has duties and rights concerning teaching and also sanctifying the faithful and providing them with a Catholic education.[91] A pastor, then, has the right and obligation authoritatively to require that parishioners or parish groups observe c. 826 §3 with regard to publishing prayer books for public or private use. He has a similar right and obligation that books to be used in the parish school or religious education programs conform to c. 827 §2 or that parish book sales conform to c. 827 §4.

Pastors of parishes are not discouraged from prudently making good and even frequent use of any or all of the various means of social communication in order to minister the word of God to all. With respect to "…any writings whatsoever which are destined for public distribution…,"[92] they are subject to the same regulations as all other members of the faithful.

---

[90] *IM*, n. 3. English translation in FLANNERY, *Conciliar and Post Conciliar Documents*, pp. 284-285.

[91] Canons 519 and 794 §2.

[92] Canon 824 §2.

2.7 — SHARING FULFILLMENT OF OBLIGATIONS AND EXERCISE OF RIGHTS

The Second Vatican Council saw that one of the ways in which the pastor would need to share in Jesus' kingly ministry of governing the parish community of God's people would be by calling on its members to grow, to recognize the rights, charisms and duties which are their own as variously gifted members of the People of God, and to share with their pastor some of his tasks as pastor in developing many aspects of parish life. Canon 519 alludes to somewhat the same idea, but focuses more on providing assistance for the pastor than developing the gifts and the participation of the laity. Chapters two, three and four will each include a segment titled *"Sharing Fulfillment of Obligations and Exercise of Rights."*

It must be carefully noted, however, that some obligations and rights of the pastor of a parish arise from his ordination as a priest and cannot be shared with others. In extraordinary circumstances, which usually arise from a scarcity of priests and deacons, lay members of the faithful may be permitted in accord with Church law to collaborate in the ministry of priests by carrying out some of the "services" usually provided by a priest or deacon, e.g., serving as an extraordinary minister of Holy Communion to the sick and aged, or in the church building. In such instances, the non-ordained licitly and with charity do help the pastor to fulfill some of his priestly obligations, but they do not share the pastor's right nor acquire a "right" of their own to serve in such a way, and may do so only when ecclesiastical authorities, acting in accord with Church law, request that they do so.[93]

The *Sharing Fulfillment of Obligations and Exercise of Rights* segment in this and the remaining chapters will treat the canoni-

---

[93] *Ecclesiae de mysterio,* Theological Principles, n. 4; art. 4, nn. °1 and °2. English translation *Certain Questions Regarding Collaboration,* pp. 8-9, 14-15. Also, c. 129 §2 stipulates "Lay members of the Christian Faithful can cooperate in the exercise of this power [the power of governance] in accord with the norm of law."

cal question whether and to what extent the fulfillment of various obligations and the exercise of the pastor's rights *can be* and/or *should be* shared with others and present some possibilities about canonical procedures which might help promote such sharing of the fulfillment of obligations, the exercise of rights and the development of the gifts God has given to members of the parish community.

In addition to the canons which touch upon this subject, the *Instruction on Certain Questions Regarding the Collaboration of the Non-Ordained Faithful in the Sacred Ministry of Priest* will be a significant authoritative source. Although titled *Instructio*, the document is far more authoritative than the *Instructiones* described in c. 34 §2. This document establishes that: "All particular laws, customs and faculties conceded by the Holy See *ad experimentum* or other ecclesiastical authorities which are contrary to the foregoing norms are hereby revoked"; the text of the document is explicitly, i.e. *in forma specifica*, approved by the Holy Father, and the Instruction's *promulgation* rather than simple publication was ordered by the Pope.[94]

2.7.1 — Sharing fulfillment of obligations and exercise of rights with respect to ministry of the Divine Word

In view of all of the canons which oblige the pastor, other clerics, religious and laity to work together to provide catechesis and Catholic education,[95] there is no question that the pastor can share almost all of his duties in this regard with any other qualified persons, and that he is encouraged by Canon Law to do so.

However, several factors which arise from the obligations

---

[94] *Ecclesiae de mysterio*, Conclusion. English translation *Certain Questions Regarding Collaboration*, p. 24.

[95] They are: cc. 211, 215, 216, 222 §1, 225 §1, 226 §2, 229 §1, 519, 528 §1, 548 §2, 757, 774, 776, 780, 785 §1 and §2.

connected to the ecclesiastical office of pastor, cannot be over-looked in the matter of sharing the ministry of the Divine Word. The pastor can only share the task of preaching homilies with other priests or deacons, and then only with those whose faculties to preach have not been restricted by the diocesan bishop or by a proper religious superior.[96]

In addition, the pastor is obliged by c. 767 §4 to see to it that certain prescriptions about when homilies are to be preached and certain general parameters about their subject matter, are observed. This law is fulfilled by supervision which may also on occasion necessitate specific action such as thanks and praise or confrontation and correction.

Other types of preaching by the lay faithful in churches and/or oratories are restricted to certain circumstances, the establishment of which requires action by the conference of bishops and the *recognition* by the Holy See of their prescriptions in the matter.

The law does not prohibit the pastor from exercising his supervision through someone else, which may even be good administrative practice. Ultimately however, the pastor must then supervise the supervisor. If a pastor legitimately shares fulfillment of some of his obligations with others, those obligations do not cease to exist. Because of the ecclesiastical office he holds, the pastor is still personally obligated to evaluate whether the people with whom he has shared his obligations are successfully fulfilling those obligations. If the obligations are not being met, the responsibility still lies with the pastor, who must find others who can share the obligations effectively, or the pastor must fulfill them personally. Concisely put, the pastor can share

---

[96] *Ecclesiae de mysterio* explicitly indicates that it is not permitted to entrust "…the preaching of the homily to seminarians or theology students who are not clerics. Indeed, the homily should not be regarded as a training for some future ministry," art. 3, n.° 1, and that "In no instance may the homily be entrusted to priests or deacons who have lost the clerical state or who have abandoned the sacred ministry," art. 3, °3. English translation *Certain Questions Regarding Collaboration*, pp. 13-14.

his supervisory duties, but he cannot entirely give them away.

By way of example, cc. 528 §1 and 776 (to cite only two canons on the subject) require that a pastor must provide Catholic education and catechetical instruction to his parishioners. If a given parish has a Catholic school and a religious education program for children who do not attend the school, a pastor may be well advised to employ the most qualified school principal and religious education professional who are available to the parish. In doing so, the pastor may entrust each with authority to make broad educational and administrative decisions. Nevertheless, in this case the pastor can only *share* his authority and responsibility with regard to the Catholic school or the religious education program; he cannot cause his ultimate responsibility for the provision of Catholic education and catechetical instruction to cease to be his and become someone else's responsibilities.

A corollary to this point is the observation that even though there is no canonical requirement that ordinary parish schools or religious education programs should have school councils, religious education councils or their own financial councils, there is no prohibition against establishing such advisory bodies. The larger the school or the religious education program is, the more such councils might prove to be useful ways of sharing authority with, and of developing the individual talents of, various members of the parish community in a systematic manner.[97] Still, the pastor can only share the responsibility, which comes with his office, he cannot abdicate it simply by delegating it.

CONCLUSION

Subject to the authority of the diocesan bishop, the pastor of the parish is, because of his ecclesiastical office of pastor, responsible for the Catholic education of everyone in the parish. The Catho-

---

[97] Such councils might prudently be modeled on cc. 536 §1 and §2, 537, 94 §1, §2 and §3, and 95 §1 and §2.

lic education which the pastor is required to provide for everyone in a parish community, is an education for dynamic Catholic living. There is an intellectual content of truth to be learned and understood, and together with that knowledge there is a person, Jesus Christ, God the Son, who is to be met and loved.

The pastor's precise obligations and rights which flow from the ministry of the Divine Word find their source not in the Divine Word alone, but also in the spiritual, intellectual, free will, emotional and physical characteristics of the nature of the human beings for whom the ministry of the Divine Word is undertaken. Thus a pastor's obligations and rights involve the content, the manner of presentation and the day to day way of life which should be among the constitutive elements of the pastor's ministry of the Divine Word.

With respect to the content of the faith, there is the necessity that the pastor accurately and integrally present the teachings of the magisterium of the Church. The same is true of the content and methods of teaching which the pastor takes part in and/or oversees by right within the parish in liturgical celebrations, organized religious education classes and presentations, in a parochial school, RCIA programs, In-Home Pre-Cana meetings and the like. The pastor has specific obligations and rights concerning the *homily*, properly so called, both with respect to its content and to its reservation to priests and deacons.

Pastors, or others assisting them in teaching the faith, are directed to teach and communicate in ways which seem most likely to help the faithful to learn thoroughly what the Catholic Church teaches and live according to it. They are also directed to take into account the "...characteristics, talents, age and conditions of life..." of each group being taught.[98]

The pastor's obligations and rights with respect to the education of children do not supersede the natural obligations and rights of parents, who are themselves bound to care for the Chris-

---

[98] Canon 799. Also see cc. 528 §1, 529 §1 and 777, °4.

tian education of their own children. Pastors along with all of the Catholic faithful are to encourage Catholic schools by assisting their establishment and continuation as their means allow.

The pastor is obligated and has the right to actualize the dynamism of the ministry of the Divine Word which goes beyond presenting correct and complete intellectual content and engages the emotions and free will of each of the faithful. Together with hearing the faith preached, the faithful need to be led to the experience of participating in living a Christian life as welcome and loved members of their family, parish and diocesan communities. To some extent this will be likely to be achieved by the liturgical experiences and organized educational efforts mentioned just above. In addition, however, participation in other parish charitable or volunteer programs could have the same effect. In all of these approaches the pastor by himself or through the assistance of others, has the obligation and the right to see that the parish community and its families are formed in the living practice of the faith.

In fine, the pastor is to teach "…so that the faith of the faithful becomes living, explicit and productive through formation in doctrine and the experience of Christian living;" and, "…he [the pastor] is to foster works by which the spirit of the gospel, including issues involving social justice, is promoted."[99]

With respect to sharing the ministry of the Divine Word, the pastor has a right to call upon all members of the parish community, clergy, religious and lay to assist him in the fulfillment of his educational obligations toward everyone in the parish. Calling for this kind of assistance is one of the ways in which the pastor recognizes the abilities, education and charisms of the lay faithful and provides them with opportunities to spread the gospel by their own example and effort. In his efforts prudently to share the fulfillment of his educational obligations and the

---

[99] Canons 773 and 528 §1.

exercise of his rights, the pastor may share almost all of his obligations — and, considering the magnitude of the tasks, he may be well advised to do so in almost all circumstances. The pastor cannot, however, cease to be personally — and ultimately — responsible that there is attentive general supervision, necessary planning, objective, effective evaluation and follow through.

The ministry of the Divine Word which announces a special way of life invites and challenges the faithful with a universal call to holiness. Chapter three will consider the obligations and rights of the pastor in the service of holiness — the ministry of sanctification.

Ministry of Sanctification

INTRODUCTION

Just as the possibility and the promise of sanctification are proclaimed and explained through the Ministry of the Divine Word, they are received and experienced within the Ministry of Sanctification. The priestly or sanctifying ministry of the pastor of a parish engenders obligations and rights in several related but different spheres of activity. Among these are the confecting and conferral of sacraments *sensu stricto*, the celebration of various liturgical ceremonies,[1] conducting or supervising prayerful paraliturgical or extraliturgical events, living Christ-like interpersonal relationships with individual parishioners and their families, recognizing and encouraging the roles of the laity as individuals and in pious associations, nourishing among the faithful true experiences of *communio* within the parish, the diocese and the universal Church, granting required delegation, dispensing from Church law in some circumstances and seeing to it that Church law is quite carefully followed in others, keeping records of the reception of sacraments or reception into full communion with the Church.

---

[1] For example: Marriage liturgies at which the Church's official minister officiates, but the bride and groom administer the sacrament to one another; praying the Liturgy of the Hours; celebrating Benediction of the Most Blessed Sacrament; conducting wake and burial services; invoking blessings according to formularies and with the ceremonies presented in approved liturgical books.

The principal consideration of this chapter will be the pastor's sharing in the priestly ministry of Jesus: the worship of God through celebratory aspects of the sacraments, the liturgy, the sacramentals of the Church and other occasions of prayer and community building. In connection with sacramental and liturgical ministry there are also some exercises of governance and various administrative activities which are proper to the pastor. Those instances of governance and administration will be considered together with broader questions of administration treated in the next chapter which considers the pastor's participation in the kingly, that is, governing, ministry of Jesus.

3.1 — THE PASTOR'S GENERAL OBLIGATIONS AND RIGHTS WITH RESPECT TO THE MINISTRY OF SANCTIFICATION

Although the pastor's obligations and rights in the ministry of sanctification are not limited to liturgical celebrations, his approach to the liturgy is of critical importance. The pastor's attitude toward liturgy will impact every liturgical celebration in the parish, many less formal prayer experiences and the spiritual lives (or lack thereof) of many parishioners. The pastor is required to know, to protect and, if necessary, even to enforce the right of the parishioners to liturgical practices that are detailed by the Church and promote true *communio* within the Church. In addition just as it is necessary for the pastor to appreciate and develop the catechetical element of the liturgy, he needs also to be attuned to the liturgy as worship.

3.1.1 — Careful adherence to approved liturgical practices

Canon 214 which enjoins: "The Christian faithful have the right to worship God according to the prescriptions of their own rite approved by the legitimate pastors of the Church…," implicitly and clearly requires that the pastor of a parish provide, among other important elements of worship within a particular rite, liturgies according to the approved liturgical books of the rite of the parish. The term "legitimate pastors" used in connection with the words "their own rite" are clear references to the hierarchies of *sui iuris* Churches, rather than parish pastors.[2] Ultimately the term "legitimate pastors" implies only those pastors who are in communion with the Apostolic See.[3]

The last phrase of c. 528 §2 concerning the sacred liturgy requires that the pastor be "...vigilant lest any abuses creep in"[4]; in addition, two specific types of liturgical abuses are legislated against in c. 846 §§1-2. Canon 846 requires faithful observance of "the liturgical books approved by the competent authority... in the celebration of the sacraments," forbids anyone to make any changes in approved liturgical books "on personal authority,"[5] and directs "The ministers are to celebrate the sacraments

---

[2] The term "rite" may also describe a liturgical rite within a *sui iuris* Church which encompasses and officially recognizes more than one distinct liturgy. See McGrath, "Christ's Faithful," in *Letter & Spirit*, n. 451, p. 122.

[3] D. Cenalmor, "Obligaciones y derechos de los fieles," Commentary on c. 214, in *Comentario exegético*, vol. 2/1, p. 101.

[4] The importance of the pastor's guarding against liturgical abuses was a serious consideration for the Pontificia Commissio Codici Iuris Canonici Recognoscendo, which reviewed cc. 362-363 of the *Schema "De populo Dei"* on May 8 and 9, 1980. In their discussions of cc. 362-363 of that Schema, which would become cc. 528 and 530 of the 1983 Code, all of the consultors agreed that the strong statement of the obligation proposed in c. 362 §2 should be retained. In addition, one of the consultors argued against the text of c. 363, because, in his view, the "reservation" of certain liturgical services to the pastor, was the best way to enable the pastor to forestall and avoid liturgical abuses. See *Communicationes*, 12 (1981), pp. 280 and 282.

[5] The seriousness of the Church's concern for a devoted, accurate and consistent use of approved liturgical texts is demonstrated by: (a) c. 214, which enunciates the right of the Christian faithful "...to worship God according to the prescriptions of their own rite as approved by the legitimate pastors of the Church"; (b) c. 383 §2, which reminds the diocesan bishop that he is to provide for the spiritual needs of the faithful of different rites within his diocese "...either by means of priests or parishes of that rite or by means of an episcopal vicar"; (c) c. 392 §2, which reminds the diocesan bishop of his obligation to prevent abuses from affecting "...the celebration of the sacraments and sacramentals, the worship of God and devotion to the saints"; (d) cc. 826 §§1-2 and 838 §§2-3, which declare the right of the Holy See to review all translations of liturgical books and require that

according to their own rite." Canon 528 §2 taken together with cc. 846 §§1-2 and 907 impose a precisely detailed obligation and confer a right identified with equal precision on the pastor of a parish carefully to supervise liturgical celebrations in the parish according to the norms of the approved liturgical texts.[6] There is also implied a right of the pastor to expect that other celebrants of liturgy in the parish will willingly accept and put into practice any needed corrections which the pastor may call for on the basis of instructions, rubrics and directions found in the approved texts.

Canon 2 also needs to be considered in conjunction with c. 528 §2.

> For the most part the Code does not define the rites which are to be observed in celebrating liturgical actions. For this reason current liturgical norms retain their force unless a given liturgical norm is contrary to the canons of the Code.

A general reading of norms and directives in liturgical texts leads to the conclusion that for the most part they are not specifically directed toward the pastor of a parish as a pastor, but address bishops, priests, deacons and other authorized ministers who celebrate, preside at or lead the liturgy. Nevertheless, in order to fulfill his obligation of guarding against abuses creeping into a parish's liturgical celebrations, a pastor has a concomi-

---

even when an episcopal conference has prepared vernacular translations of liturgical books including what that episcopal conference considers to be "appropriate adaptions," those translations and texts are to be reviewed by the Holy See prior to their publication; (e) c. 846, which requires the faithful observance of authorized liturgical books and forbids any changes "…on personal authority"; (f) cc. 850, 880 §1, 928, 998, 1119 and 1176 §2, which specifically require the use of approved liturgies at Baptism, Confirmation, Eucharist, Anointing of the Sick, Marriage and funerals.

[6] With respect to c. 907, see *Ecclesiae de mysterio*, art. 6, English translation *Certain Questions Regarding Collaboration*, p. 17.

tant obligation to be well versed in the regulations presented in the approved liturgical books and authoritative directive documents.

Several additional canons also express basic obligations of pastors of parishes with respect to their sacramental ministry. Canon 212 §2 implies an obligation of a pastor to listen to the parishioners' expression of their needs for sacramental ministry and to respond in a reasonable manner. Canon 213's reference to "...the right to receive assistance out of the spiritual goods of the Church," and c. 217's recognition of "...the right... at the same time [to] come to... live the mystery of salvation," both imply an obligation on the part of a parish pastor to work at fulfilling the needs of parishioners. Canon 519 treats explicitly, but in general terms, the pastor's obligation "of sanctifying" his community.

Canon 222 §1 explicitly states: "The Christian faithful are obliged to assist with the needs of the Church so that the Church has what is necessary for divine worship." Implicitly there is expressed the right of the pastor of a parish to expect such assistance.

Canon 276 §2, 2° invites priests to celebrate the Eucharistic sacrifice daily and deacons to participate daily in offering it, c. 904 directs that priests are to celebrate frequently and strongly recommends daily celebration "...even if the faithful cannot be present." Canon 902 allows concelebration while preserving each priest's freedom to celebrate individually, but not concomitantly with a concelebration of the Eucharist.[7] Those canons express rights of priests and deacons and the concern of the Church that they exercise those rights on a daily basis. A parish pastor would at least have the obligation of recognizing those rights of the clergy in the parish community and of not interfering with their

---

[7] Canons 902 and 904 are nuanced and restricted somewhat by c. 906: "A priest may not celebrate without the participation of at least some member of the faithful, except for a just and reasonable cause."

exercise except if a conflict of rights arises, in which case c. 223 §§1-2 should be prudently observed.

Canon 276 §2, 4° sets down the obligation of clerics to "...make a retreat according to the prescriptions of particular law." If such a particular law is in force in a diocese, that particular law read in conjunction with c. 276 §2, 4° would at least oblige a pastor to make just and reasonable efforts to establish a schedule of duties which would allow time for each of the priests and deacons assigned to the parish to comply with the law.

Among the requirements of c. 277 §2 is that clerics be prudent about associations which could endanger their observance of continence or cause scandal for the faithful. Since c. 519 establishes that according to the norm of law a pastor carries out the duty of sanctification in the parish, it appears that a pastor would have a right and a duty to address with the cleric concerned any association which the pastor judged to violate c. 277 §2.

3.1.2 — Liturgy as worship

Sacrosanctum concilium, n. 10 explained:

> ...the liturgy is the summit toward which the activity of the Church is directed; it is also the font from which all her power flows. For the goal of apostolic endeavor is that all who are made sons of God by faith and baptism should come together to praise God in the midst of his Church, to take part in the Sacrifice and to eat the Lord's Supper.
> The liturgy, in its turn, moves the faithful filled with "the paschal sacraments" to be "one in holiness"; it prays that "they hold fast in their lives to what they have grasped by their faith."[8]

---

[8] *SC*, n. 10. English translation in FLANNERY, *Conciliar and Post Conciliar Documents*, p. 6.

There is an important catechetical element of liturgy, which was considered in the previous chapter,[9] but the core of liturgy is the freely offered direct adoration of God by the faithful, who are sustained by and actively participate in Christ's redemptive life and give witness to the world by the manner in which they live their own lives.

Sacrosanctum concilium, n. 5 taught:

> He [Christ the Lord] achieved his task [the redemption of mankind] principally by the paschal mystery of his blessed passion, resurrection from the dead and glorious ascension....[10]

The *Catechism of the Catholic Church* explains:

> The word "liturgy" originally meant a "public work" or a "service in the name of/on behalf of the people." In Christian tradition it means the participation of the People of God in "the work of God." Through the liturgy Christ, our redeemer and high priest, continues the work of our redemption in, with, and through his Church.[11]

Sacrosanctum concilium provided other salient factors:

---

[9] See *SC*, n. 9. English translation in FLANNERY, *Conciliar and Post Conciliar Documents*, p. 6: "The sacred liturgy does not exhaust the entire activity of the Church. Before men can come to the liturgy they must be called to faith and to conversion.... Therefore the Church announces the good tidings of salvation to those who do not believe, so that all men may know the one true God and Jesus Christ whom he has sent and be converted from their ways, doing penance. To believers also the Church must ever preach faith and penance; she must prepare them for the sacraments, teach them to observe all that Christ has commanded, and encourage them to engage in all the works of charity, piety and the apostolate, thus making it clear that Christ's faithful, though not of this world, are to be the lights of the world and are to glorify the Father before men."

[10] *SC* n. 5. Also see *Catholic Catechism*, p. 277, footnote 3.

[11] *Catholic Catechism*, n. 1069, p. 278. Also see cc. 840 and 899.

> ...it is through the liturgy especially that the faithful are enabled to express in their lives and manifest to others the mystery of Christ and the real nature of the true Church.[12]

In partial summary, the same document taught:

> The liturgy then is rightly seen as an exercise of the priestly office of Jesus Christ. It involves the presentation of man's sanctification under the guise of signs perceptible by the senses and its accomplishment in ways appropriate in each of these signs. In it full public worship is performed by the Mystical Body of Jesus Christ, that is, by the Head and his members.[13]

In the Catholic Church the confection and ministering of the seven sacraments is tightly interwoven with the liturgy. Liturgical worship, however, includes many prayers and religious ceremonies which are not directly related to the sacraments, e.g., praying the liturgy of the hours,[14] imparting or receiving blessings and reverently using the sacramentals of the Church.[15] Even the liturgy, however, does not include all prayer or encompass all things spiritual.

The spiritual life "...is not limited solely to participation in the liturgy," e.g., a Christian is also called upon to pray to God in secret; to pray without ceasing; all of the faithful "...must always carry around in their own bodies the dying of Jesus, so that the life also of Jesus may be made manifest in our mortal flesh";

---

[12] *SC*, n. 2. English translation in FLANNERY, *Conciliar and Post Conciliar Documents*, p. 1.

[13] *SC*, n. 7. English translation in FLANNERY, *Conciliar and Post Conciliar Documents*, pp. 4-5.

[14] Canons 1173-1175.

[15] Canons 1166-1172.

various kinds of popular Christian devotion are highly recommended.[16]

In considering the text of various canons then, it needs to be borne in mind that *sacrament* and *liturgy* are not interchangeable and that liturgical obligations and rights touch many more activities of the life of the Christian faithful than do rights and obligations related to the sacraments. It is also clear that the laity have a right to participate as actively and as fully as permissible in the celebration of the liturgy, because through baptism they truly share in their own way in the priesthood of Christ, and, therefore, they have a right to exercise the priesthood to the full extent of their sharing. It also appears to be a fair judgment that all who are responsible for liturgies need to take very seriously not only the validity and liceity of their celebrations, but also whether such celebrations achieve the goals of the Council and the Catechism presented above and echoed in the words of c. 528 §2 "[the pastor] is likewise to endeavor that they [the Christian faithful] are brought to... a knowing and active participation in the sacred liturgy," and reechoed in c. 899 §2 "...and all the faithful present [at the Eucharist], whether clergy or laity, participate together, in their own way, according to the diversity of orders and liturgical roles."[17] Canons 777, 2° and 898 also underline various obligations and rights respecting preparation for, and reception and worship of the Eucharist.

---

[16] *SC*, nn. 12-13. English translation in FLANNERY, *Conciliar and Post Conciliar Documents*, p. 7.

[17] Foreseeing a possible problem in this regard, the Second Vatican Council urged: "Yet it would be futile to entertain any hope of realizing this [full and active participation in the liturgy by all the people] unless pastors of souls, in the first place, themselves become fully imbued with the spirit and power of the liturgy and capable of giving instruction about it," *SC*, n. 14. English translation in FLANNERY, *Conciliar and Post Conciliar Documents*, pp. 7-8.

3.2 — THE PASTOR'S OBLIGATIONS AND RIGHTS WITH RESPECT TO THE ADMINISTRATION OF SACRAMENTS AND LITURGICAL MINISTRY: CC. 528 §2 AND 530

Canon 528 §2 concentrates almost exclusively on the obligations and rights of the pastor of a parish with respect to the sacraments, especially Holy Eucharist and Penance, leading the faithful to a knowing and active participation in the liturgy and being watchful that no abuses creep into the liturgy. The pastor is also to encourage the practice of family prayer.[18]

In considering the text of c. 528 §2 with respect to the Holy Eucharist as center of the assembly of the faithful, the two aspects of the Holy Eucharist as *Celebration* and as *Cult* need to be kept in mind.[19] Since the general obligations set down in c. 528 §2 with respect to the Holy Eucharist bind the pastor, he will need to attend carefully to other canons which, without specifically mentioning the pastor, provide instruction and directives with respect to the Holy Eucharist and liturgy. Canon 899 §§1-2 teaches rather than commands, but the pastor must follow, preach and vitalize those teachings by good example. Canon 899 §3 presents a general requirement which binds any priest celebrating the Eucharist, or involved in planning a Eucharist, but which, read together with c. 528 §2, binds the pastor to provide a suitable arrangement so that all who take part are led through "a devout celebration…" to "receive from it [the Eucharistic Sacrifice] the many fruits for which Christ the Lord instituted the Eucharistic Sacrifice."

---

[18] At the outset it is significant to note a difference in the expression of the obligations and rights of pastors in these canons. The 1917 Code has no *single* canon which corresponds to c. 528 §§1-2. Canon 528 §§1-2 presents a general, but not taxative, description of the task of the pastor of a parish with regard to catechetics and sanctification.

[19] Because these two aspects of the Holy Eucharist are so important, the Pontificia Comissio Codici Iuris Canonici Recognoscendo removed the word "celebratio" from the text "Eucharistica celebratio" in the first sentence of the 1980 *Schema* c. 362 §2, which with several additional revisions, has become c. 528 §2 of the 1983 Code of Canon Law. See *Communicationes*, 12 (1981), n. 2, p. 279.

Canon 528 §2 calls for the pastor "to work to see to it that the Christian faithful frequently approach…" the Eucharist and Penance. One element of encouraging such an approach is the availability of the pastor, parochial vicars, deacons or other properly authorized ministers.[20] Canon 843 §1 directs: "The sacred ministers cannot refuse the sacraments to those who ask for them at appropriate times, are properly disposed and are not prohibited by law from receiving them."[21] Canon 918 establishes that: "the Eucharist should be administered outside of Mass to those who request it for a just cause…."[22] Canon 986 §1 requires:

> All to whom the care of souls is committed by reason of an office are obliged to provide that the confessions of the faithful entrusted to their care be heard when they reasonably ask to be heard and that the opportunity be given to them to come to individual confession on days and hours set for their convenience.

Also, in scheduling celebrations of Mass, the pastor must keep in mind the teaching of c. 1246 §1: "Sunday is the day on which the paschal mystery is celebrated in the light of the apos-

---

[20] A.S. Sánchez-Gil, "Parroquias y párrocos," Commentary on cc. 515-544, in *Comentario exegético*, vol. II/2, p. 1262, b), and footnote 4.

[21] Canon 467 of the 1917 Code required that the pastor was to administer the sacraments to the faithful "quoties legitime petant…," that is "as often as the faithful legitimately ask for them." The meaning of "legitimately" had to be sought from other canons, older Church documents and from commentaries. Canon 843 §1 implicitly calls on the sacred minister to judge (objectively and justly, of course) the appropriateness of the time of a request and whether the person requesting the sacraments is properly disposed. In addition, cc. 915, 1007 and a number of canons of Book VI establish specific legal prohibitions from receiving the sacraments.

[22] The term "just cause" is not defined in the Code. The words themselves and the circumstances in which the canons employ them suggest that a just cause consists of the objective facts in a specific situation, which facts, considered logically in the light of general moral and canonical principles and excluding arbitrariness or caprice, lead to a reasonable decision about the application of a particular law in that specific situation, which decision is also capable of consistent application in similar circumstances.

tolic tradition and is to be observed as the foremost holy day of obligation in the universal Church." That fact together with c. 1247's expression of the obligation of all to participate in Mass on Sundays and holy days of obligation, implicitly calls on the pastor to assist the faithful in every reasonable way by his scheduling of such celebrations.[23]

With respect to the cultic worship of the Eucharist within the parish assembly, a pastor will need to attend carefully to cc. 934 §§1-2, 937, 938 especially §§1-2, 940, 1214 and 1221 which concern reservation of, and access of the faithful to the Blessed Sacrament. In addition, c. 941 1§§-2 through 944 §§1-2 regulate exposition and benediction of the Blessed Sacrament.

Canon 528 §2 also calls on the pastor "to endeavor that they [the faithful] are brought to the practice of family prayer...." The practice of family prayer is a very broad concept. At the very least a pastor is obliged to take some form of meaningful action. If the pastor has little or no background in family prayer, he needs through prayer and study to come to some objectively based personal understanding of the practice of family prayer and then actively to lead his parishioners toward that goal.

Canon 530, in a numbered list of seven entries, established that twelve liturgical ceremonies are especially *entrusted* (Latin *"commissae"*) to the pastor of a parish.[24] A measure of the seriousness and juridic import of the "entrusting" involved can be inferred from the fact that in c. 515 the same Latin verb *"committo"* is used to indicate the entrusting of the complete pastoral care of a parish, in c. 519 the same verb is used to describe the juridic relationship of a parish to its pastor and in c.

---

[23] It is also possible, as envisioned in c. 1248 §2, that a parish pastor may be bound by particular law of a diocesan bishop in connection with making some arrangements for needs of the faithful who because of a lack of a priest or other serious reason cannot participate in the celebration of the Eucharist.

[24] The *Fontes* for c. 530 list three canons from the 1917 *Codex iuris canonici*: c. 462, which presented a similar but not identical list of liturgical celebrations *reserved* to the pastor; c. 466 §1, which concisely stated the pastor's obligation to offer the *Missa pro populo*, and 938 §2 which treated of the minister of "Extreme Unction."

534 §§1-2 it details the entrusting of the people of a parish to the pastor.

The text of c. 530 imposes on the pastor clear obligations and confers on him certain rights to celebrate the *entrusted* liturgical services for the faithful as necessary and/or beneficial to their spiritual lives.[25] Indeed, c. 515 entrusts "the pastoral care of the parish...," c. 519 outlines several general obligations, one of which is: "he carries out for his community the duties of... sanctifying...," and c. 528 §2 develops the description of works of sanctification somewhat further.

The text of c. 530 identifies what is entrusted to the pastor as "functions." Nevertheless, pointing out that each of the *functions* listed is, in fact, a liturgical celebration, one commentator holds that a preferable translation in his language, French, would be *"célébration* liturgique."[26] Once recognized as liturgical celebrations, c. 837 §1, which the commentator references, offers an additional aspect to understanding c. 530. Canon 837 §1 states:

> Liturgical actions are not private actions but celebrations of the Church itself... therefore liturgical actions pertain to the whole body of the Church and manifest and affect it, but they affect the individual members of the Church in different ways according to the diversity of orders, functions and actual participation.

From this the commentator then concludes:

> They [these terminological considerations] open up different perspectives: if these *functions* are not *"administered"* by a pastor but celebrated by the community —

---

[25] The celebration of the liturgical actions enumerated are special obligations and concerns of the pastor, "it is he who has the major responsibility to ensure that they are fulfilled." G. READ, "Parishes, Parish Priests and Assistant Priests," Commentary on cc. 515-552, in *Letter & Spirit*, n. 1052, p. 294. See also JANICKI, "Parishes, Pastors and Parochial Vicars," in *CLSA Commentary*, p. 427.

[26] BORRAS, *Les communautés paroissiales*, p. 136.

the *Church* active subject of the liturgy — it seems necessary to consider qualifying the specific function, the pastor's own proper task, in terms of his presiding at the liturgical actions.[27]

Understood in that way, the initial line of c. 530 would mean: "Presiding at the following liturgical celebrations is especially entrusted to the pastor." In such a context the pastor's more precise obligation/right would be understood as: to participate as presider, with other members of the community of the faithful, in carrying out together certain liturgical celebrations. The pastor would be seen less as solely in charge of providing certain services for the faithful and more as a necessary leader and fellow sharer in those liturgies.[28]

Another commentary notes that in the preparation of the 1983 Code of Canon Law, the Commission judged that it was suitable to stress the special obligation or responsibility of the pastor in regard to the ceremonies now listed in the text of c. 530. The commentator explains:

> Therefore, in its new canonical formulation the ceremonies especially entrusted to the pastor lose the character of personal and exclusive rights and come to be considered as ceremonies which the pastor, in virtue of his special *canonical responsibility* ought always to carry out personally when that may be possible; otherwise the ceremonies should at least be carried out under his direct supervision and with his consent. As a result it does not appear suitable that the pastor, without a just cause, habitually entrust to other priests the carrying out of those

---

[27] BORRAS, *Les communautés paroissiales*, p. 136. "Elles ouvrent d'autres perspectives: si ces *functiones* ne sont pas 'administrées' par un curé mais célébrées par la communauté — l'*ecclesia* sujet actif de la liturgie — ne faut-il pas songer à qualifier la fonction spécifique, *munus peculiare*, du curé en termes de présidence des actions liturgiques."

[28] Such a view would be solidly in line with the teachings of the Second Vatican Council on the nature of the pastor's ministry and the pastor's sharing in Jesus' priestly ministry.

ceremonies that are proper to his pastoral service and that manifest the particular relationship which exists between the parochial community — and each one of the faithful — and its own pastor.[29]

The phrases "when that may be possible" and "a just cause" are likely to have many and varied legitimate applications in practice throughout the world in parishes with different numbers of parishioners, cultures, civil jurisdictions and communication and transportation systems. The point, however, is the same everywhere; the pastor must be making a personal, good-faith effort to provide all parochial services, and especially those detailed in c. 530, for the faithful, doing what he can himself and exercising his rights implied in c. 530 to lead, delegate, authorize and supervise others, clerics and laity who assist him in disparate ways.

Still another commentary, while not mentioning an obligation of the pastor personally to celebrate the liturgies specified in c. 530 whenever possible, agrees that others need the pastor's consent to conduct those liturgies:

...it is clear that both other priests and the faithful have an obligation to see that these functions are not per-

---

[29] SÁNCHEZ-GIL, "Parroquias y párrocos," in *Comentario exegético*, vol. II/2, n. 2, p. 1265: "Por tanto en su nueva formulación canónica las funciones encomendadas especialmente al párroco pierden el carácter de derechos personales y exclusivos del párroco, y pasan a ser consideradas como funciones que el párroco, en virtud de su especial *responsabilidad canónica*, debe ejercer personalmente siempre que sea posible; en otro caso, deben ser realizadas al menos bajo su directa vigilancia y de acuerdo con él. En consecuencia, no parece conveniente que el párroco, sin una justa causa, encargue de manera habitual a otros sacerdotes el cumplimiento de aquellas functiones que son propias de su servicio pastoral y que manifestan la particular relación qui existe entre la comunidad parroquial — y cada uno de sus fieles — y su pastor propio." See also BORRAS, *Les communautés paroissiales*, p. 137. Borras makes no mention of a "special canonical responsibility" requiring the pastor personally to celebrate the liturgies mentioned in c. 530. He does, however, provide a concise theological description of how the pastor's administration of the sacrament of Baptism, celebration of the more solemn Eucharistic liturgy and presiding at celebrations of the sacrament of Matrimony give witness liturgically to the scope of the office of pastor of a parish and the significance of its full pastoral burden on behalf of the parish community.

formed at least for their canonical liceity without the consent of the parish priest, which is sometimes presumed.[30]

The pastor's right that no one perform any liturgy listed in c. 530 without at least his presumed permission is implied in c. 530's term "especially entrusted." If various specific activities are especially entrusted to some one person, that person must know, and be in a position to direct and/or reject, what is being planned in relation to those activities. Balancing the pastor's right in this regard, the rights of the faithful and the urgency of the circumstances, requires that the individual assuming the pastor's permission must act for a just cause and in a reasonable and objective manner and in accord with c. 223 §§1-2.[31] The person making the decision must also be attentive to the difference between needing permission and needing delegation; acting without the pastor's permission could result in canonical illiceity, acting without due delegation could result in an invalid act.[32]

---

[30] J. CALVO, "Parishes, Parish Priests and Assistant Priests," Commentary on cc. 515-552, in Code Annotated, p. 390. Also see c. 1114 which makes such permission a requirement, if possible, for liceity when assisting at a marriage.

[31] It is worth noting that although c. 530, 3° especially entrusts to parish pastors the administration of the sacrament of Anointing of the Sick, c. 1003 §2 establishes that the administration of the sacrament of Anointing of the Sick is an *obligation* and concomitant *right* of all priests to whom the care of souls has been entrusted. Canon 530, °3 similarly entrusts the administration of Viaticum to the pastor, while c. 911 §1 mentions that the holders of three other ecclesiastical offices also have the right and duty to administer Viaticum, and c. 911 §2 indicates that in a case of necessity or with at least the presumed permission of the pastor any other priest or other minister of Holy Communion must administer Holy Viaticum. Much the same is true with respect to "the administration of the sacrament of Confirmation to those who are in danger of death." That administration is especially entrusted to the pastor by c. 530, °2, but the faculty to do the same is given by the law itself to any priest as declared in c. 883, °3. In addition, c. 857 §2 directs: "As a rule adults are to be baptized in their own parish church and infants in the parish church proper to their parents...," but provides that a simple "just cause" allows a different venue. The precise meaning of the term "especially entrusted," therefore, seems to be less than entirely clear.

[32] Canon 558 prohibits rectors from performing the parochial functions mentioned in c. 530 unless the pastor of the parish consents, and, when necessary, delegates the rector.

3.2.1 — Administration of the Sacraments

Canon 213 declares that the Christian faithful have a right to receive the sacraments, c. 848 requires the ministers of the sacraments not to ask for more than "the offering defined by competent authority..." and warns such ministers to be careful that no one is "deprived of the help of the sacraments because of their poverty." Canon 529 §1 requires among other tasks that the pastor should both "strive to come to know the faithful..." and "make a special effort to seek out the poor." The pastor of a parish, however, may also be the person who sets stole fee and stipend policies, especially in a diocese which has no regulations about the subject, or has only rather general and unspecific directives. It would appear that an obligation arises from these canons for a parish pastor to be alert and sensitive to the needs which the poor may encounter in this regard — especially to any who may be putting off the sacrament of Baptism or Confirmation for a child or Marriage for an adult because they cannot afford the usual offering and are too embarrassed — or even ashamed — to ask for help.

Canon 847 §1 regulates the kind of oil to be used in administering the sacraments and the required liturgical preparation of that oil.[33] Canon 847 §2 requires the pastor to obtain the sacred oils from his own bishop and also to keep them with care and in a manner that is suitable. The pastor's two custodial ob-

---

[33] Canon 999, º2, referenced in c. 847 §1, provides an exception to the requirement that a bishop bless the sacred oils to be used in the administration of sacraments: in case of necessity the oil for the Anointing of the Sick may be blessed by any priest, but only in the course of celebrating the sacrament. Also, another authoritative document still in force established, "...in the case of the baptism of adults, priests have the faculty to bless [the oil of catechumens] before the anointing at the designated stage of the catechumenate," SACRA CONGREGATIO PRO CULTU DIVINO, *Order of Blessing the Oils of Catechumens and of the Sick, and of Confecting Chrism, Ordo benedicendi oleum catechumenorum et infirmorum et conficiendi chrisma*, December 3, 1970, in AAS, 63 (1971), pp. 728-730, here at n. 7, p. 729. English translation in INTERNATIONAL COMMISSION ON ENGLISH IN THE LITURGY, *Documents on the Liturgy 1963-1979, Conciliar, Papal and Curial Texts*, Collegeville, MN: Liturgical Press, 1982, n. 3867, pp. 1190-1191, here at 1191.

ligations are clear from the text of c. 847 §2.[34] In addition, c. 847 §1 also implies an obligation of the pastor of a parish to arrange that the most recently blessed oils be transported from his bishop to his parish in a timely and safe manner.

3.2.2 — The Sacrament of Baptism

Canon 850 requires that Baptism be administered according to the prescribed liturgical order, except for cases of necessity. That does not place any more obligation on the pastor than on others, but it adds specificity to the general obligation of c. 528 §2 that the pastor guard against liturgical abuses entering into the liturgy as celebrated in his parish.

The second clause of c. 851, 2° enjoins:

> … personally or through others the pastor is to see to it that the parents are properly formed by pastoral direction and by common prayer, gathering several families together and where possible visiting them.

This clause of the canon explicitly expresses a moderately detailed obligation of a pastor of a parish to be sure that the parents of infants to be baptized are themselves properly formed. It should be noted that such formation would include not only reviewing doctrine or presenting other information to the parents, but also prayer together and some community formation, presumably around the parents' common interests, e.g. their infants, their role as parents, their faith, etc. One of the *fontes*, or sources, upon which the second clause of c. 851, 2° is based, is *Pastoralis actio*, the 1980 Instruction of the Sacred Congregation

---

[34] Although c. 847 §2 declares the pastor's obligation with respect to custody of the holy oils, c. 1003 §3 also provides: "Every priest is allowed to carry blessed oil with him so that he can administer the sacrament of the anointing of the sick in case of necessity."

for the Doctrine of the Faith on infant baptism.[35] The text of n. 29 of that document envisages that the parents will contact the pastor before the infant is born; also a number of meetings would seem to be required to accomplish the various activities described in the Instruction and in the second clause of c. 851, 2°.

Canon 855 requires that the name given (or taken by an adult) in baptism is not to be "...foreign to a Christian mentality." The obligation involved specifically touches the parents, sponsors and the pastor in that order, and implicitly the person being baptized if he or she is an adult and the person administering the baptism even if a non-pastor. With respect to a pastor's obligations this canon differs in two ways from c. 761 of the 1917 Code. First, c. 855 indicates that the obligation is not solely or even primarily that of the pastor; second c. 855 does not require that a saint's name be added and recorded in the baptismal register along with the parent's choice of a name if that name is "...foreign to a Christian mentality." The parish pastor has an explicit general obligation to try to dissuade parents, sponsors, etc., from insisting on unacceptable names of the sort described.

Nevertheless, nothing in c. 855 calls for a refusal to administer the sacrament of Baptism, an extremely important sacrament, even if the parents, sponsors, etc., do not agree to the use of an acceptable name. It would be important, however, to learn the reason for insistence on an unacceptable name. If the parents and/or sponsors reveal a mindset entirely foreign to a Christian mentality, then perhaps the "founded hope" required by c. 868 §1, 2° for a licit administration of infant baptism may be lacking. A middle ground solution may also be found, since a person baptized in the name of the Father, the Son and the Holy Spirit receives his or her *name in the Church* which need not have the same function or the juridical effects proper to a

---

[35] Sacra Congregatio pro Doctrina Fidei, Instruction on Infant Baptism *Pastoralis actio*, October 20, 1980, in *AAS*, 82 (1980), pp. 1137-1156, here at n. 29, pp. 1151-1152. English translation in Flannery, *More Postconciliar Documents*, p. 112.

civil name.[36] The name given at baptism does not have to be the same as the given name in a civil record, nor the only name by which a person is known.

According to c. 858 §2, a pastor has a right to be heard by the local ordinary, before a decision is made by the latter with respect to permitting a baptismal font in another church or oratory in the parish. In view of c. 127 §2, 2°, such permission given without the pastor having been heard is invalid. Along with the explicit right to be heard, there is also an implicit obligation that the pastor base his comments regarding the *convenience* (*commoditatem*) of the faithful on the facts in the situation and a concern for the spiritual benefit of his parishioners.

Canon 861 §2 requires: "…shepherds of souls, … especially the pastor, are to be concerned that the faithful be instructed in the correct manner of baptizing." The obligation for the pastor is explicit and precise; clearly, it is also an obligation the fulfillment of which may be shared with others.

Pastors are reminded by c. 862 that outside of their own territory they are not to baptize anyone, even their own subjects, unless they have the required permission or in a case of necessity. Hence they have an obligation to refrain from such baptisms, but still in a case of necessity they have a duty and a concomitant right to baptize.

Canon 867 implies a right of parish pastors that "as soon as possible after the birth or even before it parents are to go to the pastor to request the sacrament for their child and to be prepared for it properly."[37] There is also an implication that the

---

[36] M. BLANCO, "Sacramento del bautismo," Commentary on cc. 849-878, in *Comentario exegético*, vol. III/1, pp. 461-462. See also, S. WOYWOD and C. SMITH, *A Practical Commentary on the New Code of Canon Law*, New York: Joseph F. Wagner, 1952, p. 387.

[37] The proper preparation of parents for the baptism of their children is beyond the scope of this book. It is worth noting, however, that many theoretical and practical questions about the subject and a clearer understanding of the background of the canons on Baptism, cc. 849-878, can be found in the Instruction, *Pastoralis actio*, in *AAS*, 82 (1980), pp. 1137-1156. English translation in FLANNERY, *More Postconciliar Documents*, pp. 103-115.

pastor is entitled to expect that the parents will participate actively in a parish program designed to prepare the parents for the liturgy and the responsibilities which the parents are expected to live out in raising their child as an active Catholic.

Canon 874 §§1-2 concern qualifications for a person to be admitted to the role of baptismal sponsor. Canon 874 §1, 1° places the pastor fourth in line of those who have the right to designate a sponsor. The right is explicit, but it does not seem that the circumstances required for its exercise would be fulfilled very often. A right to grant an exception, under certain circumstances, to the requirement that the sponsors have at least passed their 16th birthday, is given to the pastor by c. 874 §1, 2°. The pastor can give such an exception if the diocesan bishop has not established a different age and if the pastor judges there is a just cause for an exception.[38]

3.2.3 — The Sacrament of Confirmation

Canon 883, 3°, gives the pastor the faculty and therefore the obligation and right to administer the sacrament of Confirmation to those in danger of death and c. 530, 2° lists that liturgical ceremony among those especially entrusted to the pastor. In presenting the matter in that particular way the Church appears to be implying a preference that if the circumstances arise, the pastor of a parish should as a rule administer the sacrament of Confirmation himself rather than sending another priest, even though any priest has the same faculty in the same circumstances.

---

[38] Canon 893 §1 requires that to serve as a sponsor at Confirmation a person must fulfill the conditions listed in c. 874. The conditions of c. 874 allow the pastor to appoint a sponsor if others have failed to do so and to waive the minimum age of 16 for a just cause. Since c. 893 §1 simply accepts c. 874 as normative, the pastor would enjoy those same rights with regard to confirmation sponsors as he does to baptismal sponsors.

3.2.4 — The Sacrament of the Eucharist

With respect to the Eucharist four rather separate matters are addressed in the canons which deal with the obligations and rights of the pastor of a parish. The first is the obligation to offer the *Missa pro populo* — a weekly and sometimes more frequent Mass for the people of the parish. Canon 534 §1 legislates: "the pastor is obliged to apply Mass for the people entrusted to him each Sunday and holy day of obligation within the diocese." The obligation begins after the pastor has taken possession of the parish. If legitimately prevented, "he is to apply the Mass on these same days through another priest or he himself is to apply it on other days." The pastor cannot be freed from this obligation because of both c. 199, 3°, which rules out prescription, and c. 534 §3, which directs that he "is to apply as many Masses for his people as he has missed as soon as possible." Thus, the obligation to apply each Mass lasts until it has been individually satisfied — up to the end of the total obligation. Canon 534 §2 specifies that a pastor who is caring "for several parishes is obliged to apply only one Mass for all the people entrusted to him on those days."

Another concern addressed by these canons involves an interesting contrast which exists between c. 903 concerning even an unknown priest who wishes to celebrate the Eucharist and c. 764 which legislates about priests or deacons who wish to preach. Unless the use of the faculties of those who wish to preach is restricted in one way or another, they may preach "with at least the presumed consent of the rector." Canon 903 requires that even an unknown priest may be allowed to celebrate the Eucharist if "it can be prudently judged that the priest is not prevented from celebrating." In the case of preaching, the preacher himself could be the one who presumes the consent of the rector. Canon 903, however, appears to require that someone else, rather than the priest who wishes to celebrate, is to make a prudent judgment about allowing the priest to do so. Adding another important element to the question of whether to allow the unknown priest to celebrate, c. 904 implicitly affirms that priests have a right to celebrate the Eucharist daily by strongly recommending that priests do so, "...even if the faithful cannot be present." Who, then is to make that prudent judgment?

The question is easy enough to answer up to a point. If the pastor, or some other priest or deacon is at the church or nearby at the parish rectory or school one of them could make the required prudent decision.[39] However, where a priest shortage exists and more and more parishes are becoming *one priest parishes*, it seems clear that diocesan guidelines should be drawn up and be available in each rectory to address this point. If there are no diocesan guidelines, the pastor might be well advised to arrive at a parish policy on the question. Clearly, it would also be important for a traveling priest to become more careful about having "a letter of recommendation issued by his ordinary or superior within a year...," which is also mentioned in c. 903.

Holy Viaticum is another of the matters treated by the canons under study. Just as it was the subject of c. 530, 3°, the Holy Eucharist as Viaticum is the focus of c. 911 §§1-2. Canon 911 §1 attributes to the pastor the obligation and right of ministering Viaticum, but paragraph one mentions other ecclesiastical offices whose incumbents have the same obligation and right. Canon 911 §2 treats of Viaticum in a case of necessity, and declares that with at least the presumed permission of the pastor, any other minister of the Eucharist must provide Viaticum. It may be noted that the pastor's obligation and right in the ministration of Vi-

---

[39] If a priest, unknown to the parish staff, is known by a member of the parish who vouches for him, it would be prudent to allow him to celebrate. In addition, it might be argued that if the absent pastor had entrusted the tabernacle key to someone, he regarded that person as prudent enough to make decisions about the protection and distribution of the Eucharist, and, by extension, prudent enough to decide about allowing an unknown priest to celebrate. Another possible prudent approach in the case of an unknown priest would appear to be to contact the dean of the area, the pastor, priest or deacon of a nearby parish or the diocesan Chancery Office, so that the visitor would at least have a telephone conversation with some local member of the clergy, who could then advise the staff and the faithful on hand at the parish.

aticum is the first mentioned in c. 911 §1 and is especially entrusted to the pastor in c. 530, 3°; thus there appears to be at least a clear canonical preference that the pastor himself fulfill this responsibility whenever possible.

A concern about the pastor's obligation and right with respect to first reception of the Eucharist is also raised by the canons considered here. The final clause of c. 914 directs: "It is also for the pastor to be vigilant lest any children come to the Holy Banquet who have not reached the use of reason or whom he judges are not sufficiently disposed." In reaching a decision in such circumstances a pastor would need to consider c. 97 §2 which establishes that a person is presumed to have reached the use of reason by the completion of his or her seventh birthday. Although any canonical presumption must yield to evidence to the contrary, the burden of proof is borne by the person who would hold in any given case that a particular seven year old child does not possess the use of reason. With respect to a judgment about either use of reason or proper disposition (or both) it would also be necessary to consider c. 220 about a person's rights to a good reputation and to privacy and c. 223 §§1-2 with respect to conflicting rights. Any decision about use of reason or sufficient disposition must be based on objective facts. Prudence dictates that such a decision should be reviewed with the parents or guardians of the child involved before the child or others are informed of it.

3.2.5 — The Sacrament of Penance

The first clause of the same c. 914 declares that parents and those who take their place have the *primary* obligation to see to it that children who have reached the use of reason be correctly prepared to receive sacramental confession. Both cc. 914 and 777, 2° specifically state the pastor's obligation to prepare children to receive the sacrament of Penance. In addition, the direction of c. 914 that the pastor is "to be vigilant lest any children come to the Holy Banquet who have not reached the use of reason," implies that the pastor has an obligation to exercise the same care to be sure that children do not approach the sacrament of penance who have not attained the use of reason.

One commentary observes:

> The parish priest has a greater responsibility, but only with regard to the negative function of preventing the child from coming to first communion without adequate preparation and, having made their sacramental confession....[40]

In addition to the requirements of c. 914, the pastor is bound explicitly to the positive function called for in c. 528 §2: the pastor "is to work to see to it that the Christian faithful are nourished through a devout celebration of the sacraments." A devout celebration must include spiritual preparation as well as intellectual preparation.[41] In the case of children who are preparing to begin to make use of the sacrament of Penance as an important element of their spiritual lives and growth, accurate spiritual preparation would appear to be very important, and therefore, a pressing obligation.

---

[40] A. Marzoa, "The Blessed Eucharist," Commentary on cc. 897-958, in *Code Annotated*, pp. 587-588. The quote continues "...he [the pastor] must accept the child, however, when the parents (who have the primary obligation and right, in our opinion, that of the parish priest being subsidiary) present a child as being sufficiently prepared." Such a view seems erroneous to us. The annotator appears to hold that the order of obligation for preparing the child for the reception of the sacraments expressed in the first clause of c. 914, which order is based on the natural parent-child relationship, also applies to the second clause of c. 914, which declares the responsibility of the pastor to protect the sacredness and dignity of the sacrament, and is based on an entirely different relationship, that of the pastor, leader and guardian of liturgical worship, to the sacraments. Also, the term "negative function" seems somewhat confusing. The function of the pastor is, indeed, to fulfill his positive obligation to take positive action to prevent something which the law requires to be avoided, i.e., the approach to Reconciliation and Holy Eucharist by unprepared or ill disposed children.

[41] The pastor is bound by cc. 528 §1, 773, 776, 777, 1° and 2° to provide adequate catechetical instruction and formation in preparation for reception of the sacraments.

Canon 968 §1 declares that the faculty of the pastor of a parish to hear confessions of persons within his jurisdiction comes to him from this law itself in virtue of his office as pastor of a parish. In virtue of his office then, the pastor enjoys the faculty of hearing confessions *habitually*. Therefore then, in accord with c. 967 §2, he can hear confessions everywhere, unless in a particular case the local ordinary denies him the right.[42]

3.2.6 — The Sacrament of the Anointing of the Sick

Pastors are bound by c. 1001: "Pastors of souls and persons who are close to the sick are to see to it that they are supported by this sacrament at an appropriate time." For pastors this canon echos c. 529 §1: "...with a generous love he is to help the sick, particularly those close to death, refreshing them solicitously with the sacraments and commending their souls to God...." The obligation of the pastor is not simply to anoint the sick but to make sure that (a) the sick are supported by this sacrament, and (b) at an appropriate time. The emphasis is on early reception of the sacrament of the Anointing of the Sick so the sacrament's spiritual and physical effects may assist the seriously ill person as soon as possible and at a time when the sick person can actively participate in the liturgy. The Second Vatican Council taught:

> "Anointing of the Sick" is not a sacrament for those only who are at the point of death. Hence, as soon as any one of the faithful begins to be in danger of death from sick-

---

[42] Many other priests whose faculty to hear confessions does not come to them in virtue of an office they hold may also have the faculty to hear confessions everywhere, but for different canonical reasons. See c. 967 §2.

ness or old age, the fitting time for him to receive this sacrament has certainly already arrived."[43]

3.2.7 — The Sacrament of Matrimony

With respect to the spiritual and sanctifying aspects of the sacrament of Matrimony, c. 1063, 2°, 3° and 4° set out several general obligations of the pastor directly and the members of his parish community indirectly. The obligations imposed by c. 1063 have the same canonical binding force as most other canons which place obligations on the pastor but do not contain any special wording that expresses a particular gravity or seriousness of the obligation. Nevertheless, the importance of marriage and family to the common good of all considered together with the number of failed marriages and broken homes throughout the world, render the fulfillment of the obligations of c. 1063 an extremely important matter in practice.

The pastor is obliged by c. 1063 to lead his own parish community to provide marriage preparation so that the couple "may be predisposed toward the holiness and duties of their new state."[44] The pastor and community are also to help the couple to have "...a fruitful liturgical celebration of marriage... the spouses signify and share in that mystery of unity and of fruitful love that exists between Christ and the Church."[45] A third

---

[43] *SC*, n. 73. English translation in Flannery, *Conciliar and Post Conciliar Documents*, p. 22. Also see with respect to this sacrament *Ecclesiae de mysterio*, art. 9, n.° 1, especially: "In using sacramentals, the non-ordained faithful should ensure that they are in no way regarded as sacraments whose administration is proper and exclusive to the Bishop and to the priest. Since they are not priests in no instance may the non-ordained perform anointings either with Oil of the Sick or any other oil," English translation *Certain Questions Regarding Collaboration*, p. 20.

[44] Canon 1063, 2°.

[45] Canon 1063, 3°.

element of the obligation shared by pastor and community is to assist those already married to faithfully maintain and protect their marital covenant and "day by day… lead holier and fuller lives in their families."[46] Canon 1128 imposes an even more detailed obligation on local ordinaries and other pastors "to see to it that the Catholic spouse and the children born of a mixed marriage do not lack spiritual assistance in fulfilling their obligations and are to aid the spouses in fostering the unity of conjugal and family life."[47]

The obligations and the goals outlined are extremely challenging and certainly the pastor cannot accomplish them alone, nor are they his alone, but extend to the whole parish community and require its dedicated work. However, as serious and important as this work is, one commentary calls attention to a statement of Pope John Paul II concerning marriage preparation:

> Although one must not underestimate the necessity and obligation of the immediate preparation for marriage… nevertheless such preparation must always be set forth and put into practice in such a way that omitting it [immediate marriage preparation] is not an impediment to the celebration of marriage.[48]

---

[46] Canon 1063, 4°.

[47] Members of the community must also work with the pastor as described in cc. 1069, 1070 and 1128. Canon 1069 requires all members of the faithful to reveal to the pastor or the local ordinary any impediments they know of before a marriage is to be celebrated; the pastor has a right that the faithful act as directed. Canon 1070 requires that if someone other than the pastor has conducted the pre-nuptial investigation, that person is to notify the pastor of the results as soon as possible.

[48] J. Fornés, "Pastoral Care and Prerequisites for the Celebration of Marriage," Commentary on cc. 1063-1072, in *Code Annotated*, p. 664, quotes John Paul II, Apostolic exhortation, The Christian Family in the Modern World *Familiaris consortio*, November 22, 1981, in *AAS*, 74 (1982), pp. 81-191, here at n. 66, p. 159. English translation in Flannery, *More Postconciliar Documents*, p. 871.

The preparation and sustaining programs must exist, but the couples need to be attracted to the programs by the subject matter and the manner, both formal and informal, in which material is presented and personal experiences and prayer are shared. Simple failure to attend such programs cannot become a reason for refusing the celebration of a wedding.

Before assisting at a marriage pastors are obliged by c. 1067, to know that the norms set by the national conference of bishops concerning required pre-nuptial investigations "have been diligently observed."[49] Although pastors are specified, the importance of the matter implies that anyone assisting at a marriage as the official representative of the Church would be subject to the same requirement.

Canon 1105 §2 concerns marriages entered by proxy. According to 1105 §2, the mandate given by one of the spouses-to-be to the proxy who will represent him or her in giving matrimonial consent at the wedding ceremony is valid only if signed by the pastor or the local ordinary where the mandate was issued. It would seem that there is also an implied obligation that the pastor or local ordinary be sure that the person giving the mandate is free to marry, has been properly prepared for marriage and is acting with physical and psychological freedom in giving the mandate.

Canon 1106 obliges a pastor to refrain from assisting at a marriage which requires the services of a translator unless he is convinced of the translator's trustworthiness. By itself canon

---

[49] Texts of the norms issued by several national conferences of bishops are available in *Code Annotated*, Appendix III, "Complementary Norms to the Code Promulgated by English-Language Conferences of Bishops," pp. 1306, 1337-1414. Some general observations with respect to the approaches open to episcopal conferences by c. 1067, and some of the actions taken by the Episcopal Conference of Spain are provided by T. RINCÓN-PÉREZ, "Preparación a la celebración del matrimonio: Caput I," Commentary on cc. 1063-1072, in *Comentario exegético*, vol. III/2, pp. 1118-1120.

1106 is clear enough, but it should be kept in mind that a pastor asked to assist at such a marriage still has an obligation, despite the language problem, to be sure that there has been a proper pre-marriage investigation and spiritual and psychological preparation of the couple.

Canons 1108 through 1111 organize many aspects of the celebration of marriages of the faithful. These canons undeniably involve administrative aspects of the obligations and rights of pastors of parishes, and as such might be treated in the next chapter. However, in practice these canons also affect those who in particular will assist at and have an official ecclesiastical role in the liturgical celebration of marriage of two specific people. In addition, brides and grooms have rights of their own and perhaps also personal preferences in the particular celebration at which they are to administer the sacrament of marriage to one another. Because the pastor's authority to witness marriages and the delegation of others to do so are such important factors in the liturgical celebration of the sacrament of marriage, treatment of those elements seems best situated here within a consideration of the regular, day to day celebration of the sacramental aspects of parish life. The exceptional powers to dispense from Church laws given to the pastor and others for marriages in extraordinary circumstances are considered in the following chapter.

In virtue of their offices local ordinaries, local pastors, *personal* ordinaries and *personal* pastors have the authority to validly assist at marriages under specified circumstances. The circumstances which affect local ordinaries and local pastors are detailed in c. 1109; c. 1110 identifies the circumstances which apply to *personal* ordinaries and *personal* pastors. In accord with c. 1109, to assist at marriages validly in virtue of their office local ordinaries and local pastors must be acting within the boundaries of their territory and at least one of the contractants must be of the Latin rite. The same canon also stipulates that local ordinaries and local pastors cannot validly assist at marriages "if by *sentence* or *decree* they have been excommunicated, placed under interdict or suspended from office,[50] or if they have been *declared* to be such."[51]

Canon 1110 regulates the right of ordinaries who are *personal*, that is not local, ordinaries and of *personal* pastors to assist at marriages. A *personal pastor* is a pastor of a *personal parish*, as described in the second section of c. 518. Membership in a *personal parish* is open to persons united by some principle other than regular geographic boundaries, e.g., a campus parish, a particular rite, a parish open to all who speak a particular language or are of a particular nationality, a military ordinariate, etc. Canon 1110 directs: "In virtue of their office and within the limits of their jurisdiction an ordinary and a personal pastor val-

---

[50] Excommunication, interdict and suspension are all *censures* (cc. 1331-1335). In some cases a particular censure is attached to the *performance* of a particular act. It is then referred to as an automatically incurred censure and the term *latae sententiae — the sentence having been carried [by the act]*, is used to describe it. When a person performs an act to which an automatic penalty is attached, it is possible that no one else may know that the guilty party has incurred a censure. An automatic penalty may later be *declared*, i.e., the fact that a person has incurred a censure is stated in a *decree* by a competent ecclesiastical authority. Censures may also be called for or allowed by specific laws as due and proper *if and when* a *judicial procedure*, which results in a *sentence*, or an *administrative procedure*, which results in a *decree* has found someone guilty of particular wrongdoing. Censures applied under those conditions are said to be *ferendae sententiae — a sentence which is to be imposed*. Canon 1109 legislates that the local ordinary and the pastor excommunicated, interdicted or suspended by either sentence or decree, or declared to be such cannot validly assist at marriages.

Even without c. 1109, anyone who has been excommunicated or placed under interdiction by a *sentence* or a *decree* would *invalidly* place acts of governance (c. 1331 §2, 2°) and, therefore, cannot assist at a marriage, or delegate anyone else to do so. However, in the case of a suspension imposed by a *sentence* or a *decree*, persons thus suspended can still *validly* place acts of governance, *unless* a law or precept directs that they are unable *validly* to place such acts. In accord with c. 1333 §2, c. 1109 establishes the *invalidity* of acts of governance attempted by persons excommunicated as described in both canons.

[51] This represents a departure from the *CLSA* English translation of the Code, which is less clear than it might be. This quote, is from *The Code of Canon Law, in English Translation* (=*CLSGBI Code of Canon Law, English Translation*), translation prepared by the Canon Law Society of Great Britain and Ireland in association with the Canon Law Society of Australia and New Zealand and the Canadian Canon Law Society, London: Collins Liturgical Publications, 1983, c. 1109.

idly assist only at marriages involving at least one of their subjects." The *limits of their jurisdiction* and the elements which constitute someone as *their subject* would be found in the authentic documents issued by the competent ecclesiastical superiors who, in accord with the general laws of the Church, established either (a) the jurisdiction of the ordinaries who are *personal* (not local) ordinaries or (b) the *personal parishes*.

Priests who are not pastors and deacons may have the faculty to assist at marriages delegated to them by the local ordinary or the pastor in accord with c. 1111 §§1-2. However, local ordinaries and pastors who are not validly carrying out their offices cannot delegate others to assist at weddings. The use of such power levies on the pastor a serious obligation to use the power both justly and validly. This is so because the valid or invalid use of this power can affect the validity of a marriage, the status of other people in the Church. Nevertheless, c. 144 §1 provides: "In a common error about fact or about law, and also in positive and probable doubt about law or about fact, the Church supplies executive power of governance both for the external and for the internal forum." In addition, c. 144 §2 explicitly states that that same norm applies to c. 1111 §1. Each such instance would have to be judged on its own merits.

Canon 1109 clearly expresses the invalidity and the conditions for it, within which conditions any priest or deacon might place himself. Because c. 1109 establishes that being under such censures by sentence or decree or having been declared such is so serious that even those who have the faculty to assist at marriages in virtue of their office become unable to do so validly, the implication is clear that those who have the faculty to assist at marriage only by delegation would do so invalidly if under censure as described in c. 1109.[52]

---

[52] Depending on the actual circumstances in any given case, common error about fact or law, or possible and probable doubt about law or about fact could result in c. 144 §1 supplying the executive power of governance necessary for valid assistance at a marriage, even though c. 144 §2 does not specifically mention an application to c. 1109.

Canons 1331, 1332 and 1333, which regulate the censures of excommunication, interdiction and suspension, can apply to any priest or deacon, not just to local ordinaries and pastors. In practice, therefore, the text of c. 1109 implicitly expresses that *any* priests or deacons who have been excommunicated, interdicted or suspended by sentence or decree, or who have been declared to be such cannot be *validly* delegated either with general delegation or special delegation to assist at marriages. If any priest or deacon comes under the censures by sentence, decree or by being declared so, any general delegation he has had cannot be *validly* subdelegated by him to another; and special delegation he may have enjoyed would also become *invalid*.

The delegation treated in c. 1111 §§1-2 can be general or special. As noted above, by c. 1109 the law itself joins to the office of pastor the power to assist at marriages which take place within the boundaries of his parish and have as one of the contractants a member of the Latin rite; therefore, in accord with c. 131 §1, it is an *ordinary power* of the pastor. Canon 137 §1 allows in a general way for the delegation of ordinary power and c. 1111 §§1-2 gives specific details about the delegation of the power to assist at marriages. Ordinarily only priests or deacons are to be delegated to assist at marriages.[53] Delegation may be *special*, i.e. for a specific marriage, or *general*, for many marriages. For *validity* either special or general delegation must be *expressly* given to *specific* persons. That is: (a) delegation cannot be either simply *presumed* nor *reasoned to if the pastor does not appear to object*[54]; (b) delegation must be specific either by naming the person or per-

---

[53] Canon 1112 §1 establishes the requirements which must be fulfilled so that the *diocesan bishop* may delegate lay persons to assist at marriages "where priests or deacons are lacking." Also see *Ecclesiae de mysterio*, art. 10, n. ° 3. English translation *Certain Questions Regarding Collaboration*, p. 21.

[54] NAVARRO-VALLS, "Forma de celebrar el matrimonio," in *Comentario exegético*, vol. III/2, p. 1453, opines that while tacit and interpretative expression is insufficient for validity, *implicit* expression would seem sufficient. An example of implicit delegation might be found in a pastor saying or writing something like: "I will be happy to meet Fr. Smith, when he comes to officiate at your wedding."

sons so delegated or by indicating the office held by the specified person, or a truly unique attribute of the person.[55]

Canon 1111 §2 also requires of general delegation that "…it is to be granted in writing." At times a pastor will seek temporary assistance from priests or deacons who come from other dioceses, or from institutes of consecrated life or societies of apostolic life. In those circumstances a pastor would be prudent to learn whether such priests or deacons have been given the diocesan faculties of the diocese in which the pastor has invited them to work. If they do have diocesan faculties for that diocese, the pastor needs to know whether those faculties contain general delegation to assist at marriages within the diocese (which is possible, but seems unlikely to be granted), or within the parish in which the priest or deacon will be helping. If the visitors have no such faculties, the pastor may then wish to give them either special delegation, which can be done *viva voce*[56] for *specific* marriages at which the pastor wishes them to assist, or the pastor might wish to give them general delegation, which must be done in *writing*, to assist at any marriages during their stay.[57]

---

[55] The more specific the delegation the less chance there would be for it to be invalid. If the persons' names are known, it would be best to use them in granting delegation. Specifying by some other distinctive *attribute* increases the chance of not accurately specifying at all and such a case would result in invalid delegation.

[56] However, if there is no written record that delegation had been granted, then in accord with c. 131 §3, the burden of proof that delegation had been granted "rests with the person who claims to have been delegated." That burden of proof exists in the case of establishing the existence of either general or special delegation. With records as important as marriage records it is clearly a prudent practice to note in the marriage register the source of delegation for every "visiting" priest or deacon who assists at a marriage.

[57] It would also seem prudent to clarify the status of any priest living in a parish rectory, retired pastors, residents carrying out other ministries in regard to delegation to assist at marriages. This is so because unplanned for situations arise as a result of which, a priest who lives in a rectory but is not the pastor or parochial vicar, may be asked to fill in and assist at a marriage. If such a priest does not clearly know his status with respect to marriage delegation, he may make the wrong guess — or may not think about the matter at all, especially if the request is immediately pressing and has taken him by surprise. Although trying to help, he may invalidly assist at a marriage without proper delegation himself, or he may invalidly subdelegate someone else for a particular marriage.

In relation to different aspects of marriage cc. 1114, 1115 and 1118 §1 each mention a need for the pastor's permission. Canon 1114 implicitly expresses a right of the pastor, that his permission should be obtained, if possible, in order for a minister, who is functioning in virtue of general delegation, licitly to assist at each marriage he celebrates in the parish.[58] That requirement is not surprising in view of c. 530, 4°, which especially entrusts to the pastor "the assistance at marriages and the imparting of the nuptial blessing." The requirement to seek the pastor's permission seems to be simply a further explication of marriages being especially entrusted to the pastor. The pastor would also have the obligation and the correlative right, to be used with justice and prudence, to withhold such permission for a serious reason.

With respect to cc. 1115 one commentary notes: "...can. 1115 determined the place of marriage in broad terms...."[59] Canon 1115 deals with a geographical location and explicitly requires permission of a *proper* ordinary or a *proper* pastor. Canon 1115 regulates in what parish a marriage should ordinarily take place, but also provides that "...marriage can be celebrated elsewhere with the permission of the proper ordinary or proper pastor." The present law allows more freedom of choice for the bride and groom than did c. 1097 of the Code of 1917. Canon 1115 also provides equal recognition of the importance of the groom's or the bride's own, or *proper*, parish, or *ecclesial community*. In *addition to* parishes where either bride or groom has a domicile or quasi-domicile (and, therefore, a proper pastor),[60] a

---

[58] Since c. 1114 requires for liceity that a person functioning in virtue of general delegation ought to obtain, if possible, the pastor's permission before assisting at a marriage, *a fortiori* but implicitly, a person who has been subdelegated to assist at a particular marriage would be bound by the same requirement.

[59] KELLY, "Marriage," Commentary on cc. 1055-1165, in *Letter & Spirit*, n. 2255, p. 629.

[60] As established in c. 107 §1, the usual canonical basis for acquiring a proper pastor is domicile or quasi-domicile. Canon 107 §2 makes provision for those who have neither domicile or quasi-domicile.

marriage may also be celebrated in a parish in which either the bride or groom has resided for a month.

In practice, with respect to c. 1115 ordinarily three principles need to be kept in mind with respect to the geographical location of the marriage: (a) there is no canonical preference between the *proper* parish of the bride or of the groom, (b) each of the contractants may have more than one *proper* parish and, therefore, more than one *proper* pastor, (c) the pastor of *any* of the *proper* parishes can give permission that the marriage be celebrated elsewhere, i.e., outside of any of the *proper* parishes of the bride and groom.

Canon 1118 §§1-3 addresses the character of the *place of marriage* and requires permission of a *local* ordinary or a pastor.[61] In accord with c. 1118 §1, a pastor can only permit a marriage between two Catholics or a Catholic and a baptized non-Catholic to take place in a parish church, or another church or oratory.[62] In the case of a Catholic and a non-baptized party, a pastor can permit the marriage in a church or some other suitable place as allowed by c. 1118 §3. Since the Code contains canonical definitions of the words *church* and *oratory*, they are to be understood as defined unless something different is noted or obvious from the context. These words as used in c. 1118 §1 mean a Catholic church or a Catholic oratory. The term "other suitable place" could be a church of the baptized non-Catholic.[63]

A canonical conundrum has arisen relative to c. 1118 §§1-2. A bride and groom, one Catholic the other Catholic or baptized non-Catholic, obtain the permission of the proper pastor

---

[61] KELLY, "Marriage," Commentary on cc. 1055-1165, in *Letter & Spirit*, n. 2255, p. 629.

[62] See c. 1214 for definition of "church"; c. 1223 for definition of "oratory."

[63] Indeed, c. 993 allows the local ordinary, with no mention of the pastor, even to give permission for the celebration of the Eucharist in "a sacred edifice of another church or ecclesial community that does not have full communion with the Catholic Church...."

of either the bride or groom to be married outside of that proper pastor's parish boundaries in accord with c. 1115. Canon 1118 §1 stipulates that marriage of a Catholic and a baptized non-Catholic is to be celebrated in a *parish* church, but with the permission of the local ordinary or the pastor it can be celebrated in another church or oratory. The couple in question wish to be married in a church which is not a parish church, or in an oratory. Which *is the pastor* of c. 1118 §1 whose permission is necessary? Is it the permission of (a) the pastor of the parish in which the non-parish church or the oratory exists, or (b) the proper pastor who originally gave permission under c. 1115 so that the couple could marry outside of the proper parish of at least one member of the couple, or (c) still another proper pastor one member of the couple might have — or both might have because of multiple domiciles or quasi-domiciles? If both the *a quo* pastor and the *ad quem* pastor are within the territory of the same local ordinary, that local ordinary could give permission under c. 1118 §1 and the question would become moot. If, however, the parishes are under the jurisdiction of different local ordinaries, the problem becomes compounded: whether it is the permission of the *a quo* or *ad quem* local ordinary or pastor which is required for the marriage at the other church or oratory. The Code does not seem to contain an apodictic answer.[64]

Canon 1118 §3 indicates that a marriage between a Catholic and an unbaptized person "...can be celebrated in a church or in some other suitable place." In either instance it is possible,

---

[64] T.P. Doyle, "Marriage," Commentary on cc. 1055-1165, in *CLSA Commentary*, p. 798 notes: "...the permission of the pastor of one of the parties [is required] to celebrate a marriage in another parish church (and presumably that of the pastor of the other church) and the local ordinary's permission to celebrate in a non-parochial church or oratory." A.M. Vega, "Forma de celebrar el matrimonio," Commentary on cc. 1118-1123, in *Comentario exegético*, vol. III/2, p. 1476 concludes: "In our opinion the Code does not offer any criterion which would enable the doubt to be resolved. It belongs to particular law, then, to decide what should be done in each place."

even likely, that there may be diocesan regulations and perhaps particular law which need to be obeyed as the pastor determines whether or not to agree to assist at marriages in the place where the couple wish to wed. Agreeing or declining to assist in each case should be based on objective facts, arrived at justly and prudently and communicated to the parties with sensitivity. Finally, it is to be noted that c. 1115 provides also for marriages of transients. Canon 100 declares that a transient, *vagus* in Latin, is "one [who] has neither domicile nor quasi-domicile anywhere." Their marriages are to be celebrated in the parish where one or both actually reside. The rule of c. 1071 §1, 1° must be kept in mind, however, that except in case of necessity, no one is to assist at the marriage of transients without the permission of the local ordinary.

3.2.8 — Ecclesiastical funeral rites

Canon 1176 §1 directs that: "The Christian faithful departed are to be given ecclesiastical funeral rites according to the norm of law." By its wording c. 1176 §1 simultaneously declares a right of each Christian and an obligation of the Church. The right to ecclesiastical funeral rites and the obligation of the Church to provide them are set aside only by c. 1184, which enumerates conditions under which the right to an ecclesiastical funeral is to be denied to members of the faithful. The pastor of the parish has an implied obligation arising from c. 1176 §1 to see to it that the decedent's right is respected and observed by ecclesiastical funeral rites which are carried out according to the proper liturgical norms. The decedent's family and/or heirs would also have a responsibility to respect the right of the deceased. If a pastor receives requests to do less than celebrate the full funeral rites for the deceased, he has an obligation to try his best to instruct those who make such a request about the rights of the deceased (which his or her survivors should exercise) and his own obligation to follow Church law.[65]

Canon 1177 §§1-2 uses the terms "own parish church" and "person's pastor." According to c. 107 §§1-3, ordinarily a person acquires a proper pastor by either parish domicile or parish quasi-domicile. A person with only a diocesan domicile or quasi-domicile and/or a transient acquire a proper pastor by the place in which she or he is then and there living. Canon 1177 §1 provides the general rule that a person's funeral must be celebrated in his or her own parish church. Very often a person's *own parish church* would be the church of the parish within the boundaries of which the person lives. Although the Latin word *"debent"* used in c. 1177 §1 is correctly translated "must," or "ought," c. 1177 §§2-3 offers wide options. If a legitimate decision has been made by the decedent or those responsible for his or her funeral in accord with Church law that a funeral will take place in a church other than that of a person's proper parish, the only right that the proper pastor has is that he be informed in what church the funeral rites will be celebrated. The pastor or rector of any other church chosen by the decedent or those responsible for his or her funeral has the right to consent or not to celebrate the funeral. As with other decisions, in order to refuse consent there

---

[65] With the dearth of priests in many places and the concomitant existence of many parishes with very large Catholic populations, full ecclesiastical funeral rites, wake services, Mass of Christian Burial and interment present a tremendous problem for many pastors. *Ecclesiae de mysterio*, art. 12, notes that "...death and the time of obsequies can be one of the most opportune pastoral moments in which the ordained minister can meet with the non-practicing members of the faithful. It is thus desirable that Priests and Deacons, even at some sacrifice to themselves, should preside personally at funeral rites...." English translation *Certain Questions Regarding Collaboration*, p. 22. In view of the various circumstances possible in any given area of a diocese, it would seem prudent for the diocesan bishop and presbyterate, recalling the teaching of c. 223 §§1-2 with respect to the exercise of rights, the common good of the Church and the rights of others, to study their situation and how best to weigh this obligation, which is one obligation among many others, and determine together a unified, reasonable and public course of action.

should be objective facts, justice and prudence in the decision and concern in the act of informing the parties involved.

With respect to funerals which are taking place in his parish, the pastor has an implied right from c. 530, 5° that, since the performing of funerals is especially entrusted to the pastor, his permission should be obtained by another priest who might wish to celebrate that liturgy.

Canon 1177 §3 provides that funeral rites are to be celebrated in the church of the parish where the death occurred if ordinary procedures are not otherwise being followed and particular law has no other provision. Providing for the proper funeral liturgy then becomes the obligation/right of the pastor of the parish in which the person died.

Canons 1183 and 1184 concern those to whom ecclesiastical funeral rites are to be granted or to be denied. Those canons are not addressed specifically to pastors; nevertheless, since the application of these canons is always connected with funerals, pastors are likely to be the first persons asked for a decision about granting or denying ecclesiastical funeral rites. Unless there are guidelines covering the *granting* of ecclesiastical funeral rites, as treated in c. 1183 §§1-3, pastors must always refer questions, together with all available information about the people and circumstances involved, to the local ordinary, who is the only one authorized by that canon to decide what is to be done about *granting* ecclesiastical funeral rites in any questionable case.

Canon 1184 §1 concerns *deprivation* of ecclesiastical funeral rites and does not require that the matter be referred to the local ordinary unless there are doubts. The pastor of a parish should, however, always exercise great care in such circumstances, because the point at issue is whether or not to deny a right. Canon 18 directs: "Laws which establish a penalty or restrict the free exercise of rights... are subject to a strict interpretation." That means that each word in the text cannot be extended beyond its strictest, most precise — and thus most limited — meaning.

If persons otherwise liable to suffer the effects of c. 1184 §1 "...have given some signs of repentance before their death...," then denial of ecclesiastical funeral rites is not applicable. What kind of sign? "Almost any positive sign which would indicate continued belief in God's mercy, however apparently flawed by previous personal conduct, would suffice — even by his or her making the sign of the cross, by responding to an invocation of God's mercy, or the like."[66] Other signs could be asking for the sacraments of Reconciliation or Anointing of the Sick, having insisted on the Christian education of one's children, etc.[67]

Persons cannot be judged to have been guilty of apostasy, heresy and schism unless they have done *exactly* the actions described in defining those terms in c. 751. In addition, the guilty actions of such persons must be "notorious," that is "either in some way publicly declared by ecclesiastical authority, or in fact so well known that it would be impossible to deny or doubt...."[68]

In accord with c. 1184 §1, 2°, cremation is not grounds for deprivation of ecclesiastical funeral rites except in the case of "persons who had chosen the cremation of their own bodies for reasons opposed to the Christian faith." Even if such reasons were the person's bases for choosing cremation, that fact would have to be notoriously known for denial of ecclesiastical funeral rites to be imposed.

"Other manifest sinners..." referred to in c. 1184 §1, 3° are not even to be denied the right to ecclesiastical funeral rites *unless* such rites "...cannot be granted without public scandal to the faithful." At times some of the Catholic faithful may be living in what is certainly a sinful situation, but may have otherwise preserved their allegiance to the Church. With respect to the possibility of avoiding or mitigating scandal when a Catholic dies in such circumstances *and* has also given some sign of penitence a *private* letter issued by the Sacred Congregation for

---

[66] B. McLean, "Church Funerals," Commentary on cc. 1176-1185, in *Letter & Spirit*, n. 2390, p. 672.

[67] J.L. Santos, "Concesión y denegación de las exequias," Commentary on cc. 1183-1185, in *Comentario exegético*, vol. III/2, p. 1708.

[68] McLean, "Church Funerals," in *Letter & Spirit*, n. 2391 (a), p. 672.

the Doctrine of the Faith made a suggestion about a possible approach to mitigating scandal:

> ...to the extent that pastors will explain the viewpoint which befits the meaning of Christian obsequies and in which many see an appeal to the mercy of God and a testimony of the community's faith in the resurrection of the dead and of eternal life.[69]

Although the situation described in c. 1184 §1, 3° does not include someone who has given some sign of penitence, scandal might still be obviated by the explanation suggested by the Sacred Congregation for the Doctrine of the Faith, since the mercy of God cannot be ruled out in any case.

3.3 — SHARING FULFILLMENT OF OBLIGATIONS AND EXERCISE OF RIGHTS

The pastor of a parish has many and varied obligations to fulfill as he strives to make the means, motives, example and experience of sanctification available to everyone within the parish community. Some sacraments simply do not exist in a parish unless a priest is present to celebrate them. Celebrating the sacrament of the Eucharist as the liturgical offering of Christ's one sacrifice on the Cross, Penance or Reconciliation, Anointing of the Sick and Confirmation are elements of the pastor's ministry which require priestly ordination. The pastor may share his obligations in these areas only with other priests.

The celebration of the sacrament of Baptism and assisting at the sacrament of Marriage are ministerial actions usually performed only by priests and deacons, unless because of a dearth of clergy, the Code itself, the diocesan bishop or the local ordi-

---

[69] *CLD*, vol. 8 (1973-1977), p. 863.

nary has made extraordinary arrangements.[70] Also, the preaching of a homily, *stricto sensu*, is reserved by canon law to a priest or deacon.[71]

With special terminology c. 530 identifies twelve specific liturgical ceremonies which are *especially entrusted* to the pastor. By c. 530 an explicit obligation is placed on the pastor to see to it that the liturgical ceremonies identified are available to his parishioners when they are needed; less clear but still implicit is an obligation not to be indifferent to the minister by whom and the manner in which such liturgies are carried out. Perhaps because c. 530 implies the Church's evident interest in linking the pastor to these ceremonies which would bring him into contact with the faithful at some of the most meaningful moments of their lives, it also implies an obligation that the pastor ordinarily carry out these celebrations in person, unless he has a just cause not to do so. The expression *especially entrusted* is also broad enough to support the interpretation that the pastor may at times enlist the aid of members of the faithful, clergy and lay, as the situation may require and applicable norms permit, in carrying out the functions with which he is especially entrusted. The pastor may actually find that, in various circumstances, he must share the conducting of the liturgical ceremonies especially entrusted to him, because otherwise he could not possibly meet the

---

[70] Assisting at (or simply witnessing) the sacrament of Matrimony by someone other than a priest or deacon is regulated by cc. 1112 §§1-2, 1116 §§1-2 and 1127 §§1-2. Administration of the sacrament of Baptism by someone other than a priest or deacon is regulated by c. 861 §2. *Ecclesiae de mysterio*, art. 11 declares: "Thus, for example, the absence or the impediment of a sacred minister which renders licit the deputation of the lay faithful to act as an extraordinary minister of Baptism, cannot be defined in terms of the ordinary minister's excessive workload, or his non-residence in the territory of the parish, nor his non-availability on the day on which the parents wish the Baptism to take place. Such reasons are insufficient for the delegation of the non-ordained faithful to act as extraordinary ministers of Baptism." English translation *Certain Questions Regarding Collaboration*, p. 21.

[71] Canon 767 §1.

needs of all of the faithful who comprise and worship in the parish community.[72]

Although only a priest can offer the Eucharistic sacrifice, administer the sacraments of Confirmation, Reconciliation and Anointing of the Sick, and only a priest or deacon is an ordinary minister of Baptism or an ordinary official Church witness for the sacrament of Marriage, still the celebration of each sacrament is a part of the liturgy of the Universal Church and, therefore, both clergy and laity have a proper role in all of those liturgical celebrations. Even in the case of the homily, the preparation of homilies may involve consultation with, and the ideas, questions and suggestions of laity as well as clergy.

Overall, it would not be easy to find any obligation of sanctification placed on the pastor the fulfillment of which he cannot share in various ways and to different degrees with other members of the faithful. This should not be surprising in view of the teachings of the Second Vatican Council that the great work of the pastor is to be the servant leader of the parish community, and that all of the baptized have become sharers in Christ's priestly, prophetic and royal office in their own manner.[73] It should also not be surprising in view of the numerous and far reaching obligations of the pastor to provide and organize the varied facets of the task of sanctification for the parish community.

Several canons clearly oblige pastors of parishes to share their task of sanctification in ways which obviously involve a sharing with other members of the faithful. Canon 528 §2 directs: "He [the parish pastor] is likewise to endeavor that they [the

---

[72] Canon 548 §2 envisions broad assistance of parochial vicars "Unless... the diocesan bishop expressly states otherwise the parochial vicar is obliged by reason of his office to assist the pastor in fulfilling the total parochial ministry...." In addition, the diaconate has been restored in the Church, and in various circumstances lay catechists or other well instructed laity are authorized to baptize and to witness marriages.

[73] Which teachings are reflected especially in cc. 519 and 204 §§1-2. Also see *Lumen gentium*, n. 31.

Christian faithful] are brought to the practice of family prayer as well as to a knowing and active participation in the sacred liturgy...."[74] Canon 230 §§1-3 explicitly treats, but does not exhaust, various ways in which the laity may exercise proper liturgical functions within various celebrations. The same canon implicitly suggests comparable and perhaps even broader roles in paraliturgical and extraliturgical prayer services and similar activities.

Canon 529 §1 rules: "He [the parish pastor] is also to labor diligently so that spouses and parents are supported in fulfilling their proper duties and he is to foster growth in the Christian life within the family." A wider view is presented in c. 529 §2:

> The pastor is to acknowledge and promote the proper role which the lay members of the Christian faithful have in the Church's mission by fostering their associations for religious purposes... so that the faithful be concerned for parochial communion and that they realize they are members both of the diocese and of the universal Church and participate in and support efforts to promote such communion.

---

[74] See also SACRA CONGREGATIO PRO CULTU DIVINO, *General Instruction on the Roman Missal Cenam paschalem*, March 26, 1970, in *Missale Romanum ex decreto sacrosancti oecumenici concilii Vaticani II instauratum auctoritate Pauli PP. VI promulgatum*, editio typica altera, Libreria editrice Vaticana, 1975, pp. 19-92, here at p. 46, n. 73. English translation in *The Roman Missal: The Sacramentary*, Revised by decree of the Second Vatican Council and published by authority of Pope Paul VI, approved for use in the Dioceses of the United States of America by the National Conference of Catholic Bishops and confirmed by the Apostolic See, English translation prepared by the International Commission on English in the Liturgy, New York: Catholic Book Publishing Co., 1974, General Instruction of the Roman Missal pp. 17*-52*, here at 29*, n. 73: "All concerned should work together in preparing the ceremonies, pastoral arrangements, and music for each celebration. They should work under the direction of the rector and should consult the people about the parts which belong to them." It may also be noted in passing, that all priests, including the pastor, are reminded by c. 909 that they are "...not to fail to make the required prayerful preparation for the celebration of the Eucharistic Sacrifice...."

Canon 210 speaks of the obligation of all Christian faithful "to live a holy life and to promote the growth of the Church and its continual sanctification." In those words the canon implies an obligation on the part of the faithful to share in the Church's works of sanctification, which for many, if not most, must include their lives as members of a parish community. Canon 212 §3 indicates a general obligation/right which lay people have to present advice to pastors "in accord with the knowledge, competence and preeminence which they possess..."; c. 228 §§1-2 points out that the lay people may hold ecclesiastical offices and: "Lay persons who excel in the necessary knowledge, prudence and uprightness are capable of assisting the pastors of the Church as experts or advisors...." As the Code sets down that lay people may counsel pastors, pastors may certainly seek their advice.

A special case is noted in c. 526 §1 which treats of the possibility of a pastor being required to take on the spiritual care of more than one parish because of a severe lack of priests or for other reasons. A pastor in that position would need to share with lay faithful the fulfillment of a great portion of his obligations and the exercise of his rights, probably even in some of the extraordinary ways in which the Code permits such help.

Nevertheless, the pastor cannot share the fulfillment of his obligations and the exercise of his rights to the extent that he no longer has canonical responsibility for doing all that he can to carry out all of the requirements of each canon. Where the pastor shares the fulfillment of his obligations and the exercise of his rights he must continue to evaluate the tasks done by those sharing his work and make corrections or revisions of his sharing as necessary to assure the accomplishment of the complete work for which he is responsible. In all candor it must be noted that except in the cases of parishes which are both small in population and compact in geographical area, it does not seem that any one individual working alone could ever manage all of the liturgies, liturgical training, sacramental preparation, preaching, prayer group organization and other tasks which the canons place at the pastor's door. Considered all together the canons concerning the pastor's obligations and rights with respect to the sanctification of the members of the parish community imply that the pastor will need and would be wise to accept a large amount of good help from the rest of the faithful.

CONCLUSION

Drawing on the teachings of the Second Vatican Council, the canons of the Code which establish the obligations and rights of parish pastors with respect to their participation in Jesus' priestly work of sanctification lead to several general conclusions about the pastor's ministry of sanctification and his interrelations with the faithful, clergy and laity, of the parish. Concisely put, the pastor is to share, prepare, protect and make decisions about the liturgy/means of sanctification; the obligation to prepare the faithful concerning the liturgy/means of sanctification calls for both specific preparation and general preparation.

With respect to works of sanctification, the pastor's principal obligations and rights range around his service of leadership in parish liturgies. That service of leadership includes not only sharing liturgical celebrations with the faithful, but also preparing parishioners through spiritual formation to fulfill their own liturgical roles. The canons do not present the pastor as what might be called the *provider of the sacraments* for the laity, but rather as the parish community's *leader in their sharing together* the liturgical celebrations of the sacraments.

The pastor's specific duties with respect to the spiritual formation of parishioners for their sharing in the sacramental/ liturgical life of the parish, includes, but is not limited to, developing parishioners' awareness of the spiritual dimensions of serving as extraordinary ministers of Holy Communion, lectors, musicians, choir members, acolytes, ushers, greeters, liturgical committee members and planners.[75] At one time or another, all need to be prepared spiritually for special experiences of sharing in the liturgy: their first reception of the sacraments of Penance or Eucharist or for their reception of Confirmation. Parents and prospective godparents are in need of special spiritual formation for their roles not only within the actual celebration of the sacrament of Baptism, but also for living lives worthy of the new responsibilities, which they will be taking upon themselves, to guide and introduce the child more and more completely as she or he grows and develops a personal spiritual life. Adults approaching baptism or reception into full communion with the Catholic Church also need special spiritual formation. Parishioners who are planning to marry need spiritual formation to understand and knowledgeably embrace the vocation and sacrament of marriage, and to continue to be faithful in marriage and in family life.

The pastor also has a general obligation with respect to spirituality. A pastor is charged not with *giving the sacraments* to parishioners, but with doing all in his power to motivate, inspire and organize parishioners so that they will in fact be *living the sacraments*. Efforts in this area would include, among many other worthwhile possibilities, encouraging family prayer, fostering religious vocations, founding parish units of pious societies, such as the Nocturnal Adoration Society, Society of St. Vincent de Paul, Rosary Societies, Confraternity of Christian Doctrine, promotion of evangelization and missionary activities.

The pastor is also required to use liturgical texts properly approved by competent ecclesiastical authority and carefully to keep any abuses from creeping into liturgical celebrations. Those same canons establish, by implication, that the pastor has a right

---

[75] With respect to the role, appointment, activity and liturgical actions of *extraordinary ministers of Holy Communion* a number of authoritative norms are reprised or newly established in *Ecclesiae de mysterio*, art. 8, nn. °1 and °2, English translation *Certain Questions Regarding Collaboration*, pp. 17-19.

to receive full and willing cooperation from all of the faithful, clergy and laity, as he carries out his obligation in this regard.

Various canons concerning the means of sanctification require, either explicitly or implicitly, that before one action or another is taken, the pastor is to be asked to give his consent or permission. In various circumstances the Code of 1917 had similar requirements. The 1917 Code, however, was not nearly as clear about the rights of individual members of the faithful. If it was not clear previously, it is reasonably clear in the Code of 1983 that the pastor's decision to grant or deny consent or permission in one case or another is not to be some vagary of his, but a reasonable and responsible decision which recognizes the rights of others and has an objective basis for giving or withholding consent.

Just as there are canons which require and authorize the pastor to make administrative decisions about works of sanctification, there are many other canons in the Code which charge the pastor with carrying out administrative duties, some spiritual and some material. In discharging these obligations the pastor's service of leadership shares in Jesus' kingly or governing ministry. The pastor's obligations and rights with respect to parish administration are treated in the following chapter.

CHAPTER FOUR

Ministry of Governing

INTRODUCTION

The pastor of a parish shares in the governing ministry of Christ, working as Jesus did while he was on earth, as one who came not to be served but to serve. The pastor's service is one of leadership. The pastor's leadership calls for many decisions and actions spanning the gamut from matters which are obviously and essentially spiritual to others which are thoroughly material, but which must, nonetheless, be faced and dealt with by a pastor in a Christ-like way. Although the administrative obligations and rights of pastors may seem less significant than his share in the prophetic and priestly roles of Jesus, it is important to realize that as preaching and liturgical worship bring a Christian community into existence and enable it to grow, that growing community will have the same human needs for administration of communal interests, good order and activities as does any other cohesive and productive society.

The subject matter of this chapter will be approached first by a concise review of the theological question of the source of a parish pastor's canonical power or authority and a consideration of the terms *the ministry of governing* and *the power of governance*. Next the pastor's general obligations and rights with respect to the Ministry of Governing will be reviewed. Separate sections will follow treating: the Service of Leadership, the

Pastor's Care of Parish Temporalities and Sharing Fulfillment of Obligations and Exercise of Rights.

4.1 — MINISTRY OF GOVERNING AND THE POWER OF GOVERNANCE

Canon 519 establishes that an element of the ecclesiastical office of pastor is that a pastor is to carry out the function of governing (*munus regendi*) within his parish and c. 129 §1 stipulates that clerics are capable of a power, which exists in the Church by divine institution and which is called either the power of governance (*potestas regiminis*) or the power of jurisdiction (*potestas iurisdictionis*).

Whether a pastor is capable of the power of governance because of his sacred ordination or because of the office he holds, or both, does not alter his canonical obligations or rights as pastor. There is, however, a basic and presently unsettled theological question about the precise manner or manners in which power is present in the Church. As a result, the canons relating to questions of power in the Church attempt to present a practical way of acting which encompasses both sides of the question without choosing between them. One commentator, although not writing on the subject of pastors, deals concisely with the elements and the unfolding canonical history on two different sides of this question.[1] All agree that ultimately God is the source of power in the Church. Some hold that within the Church there is only one power, "sacred power" (*sacra potestas*), and it is conferred with Holy Orders but in differing degrees. Others argue that God provides through divine natural law a power of jurisdiction, which any society has and, in addition, another power,

---

[1]   See J.H. Provost, "The Participation of the Laity in the Governance of the Church," in *Studia Canonica*, 17 (1983), pp. 417-448.

the power of orders (*potestas ordinum*), with the result that the Church can in varying degrees attach the exercise of legislative, judicial and executive power to ecclesiastical offices and/or provide for the delegation of the exercise of such powers to other individuals.

Theologically (and possibly sociologically) the concept of the ministry of governing appears broader than the power of governance, because a leader can and often does *govern* others by example, moral suasion, innovative ideas and perhaps charisms, aside from whatever legal power the leader may have to legislate, judge or exercise executive authority. This would seem to be especially true of one whose ministry of governing is to be modeled on and is a true sharing in the governing ministry of Jesus.

Since the pastor of a parish must be in sacred orders (c. 521 §1) he is, therefore, capable of the power of governance, which is distinguished as legislative, executive and judicial (c. 135 §1). However, in Canon Law neither legislative power nor judicial power are proper to, that is, are elements of, the office of pastor of a parish (c. 135 §§ 2-3).[2] In accord with c. 519 a pastor's care for his parish community does include the function of governing (*munus regendi*) under the authority of the diocesan bishop and in accord with the norm of law; in other words, in order to fulfill his responsibilities, the pastor has some share in the exercise of the executive aspects of the power of governance.

"*Executive power...* is that which is required for ordinary administration or the application of the law."[3] The extent of executive power, or the power of jurisdiction, is generally related to a territory; in the case of a pastor's executive power its extent

---

[2] A. McGRATH, "*Title VIII Power of Governance,*" Commentary on cc. 129-144, in *Letter & Spirit*, nn. 295-297, p. 81.

[3] A. McGrath, "*Title VIII Power of Governance,*" Commentary on cc: 129-144, in *Letter & Spirit*, n. 298, p. 81.

is the parish boundaries.[4] The extent of executive power of pastors of *personal*, that is non-territorial, parishes and the unifying characteristic of his subjects, would have to be learned from the decree which canonically established the personal parish.

The norm of law with regard to the exercise of executive power is both general as found in cc. 135 §4-144, and particular in various canons which empower the pastor to exercise executive power in special situations, which are treated later in this chapter.[5]

4.2 — THE PASTOR'S GENERAL OBLIGATIONS AND RIGHTS WITH RESPECT TO THE MINISTRY OF GOVERNING

By establishing that the faithful have the right to make their pastors aware of especially their spiritual needs, c. 212 §2 implies that there is also a right to make their temporal needs known to pastors. The same canon implies that pastors must at least listen to the non-spiritual perceived needs manifested by the faithful and to offer some honest and responsible answer. There is no suggestion in the law that pastors can fulfill every need (not even every spiritual need) brought to their attention, but there is an implication that the pastor should do what he

---

[4] The fact that *executive power* is described as being "related to a territory" does not, however, mean that such power cannot be exercised outside of a particular place. For instance, a Latin rite Catholic having a domicile or quasi-domicile in a Latin rite parish is a *subject* of the pastor and, with due respect for universal or particular law, a pastor can legitimately exercise executive power over his own subjects even when they are or he is outside of the boundaries of the parish. A. McGrath, "*Title VIII Power of Governance*," Commentary on cc: 129-144, in *Letter & Spirit*, n. 299, p. 81.

[5] For example, the faculty to assist at marriage, cc. 1109-1111; dispensing from certain matrimonial impediments, cc. 1078-1180; dispensing from or commuting vows, cc. 1196-1197, and promissory oaths, c. 1203; commuting or dispensing from observance of feast days and fast and/or abstinence, c. 1245.

reasonably can to help the faithful when they are in need.

The faithful, clergy and lay, have more to talk to the pastor about than simply their own needs. Canon 212 §3 directs[6]:

> In accord with the knowledge, competence and preeminence which they [the faithful] possess, they have the right and even at times a duty to manifest to the sacred pastors their opinion on matters which pertain to the good of the Church....

It is possible that the term *sacred pastors* as used here principally refers to bishops, but the general context would not exclude pastors of parishes. Here, the pastor's obligation is to recognize the rights of other members of the faithful in accord with the qualifications set down, to listen attentively and to consider, perhaps also consulting with others, the significance of the opinions offered. This paragraph of c. 212 should have a bearing on the pastor's leadership of parish pastoral councils, parish finance councils and other boards and committees.

A general right of the pastor is implied in c. 222 §1 which states:

> The Christian faithful are obliged to assist with the needs of the Church so that the Church has what is necessary for divine worship, for apostolic works and works of charity and for the decent sustenance of ministers.[7]

The pastor therefore has the right reasonably to ask for and receive these kinds of assistance, which are not in any way lim-

---

6 In addition to manifesting their opinions in accord with c. 228, qualified lay persons may serve in certain ecclesiastical offices and functions and also serve as experts or advisors to pastors of the Church, even in councils as permitted by law.

7 Also see c. 1254 §2.

ited to financial assistance; nor is the application of the canon limited to lay members of the faithful.[8]

Canon 223 §§1-2, which was treated earlier, respectively sets down a general obligation and a general right of the pastor of a parish. The pastor, as are all of the faithful, is obliged to exercise personal and social responsibility, recognize the rights of others and consider the common good of the Church in his exercise of pastoral governing. The pastor, in addition, holds an office of "ecclesiastical authority" and has, therefore, "competence to regulate the exercise of the rights which belong to the Christian faithful."[9] In making such judgments, the prudent pastor of a parish will be aware that while he is *an* ecclesiastical authority, there are not lacking other ecclesiastical authorities to whom recourse can be had to provide support for his decisions, or to protest against them.[10]

It may also be noted here that c. 231 §2 expresses a general right of lay persons employed by the Church to a decent remuneration. This in turn implies a general obligation of the pastor to provide such a remuneration for persons employed by the parish. Remuneration of parish employees will be treated in this chapter in the section on the pastor's obligations and rights with respect to temporalities. There are other canons which indicate obligations and rights of clergy who are not pastors, while also implying general obligations or rights of pastors. Those canons will be treated in this chapter in the section: **4.3.1 — Governing: working with other clergy members of the parish community.**

Canon 529 §§1-2 provides broad outlines for the governing work of the pastor. Paragraph §1 requires that the pastor should come to know the faithful, visit families, share their cares, strengthen the faithful in the Lord, correct them prudently when

---

[8] For additional applications of c. 222 §1, cf. McGRATH, "Christ's Faithful," in *Letter & Spirit*, n. 468, p. 125.

[9] Canon 223 §2. Also see *AA*, n. 3. English translation in FLANNERY, *Conciliar and Post Conciliar Documents*, p. 769.

[10] Canons 1732-1739: *Recourse against Administrative Decrees*.

necessary, provide spiritual help for the sick, seek out those enduring special difficulties, support spouses and parents in fulfilling their duties and foster the growth of Christian life within families. Nine general activities are identified which "in order to fulfill his office in earnest the pastor should strive" to accomplish. Each of these general activities provides a separate example of how a pastor is to interact with individual parishioners on a person to person level as he conducts the parish affairs on their behalf. In fine, the pastor is called upon to be in close, personal contact with his parishioners as individuals as well as members of families and organizations.

In addition, the nine general requirements of c. 529 §1 could be analyzed into many sub-species of obligations. Nevertheless, each obligation specified by c. 529 §1 also implicitly confers on the pastor the right reasonably to share the fulfillment of his obligations, to carry out these many tasks *per se vel per alios*. Such others would especially be members of the faithful, clergy and laity, who have various canonical obligations to assist the pastor and those who volunteer to do so. When a pastor cannot find time (or stamina) for all such personal contact, he has an obligation to be as personal as possible through the work of others, clergy, religious and dedicated lay people, whom he organizes and sends in his place to reach each of the parishioners in as personal a manner as can be achieved.

The pastor's obligations detailed in c. 529 §2 are no less demanding, but are oriented toward guiding the faithful into various associations and/or programs which provide experiences not only of the parish as a true community, but also of communion within the diocese and the Church universal.[11] There is also an obligation that the pastor work in cooperation with his

---

[11] READ, "Parishes, Parish Priests and Assistant Priests," in *Letter & Spirit*, n. 1051, p. 294, points out that the laity do not require the pastor's consent to join or form associations for religious purposes (cc. 211, 215, 216), but that the parish pastor is to encourage their efforts and to coordinate them in order to avoid friction or wasted effort (c. 223).

bishop and the presbyterate of the diocese to promote the realization of universal communion. In accord with c. 532, it is the pastor who "represents the parish in all juridic affairs" and is responsible for the administration of the parish goods.[12] These obligations, although they are more general, present the pastor with the same kind of rights noted above with respect to c. 529 §1.[13]

4.3 — MINISTRY OF GOVERNING: THE SERVICE OF LEADERSHIP

The Code is quite clear that, subject to the authority and supervision of the diocesan bishop, the pastor is canonically in charge of the parish and that he is to govern it.[14] Canon 515 §1 establishes that the pastoral care of the parish is entrusted to the pastor and refers to the pastor as the parish's own shepherd; c. 519 sets down that the pastor is the proper shepherd of the parish and that the pastor has been called to share the bishop's minis-

---

[12] It may also be noted that the pastor enjoys canonical stability in office and cannot be removed from office unless the procedures set down in cc. 1740-1747 are meticulously followed (unless he is a religious in which case c. 682 §2 would apply). A parochial vicar can be removed for a just cause by the diocesan bishop, diocesan administrator, or, if he is a religious, by his religious superior (cc. 193 §3, 552 and 628 §2). Canon 532, with specific reference to the pastor representing the parish in all juridic affairs, does not confer an unlimited authority, as c. 1288 indicates: "Administrators [of the temporal goods of the Church] are neither to initiate nor contest a lawsuit on behalf of a public juridic person in civil court unless they obtain the written permission of their own ordinary."

[13] J. Calvo, "Parishes, Parish Priests and Assistant Priests," in *Code Annotated*, p. 389, notes that c. 529 is "...an exhortatory legal text, but its contents can be fully enforceable as a particular obligation."

[14] Canon 510 §3 provides that in a church which is both parochial and capitular the bishop should set up definite norms to properly integrate the pastoral and capitular responsibilities in such a way that they will not impede one another. In resolving conflicts the bishop's first concern is to be the pastoral necessities of the faithful. For pastors of parishes of this type c. 510 §3 implies an obligation to observe the bishop's norms and explicitly obliges the bishop to truly hold the pastoral necessities of the faithful as his first concern.

try of Christ including the ministry of governing.[15] Canon 1279 §1 establishes that "the administration of ecclesiastical goods is the responsibility of the individual who immediately governs the person to whom the goods belong," and c. 1741, 5° leaves no doubt that the pastor is thus responsible in the case of a parish. Nevertheless, a broad view of the importance, diversity, size and number of the obligations of the pastor of a parish leads almost ineluctably to the conclusion that the pastor is going to need help to carry out his duties, some specific help that can be provided only by other clergy, but much that can be supplied by lay persons, both paid and volunteer workers.

Given the fact that the pastor *governs*, does the Code direct what the process or characteristics of such governing should be? Often the Code does employ the words *cooperate, cooperating, cooperation, co-worker* to describe a general *modus operandi* of governing in various circumstances by the Supreme Pontiff, bishops, dioceses, major superiors, faculties within ecclesiastical universities, priests with bishops, pastors with their diocesan bishops and their parochial vicars.[16] Canon 519 indicates that other priests and deacons in a parish are to cooperate with the pastor, which implies that the pastor is also expected to engage in cooperation with them, and c. 545 §1 identifies the pastor and parochial vicars as "co-workers." The words *coordinate, coordination, coordinated,* also appear in the Code describing one or another activity of bishops, vicars general, episcopal vicars and major superiors as they carry out different governing activities.[17] Canon 495 §1 mandates that each diocese is to have a presbyteral council to aid the diocesan bishop in the governance of the diocese; also there are twenty-three other specific references in the

---

[15] *Ecclesiae de mysterio,* art. 4 and art. 5, nn. °2 and °3 also makes it clear that the pastor is to govern the parish. English translation *Certain Questions Regarding Collaboration,* pp. 14-16.

[16] OCHOA, *Index verborum ac locutionum,* p. 115.

[17] *Ibid.*

Code to the "*consultative*" activity of that college of consultors.[18] A cooperative style of governing is, then, sometimes canonically required of pastors and in various other instances is called for, along with coordination and consultation, by the Code. Yet, if an approach to governing is to comprise cooperation, coordination and consultation, it must also imply *communication,* since not a single one of the other three elements can exist or function without communication.[19]

This in turn suggests the practical conclusion that the pastor may govern most effectively by a style that is cooperative, coordinating, consultative and communicating, working together with other informed persons and groups by means of planned and well organized powers, abilities and talents to achieve common goals. A governing style of this kind would seem well suited to the pastor's task of serving the parishioners by leading them, striking a proper balance between the pastor's knowledge that he has the obligation and the right to govern the parish and the pastor's realization that he has the obligation to serve by exercising leadership, which, among other goals, is to recognize and foster the charisms of the laity.[20] In the following subsections consideration is given to the pastor governing by working with other parish clergy, persons living in a religious state approved by the Church and parish and non-parish organizations. The pastor's governing obligations and rights with respect to individual members of the faithful have already been treated.

---

[18] *Ibid.,* p. 85 "collegium consultorum."

[19] *Ibid.,* pp. 80, 232, 274. Interestingly, the Code's use of *communicatio, communicatus* and *communico* refers to means of social communication 14 times, the presentation or transmittal of official notices or documents 12 times, reception of the Eucharist 2 times and with the general meaning of being in contact only once.

[20] *PO,* n. 9. English translation in Flannery, *Conciliar and Post Conciliar Documents,* pp. 880-881; canon 529 §2.

4.3.1 — Governing: working with other clergy members of the parish community

The working relationship of a pastor and a parochial vicar is first directly treated in c. 545 §1, which mandates that: (a) they are to be "co-workers," (b) they are to work "in common council" and (c) the parochial vicar serves under the authority of the pastor.[21]

In respect to being co-workers, c. 548 §2 requires that a parochial vicar is bound by his office "to assist the pastor in fulfilling the total parish ministry,"[22] while c. 548 §3 states plainly that both pastor and parochial vicar are "responsible together" by their collaboration to provide the needed pastoral care for the parish. The requirement of common council is repeated in c. 548 §3. It is worth noting that the explicit requirement in c. 548 §3 is that the parochial vicar consult with the pastor "on planned or existing programs." Since the text does not specify that the planned or existing programs which are to be consulted about are *only* those of the parochial vicar, but rather describes them as productive of "pastoral care for the parish," there is implicitly expressed a requirement that *the pastor also consult* the parochial vicar about *the pastor's* parochial plans.[23] Fundamentally,

---

[21] It is also possible that some or all of the clergy serving a parish may be members of a religious institute or a society of apostolic life. Their special consecration to God and the proper law of their own institutes or societies need to be acknowledged and respected, but their special dedication and status do not modify the universal law regarding the rights and obligations of pastors as pastors nor the tasks required by the Church of priests who serve Christ's faithful in a parish.

[22] Canon 548 §2 also indicates that if the letter of assignment from the diocesan bishop states otherwise, then a parochial vicar is not obliged to assist in fulfilling the total parochial ministry. In addition, c. 548 §2 establishes that the parochial vicar does not share the pastor's obligation of applying the Mass for the people.

[23] The kind of working relationship and consultation required of pastor and parochial vicar has certain analogies with c. 407 §§1-3, which sets down directives for the interaction of diocesan bishop, coadjutor bishop and auxiliary bishop.

the consultation and cooperation need to be thorough, honest and reciprocal.[24]

Canon 275 §1 requires that all clerics, since they work to build up the Body of Christ, should be "united among themselves by the bond of brotherhood and of prayer; they are to strive for cooperation among themselves in accord with the prescriptions of particular law." All clerics are called upon "faithfully and untiringly to fulfill the duties of pastoral ministry" by c. 276 §2, 1°. By c. 287 §1 all clerics are "most especially" reminded of their duty "always to foster that peace and harmony based on justice which is to be observed among all persons."

Both pastor and parochial vicar have a general obligation to reside within the parish, the pastor in a parish house close to the church, the parochial vicar simply within the parish, or at least in one of the parishes, if he has been assigned to simultaneous service in more than one. The local ordinary can permit both pastor and parochial vicar to live elsewhere "especially in a house shared by several priests" (c. 533 §1), provided there is a just cause and the parochial needs of their parishioners are cared for properly.

Canons 281 §1-2, 1254 §1, 1274 §1-2 raise various points about compensation and support for the clergy. Since those canons are of such a general nature, it is likely that diocesan statutes will provide more exact directions about the duties of a pastor in fulfilling them; a pastor has the obligation to observe such regulations. Even when there are not precise rules about some particular situation, e.g. clergy, priests or transitional deacons helping for the summer in a parish or filling in while another priest is on sabbatical or ill, or a transitory deacon serving

---

[24] Canon 550 §2 establishes for a local ordinary an obligation which is indicative of the mind of the Church about the relationship of pastor and parochial vicar; it is this: "...to see to it that some community of life is fostered between the pastor and the parochial vicar within the rectory...." Canon 280 states that for the clergy: "Some community of life is highly recommended to clerics; wherever such a practice exists, it is to be preserved to the extent possible."

in a parish in one way or another, the pastor has an obligation to provide for their remuneration as sketched out in c. 281 §1 and §2. In the matter of the duration of annual vacation, bishop, pastor and parochial vicar possess the same rights (cc. 395 §2, 533 §2 and 550 §3). Canon 533 §3 specifies that the diocesan bishop is to issue norms for the care of a parish by a priest with proper faculties during the absence of a pastor. By establishing that responsibility of the bishop, which would include care of the parish during the pastor's absence on vacation, c. 555 §3 implicitly expresses the pastor's right that the bishop help him in this way. Whether with respect to an annual vacation or any other absence from the parish c. 533 §2 mandates that "if the pastor is to be absent from the parish beyond a week he is bound to inform the local ordinary of such an impending absence before he leaves." Other clerics have the right to "a due and sufficient period of vacation each year" as such may be determined by universal or particular law (c. 283 §2). By analogy with the canons on priests residing outside of the parish they serve, vacation time would need to be arranged in a fair and reasonable way so that the parochial needs of their parishioners are properly cared for. Since the pastor is the shepherd of all of the faithful in the parish and is to govern the parish in accord with the law, one of his obligations would appear to be to recognize the vacation rights of parochial vicars and to do all that is reasonably possible to enable the parochial vicar to exercise those rights.[25]

Balanced together with the spirit of cooperation and consultation is the canonical fact, which both pastor and parochial vicar need to understand, that the pastor is in charge, he is the proper shepherd of, and governs the parish (c. 519). Within the parameters of canon law, the diocesan statutes and the bishop's

---

[25] *PO*, n. 20, taught: "Moreover, priests' remuneration should be such as to allow the priest a proper holiday each year. The bishop should see to it that priests are able to have this holiday." While the *fontes* for c. 283 §2 include a reference to *PO*, n. 20, those for cc. 395 §2, 533 §2 and 550 §3 do not.

letter appointing a parochial vicar, it is the pastor who specifies the parochial vicar's obligations and rights within the parish (c. 548 §1). After consultation, decisions on parochial ministry are the responsibility of the pastor.[26]

In addition to parochial vicars, other priests engaged full time or part time in other kinds of ecclesiastical assignments, or retired, may reside in a parish rectory or at least within the boundaries of a parish.[27] It would be prudent to have the relationship between the pastor of the parish and such priests as well

---

[26] *CD*, n. 30, (3) presented the relationship in these words: "Curates, as co-workers with the parish priest, should be eager and fervent in their daily exercise of their pastoral ministry under the authority of the parish priest. There should be a fraternal relationship between the parish priest and his curates; mutual charity and respect should prevail, and they should assist each other by advice, practical help and example, providing with harmonious will and a common zeal for the needs of the parish." English translation in FLANNERY, *Conciliar and Post Conciliar Documents*, p. 582.

[27] Canon 776 mandates that the pastor "…is to employ the services of the clerics attached to the parish…" in providing for the catechetical formation of parishioners. Some clerics who have other kinds of ecclesiastical assignments may have been assigned to live in the rectory of a particular parish or at least within the parish boundaries. Are such clerics "attached (*addictorum*)" to the parish in the sense of c. 776? It seems clear that they are not attached to the parish in that way, unless the diocesan bishop's letter assigning them to live in a particular parish specifically indicates that they are to assist the parish in its catechetical programs. This is so because c. 776 replaces c. 1333 of the 1917 Code, which in paragraph §1 explicitly required that, if the pastor was unable to provide the requisite instruction, he was to use the assistance of other clergy "dwelling in the parish;" paragraph §2 of that same c. 1333 authorized the bishop to inflict ecclesiastical penalties on clerics who refused to help although they were not legitimately impeded from helping. The difference in the text of c. 776, which has replaced "dwelling in" with "attached to" indicates a different requirement than did c. 1333 of the 1917 Code. Canon 757's direction that "…pastors and others entrusted with the care of souls are especially bound to this office [Ministry of the Divine Word: preaching and catechetical instruction] as regards the people entrusted to them…," seems to indicate the obligation arises from a more official relationship than merely living in a particular parish. If, then, the diocesan bishop's letter directing a cleric who has a different kind of ecclesiastical assignment to live in a particular parish, does not express some other specific attachment to the parish, no such attachment is established precisely because the cleric has another kind of ecclesiastical assignment; or, if the letter assigning a residence in a parish does detail specific attachment between the cleric and the parish, but helping with catechetical formation is not specified, then the cleric would not be attached to the parish in such a way as to require that he help in that way.

as their participation in any parochial ministry determined by individual letters from the diocesan bishop to the priests and the pastor involved. Detailed diocesan statutes could also legitimately provide for such situations. Lacking any particular law or diocesan directives about respective obligations and/or rights, it might be advisable for the individual priests and the pastor to work out, and write out, a *modus vivendi et operandi* which each can accept.[28] Such agreements, however, would not bind a new pastor, nor prevent the diocesan bishop from later setting up other statutes or issuing different directives addressed to the priests involved.

There may also be chaplains living within the boundaries of a parish. The ecclesiastical office of chaplain is treated in cc. 564 through 572. Among those canon 571 directs: "In exercising his pastoral office a chaplain is to maintain an appropriately close relationship with the pastor." The text of c. 571 implies correlative obligations and rights for both the pastor and the chaplain — cooperating to achieve a good working relationship.

In many parishes the pastor may also have one or more deacons assisting him in some aspects of the parochial ministry. As established by c. 266 §1, "a person becomes a cleric through the reception of diaconate." Reception of the diaconate constitutes a sharing in the sacrament of Holy Orders, as is clear from c. 1009 §1. Any deacon, therefore, whether *transitional,* as he continues formation for priestly ordination, or *permanent,* as he intends to serve the community in that role, is a member of the clergy in virtue of his ordination. By ordination deacons become *ordinary* ministers of Baptism and Holy Communion; they may be delegated to assist at marriages and enjoy the same faculty as priests to preach, including the homily; just as a priest, a deacon is a "minister of exposition of the Most Blessed Sacra-

---

[28] Thus acting in a manner somewhat analogous to that required by *CIC* c. 520 §2 and *CCEO* c. 282 §2 when a parish is entrusted to a clerical religious institute or to a clerical society of apostolic life.

ment and the Eucharistic benediction."[29] By explicitly stating that clerics "are to nourish their spiritual life from… the Eucharist" and that "deacons are earnestly invited to participate daily in offering it [the sacrifice of the Eucharist]," c. 276 §2, 2° implicitly indicates that deacons are entitled to exercise their diaconal ministry at Mass on a daily basis. In working with a married deacon, the pastor's obligations to provide remuneration are set out in c. 281 §3, and perhaps in more exact detail in particular law.[30]

As clerics, deacons are directed by c. 276 §2, 1° "…faithfully and untiringly to fulfill the duties of pastoral ministry." They are to cooperate with the pastor according to c. 519 and, by analogy with c. 545 §1, deacons exercise their ministry under the authority of the pastor of the parish in which they serve. Since the deacons are directed to cooperate with the pastor, there is an implication that both are expected to engage in sincere and thorough communication. Nevertheless, as noted above, any other clergy in the parish must acknowledge that the pastor is in charge and has the authority to make decisions governing pastoral ministry and administration in the parish.[31]

---

[29] For the deacon as ordinary minister of Baptism, see c. 861 §1; of Holy Communion see c. 910 §1. With respect to Marriage, c. 1108 §1 provides that a deacon may be delegated to assist at marriages; in accord with c. 137 §3, if such delegation to assist at marriages was general, i.e. for all cases, the deacon can subdelegate another priest or deacon for a particular marriage; a delegated deacon may also dispense from matrimonial impediments in accord with c. 1079 §2. The deacon has a general faculty to preach in accord with c. 764 and particular reference to the homily is found in c. 767 §1; also see cc. 757 and 835 §3. The deacon as minister of exposition and benediction of the Blessed Sacrament is set forth in c. 943.

[30] Although c. 281 §3 does not treat specifically of permanent deacons who are unmarried, it appears that an application of c. 19 would result in a similar regulation for the remuneration of those unmarried permanent deacons who work full time for the Church.

[31] Note should be taken that the vicar forane, or dean, in carrying out a number of the tasks assigned to him by c. 555 §§1-4 will need the cooperation of the pastors of the deanery. As a result, c. 555 implies a general obligation of pastors to participate in the dean's efforts.

4.3.2 — Governing: working with members of the parish who are also members of Institutes of Consecrated Life or Societies of Apostolic Life

Although each institute of consecrated life and society of apostolic life has its own constitution and proper laws concerning its legitimately constituted houses and the ministry of its members, it appears that a pastor will most often have obligations and rights with respect to members of institutes of consecrated life or societies of apostolic life either because those members serve on the parish staff as *employees,* or because, although serving elsewhere, they live in the parish and are parishioners, or because they are both parish staff members and parishioners. In any of those circumstances they might also be members of the parish pastoral council.[32]

Whether staff members, parishioners, or both, members of institutes of consecrated life and societies of apostolic life belong to a "a religious state approved by the Church."[33] The Second Vatican Council taught that they "are called by God so that they may enjoy a special gift of grace in the life of the Church and may contribute, each in his [or her] own way, to the saving mission of the Church."[34] As noted above, one of the duties of pastors (and parochial vicars) is to acknowledge and promote the proper role of the laity, which would include the religious vocations of such staff members and parishioners.[35] On their part, members of institutes of consecrated life and societies of apostolic life should bear in mind c. 776's directive that the pastor of

---

[32] Canon 512 §§ 1-3 as applied to *parish* pastoral councils by *Ecclesiae de mysterio,* art. 5, n.°2, footnote 85; English translation *Certain Questions Regarding Collaboration,* p. 16.

[33] *LG,* n. 31. English translation in FLANNERY, *Conciliar and Post Conciliar Documents,* pp. 388-389.

[34] *LG,* n. 43. English translation in FLANNERY, *Conciliar and Post Conciliar Documents,* pp. 402-403.

[35] Canon 529 §2; *PO,* n. 9. English translation in FLANNERY, *Conciliar and Post Conciliar Documents,* pp. 880-881.

a parish in his efforts to provide catechetical formation for parishioners is, among others, to call the members of institutes of consecrated life and societies of apostolic life to assist him "with due regard for the character of each institute..." and that those members "are not to refuse to furnish their services willingly unless they are legitimately impeded." Beyond those specifics, the pastor's obligations and rights with respect to non-clerical members of institutes of consecrated life and societies of apostolic life would be much the same as those toward lay members of the parish community.

4.3.3 — Governing: working with the Parish Pastoral Council, other Parish and non-Parish organizations

Canon 536 §1 requires that if the diocesan bishop considers it opportune after having heard the presbyteral council, a pastoral council is to be established in each parish. The same canon in paragraphs §§1-2 identifies the *reason for the existence* of the pastoral council and establishes *three parameters of its modus operandi*.

Canon 536 §1's reason for the existence of the pastoral council implies helpful cooperation: "...through it [the pastoral council] the Christian faithful *along with* those who share the pastoral care of the parish, in virtue of their office give their help"; in addition, a focus is specified: "in fostering pastoral activity."[36] It appears that the pastor, by law the presider over the pastoral council, has some obligation to preside in a cooperative, coordinating, consultative and communicative way, which acknowledges and promotes the council's reason for existing. If that cooperation cannot be brought about and/or pastoral activity is not fostered by a parish pastoral council, the pastor, the presider,

---

[36] Canon 536 §1 (emphasis added).

has an obligation to recognize that something is wrong and to work to set it right. In some cases it may be prudent (and necessary) for a pastor to seek assistance from communication or organizational professionals.

The three parameters of the pastoral council's modus operandi stipulated by c. 536 §1 and §2 are: (a) "the pastor presides over it [the pastoral council]," (b) "This pastoral council possesses a consultative vote only, and [(c)] is governed by norms determined by the diocesan bishop."

Canon 213 §§2-3 makes no specific reference to parish pastoral councils, but it expresses the rights of all of the faithful not only to make their needs, especially spiritual needs, and their desires known to their pastors, but also:

> ...In accord with the knowledge, competence and preeminence which they possess, they have the right and even at times a duty to manifest to the sacred pastors their opinion on matters which pertain to the good of the Church, and they have a right to make their opinion known to the other Christian faithful.

The pastor/presider when setting an agenda or conducting a parish pastoral council meeting would have an obligation to keep those rights in mind and take care that they are not denied. The pastor would also have the obligation and the right based on the final lines of c. 213 §3 and c. 223 §§1-2 to be sure that those rights not be overstepped to the detriment of the common good.

In addition to the general reference in c. 536 §1 to the pastor presiding over the pastoral council, the 1997 *Instruction on Certain Questions Regarding the Collaboration of the Non-Ordained Faithful in the Sacred Ministry of Priest* authoritatively directs:

> They are to be considered invalid and hence null and void, any deliberations entered into, (or decisions taken), by a parochial council which has not been pre-

sided over by the Parish Priest [Pastor] or which has assembled contrary to his wishes.[37]

This detailed and specific presentation of the understanding of a pastor's authority as presider over the pastoral council does emphasize the pastor's right, but, as always, rights impose obligations. The more power the pastor has over the pastoral council, the greater his personal responsibility to lead it successfully to achieve its goal as stated in c. 536 §1.

According to c. 536 §2, the parish pastoral council has only a consultative vote. However, a consultative vote should not be considered a meaningless exercise.[38] The pastor and the parish pastoral council have a common goal to achieve, in addition to which, the pastor shares Christ's task of servant leader. Sincere persons can have honest differences of opinion on any number of topics, nevertheless, in such circumstances each would appear to have an obligation to explain the facts and reasoning which she or he believes support an opinion or decision.

According to c. 536 §2, the parish pastoral council "is governed by norms determined by the diocesan bishop." While the diocesan bishop is not free to determine norms which contravene universal Church law, this canon neither requires nor forbids the diocesan bishop to establish one standard set of norms for parish pastoral councils in his diocese, nor does this canon restrain the diocesan bishop from determining or authorizing

---

[37] *Ecclesiae de mysterio*, art. 5 n.° 3. English translation *Certain Questions Regarding Collaboration*, p. 16. In art. 5, n. °2 of *Ecclesiae de mysterio* the reference in c. 536 §2 to the purely consultative vote of the pastoral council is emphasized with these words: "Diocesan and parochial Pastoral Councils and Parochial Finance Councils, of which non-ordained faithful are members, enjoy a consultative vote only and cannot in any way become deliberative structures."

[38] Canon 127 §2, 2° establishes that "if counsel is required, the action of a superior is invalid if the superior does not listen to those persons; although in no way obliged to accede to their recommendation, even if it be unanimous, nevertheless the superior should not act contrary to it, especially when there is a consensus, unless there be a reason which, in the superior's judgment, is overriding." No canon requires a pastor to consult the parish pastoral council on a specific matter, but it would not be impossible for a particular law to do so. In any case, a pastor might find useful, although analogous guidance in c. 127 §2, 2°.

different norms for the parish pastoral councils of different parishes. The latter approach could enable each parish to have the experience of formulating its own council with a knowledge of its own strengths and weaknesses and its commonly held goals; such a variety of possibilities might also meet the needs of a diocese with a mix of urban, suburban and rural parishes.

One commentary presents an insightful observation concerning the interaction of the diocesan bishop and members of a parish pastoral council:

> It is clear that, in this context — as in so many others — the most sensitive care must be exercised to accommodate, and to develop a genuine ecclesial understanding of, on the one hand the indisputable authority of the diocesan Bishop and, on the other, the right of his flock to express their views precisely in order to assist him in fulfilling his apostolic office. This was very much the theme of Vatican II.[39]

Canons 223 §§1-2 and 529 §2 call on the pastor of a parish to exercise an important role in helping the faithful to develop a genuine concern for the common good in general, the common good of the Church in particular and for ecclesial communion within the parish, diocese and universal Church.

In accord with c. 537[40] each parish is required to have a finance council. The parish finance council is a consultative body.[41] The pastor's interaction with that council must obviously

---

[39] READ, "Parishes, Parish Priests and Assistant Priests," in *Letter & Spirit*, n. 1066, pp. 298-299.

[40] Canon 537 is specific to the juridic person which is a parish. Canon 1280 states a broader requirement that every juridic person have its own finance council.

[41] The Code does not specifically state that the parish finance council is simply consultative, but c. 537 makes reference to "due regard" for c. 532 which establishes that the pastor is to see to the administration of parish goods and, the Code makes no mention of that council having any determinative authority. In addition, *Ecclesiae de mysterio*, art. 5, °2, plainly states that "Parochial Finance Councils... enjoy a consultative vote only and cannot in any way become deliberative structures." English translation *Certain Questions Regarding Collaboration*, p. 16. Also see art. 5 *in toto*, pp. 15-16.

be thorough, honest and reciprocal if it is to accomplish its goal. The operation of the parish finance council is "regulated by universal law as well as the norms issued by the diocesan bishop" as required by c. 537. In addition to c. 537, it is not clear that any other canon refers specifically to a pastor consulting with the parish finance council. Particular laws, differing from diocese to diocese, may impose obligations upon and give rights to pastors with respect to the parish finance council. Nevertheless, particular laws cannot alter the specific legislation of the *Instruction on Certain Questions Regarding the Collaboration of the Non-Ordained Faithful in the Sacred Ministry of Priest* which sets down that parish finance councils are only consultative and cannot become deliberative.[42]

What of the pastor's interaction with other parish and non-parish organizations? The pastor's general obligations in this regard have been considered previously, especially with reference to c. 529 §2 and the fostering of associations for religious purposes. In addition, as also treated earlier, c. 1063 obliges pastors of souls "to see to it that their own ecclesial community" provides in a number of ways to assist the faithful to prepare for marriage and to lead full and holy lives in their families. Fulfillment of that canon requires pastoral organization and co-operation on several levels.

Many parishes have variously titled, organized groups, which provide religious education, care for the appurtenances of the Church and liturgical worship, serve the needy, assist the spiritual and physical needs of the sick and aged, conduct sports and other wholesome activities for the youth of the parish, provide social gatherings for parishioners, raise money for parish projects, etc. The Code does not present specific regulations about every imaginable organization, but c. 519 establishes that the pastor of a parish is the proper shepherd of the parish and that, according to the norms of law, he governs his community.

---

[42] *Ibid.*

It seems that the least this could mean about the pastor's leadership role vis-à-vis organizations regarded as parish organizations would be that the pastor have a clear line of communication with each organization, be aware of their plans, recognize and encourage the good they may be doing, and/or warn them away, with a clear and detailed explanation, from activities which he judges to be unacceptable for a group associated with the parish, and in many cases using the parish's name.

Depending on the size of the parish, the number of organizations and the number and duties of the parish staff, the pastor may be personally able to attend meetings of all or some of the organizations, or the pastor may be able to have other staff members provide a personal presence at such meetings. Canons 528 and 529 in their entirety establish both general and specific obligations and rights for the pastor (either in person or through co-workers) to have as much contact as possible with parishioners, individually or in groups.

The pastor may also come in contact with non-parish organizations, perhaps groups from other Catholic parishes, or ecumenical religious groups, or organizations of members of other faiths, or civic groups and even pressure groups of one kind or another. Canon 519 directs that the pastor is to fulfill his task "exercising pastoral care in the community entrusted to him." The term *pastoral care* implies, at least, a duty to lead with foresight and prudence. Foresight and prudence in turn place an obligation on the pastor to learn about the goals, philosophy, methods and leadership of previously unknown organizations which may approach him or his parishioners. With regard to ecumenical efforts a pastor must follow the directives of the Holy See and his diocesan bishop.[43] In general, the pastor should prudently promote those organizations which he judges will help his parishioners and explain to his parishioners what is wrong with or dangerous about those which he judges will harm them.

---

[43] *CIC* c. 755 §1-2 and *CCEO* cc. 902-908.

4.3.4 — The pastor and the exercise of the executive power of governance

Executive power is required for and exercised in the ordinary administration and application of the law. There are also particular circumstances and specific conditions in which a pastor can exercise the executive power of governance in special ways, some more common than others. The pastor does this in relation to delegating others to assist at marriages and in dispensing from matrimonial impediments; he may also dispense or commute private vows, obligatory Mass attendance on Sundays and feast days and the obligation to fast and/or abstain on days of penance.

4.3.4.1 — The pastor's faculty to dispense from matrimonial impediments

The obligations and rights of the pastor with respect to marriage delegation are presented in cc. 1108 through 1111 and were treated in the previous chapter.

Canon 1073 establishes: "A diriment impediment renders a person incapable of contracting marriage validly." Diriment impediments may be of divine positive law, or natural law, or ecclesiastical law.[44] Only the supreme authority of the Church

---

[44] The Code of 1917 used the terms *diriment impediment* to identify an impediment which rendered a marriage invalid and *impedient impediment* to describe an impediment which rendered a marriage illicit but not invalid. During the consultations for the formulation of the 1983 Code the term *impedient* was initially changed to *prohibitive* and later completely eliminated. See J. FORNÉS, "Diriment Impediments," Commentary on cc. 1073-1094, in *Code Annotated*, pp. 667-668. It may be well to note that 1983 *CIC* continues to use the term *diriment impediment* in reference to marriage impediments even though the term *impedient impediment to marriage* does not appear in the 1983 Code. It is also interesting to note that c. 1085 §2 considered in conjunction with c. 10 declares the existence of a circumstance in which a marriage would be illicit, but not invalid; c. 1127 §1 admits of another case which would produce the same result.

can authentically declare when divine law, whether natural or positive, prohibits or voids a marriage; additionally, only the same authority can establish other impediments for the baptized.[45]

Canons 1079 §2 and 1080 §§1-2 set down two sets of circumstances and conditions within which a pastor is empowered by the law to dispense from certain matrimonial impediments.[46] For ease of reference the first situation will be called a *danger of death case*. Canon 1079 §2 requires two circumstances: danger of death *and* inaccessibility of the local ordinary.[47] In such circumstances c. 1079 §2 confers on the pastor the faculty to dispense from "each and every impediment of ecclesiastical law, whether public or occult, except the impediment arising from the sacred order of presbyterate." Since the *sacred order of presbyterate* is specified rather than the broader *sacred orders*, in a *danger of death case* the pastor can even dispense from the impediment arising from the reception of the diaconate.

The second situation will be termed an *everything ready for the marriage case*; c. 1080 §§1-2 requires three circumstances: that the impediment to be dispensed "is discovered *after* all the wedding preparations are made *and* the marriage cannot be deferred without probable danger of serious harm until a dispensation can be obtained from competent authority *and*, that the case is

---

[45] Canon 1075 §1-2. Also see c. 199, 1° which witnesses canonical use of the term "divine law" as including "divine natural or positive law" and c. 1399 which does the same, but less clearly.

[46] These canons empower not only the pastor but also: "…the properly delegated sacred minister and the priest or deacon who assists at matrimony in accord with the norm of can. 1116 §2.…" A lay person validly delegated by the diocesan bishop in accord with c. 1112 §1 to assist at marriages can also dispense from the same impediments under the conditions required by cc. 1079 §2 or 1080 §1-2. Their power to do so is provided by c. 138 in view of their valid delegation: "…a person who has received delegated power is understood to have been granted whatever is necessary to exercise that power."

[47] Canon 1079 §4 provides that in danger of death circumstances "the local ordinary is not considered to be accessible if he can be contacted only by means of telegraph or telephone."

an occult one. In such circumstances c. 1080 §1 confers on the pastor the power to dispense from all the impediments except "the impediment arising from the reception of sacred orders, or from a public perpetual vow of chastity in a religious institute of pontifical right."[48]

Canon 1079, which treats *danger of death cases*, provides for dispensations from "each and every impediment of ecclesiastical law." Canon 1080, the *everything ready for the marriage case*, grants authority to dispense from "all the impediments." A previous canon, 1078 §1, uses the broad term "all the impediments of ecclesiastical law" to describe the local ordinary's power to dispense from diriment impediments. Aside from the distinct exceptions that each of these canons establish in the particular circumstances which they specify, what do the terms *each and every impediment of ecclesiastical law, all the impediments* and *all the impediments of ecclesiastical law* mean? According to c. 1075 §§1-2, all diriment impediments are either of divine law or ecclesiastical law. Since the more serious *danger of death cases* of c. 1079 §§1-2 only allow dispensations from "each and every impediment of ecclesiastical law" it must be concluded that, although c. 1080, which provides for the less serious *everything ready for the marriage cases*, uses the term "all the impediments" it can only mean all of the impediments of ecclesiastical law and does not in any way express a faculty to dispense from impediments of divine law. In practice, then, there is no difference in the meaning of the three formulations.[49]

---

[48] Canon 1078 §2, 1º.

[49] Distinguishing diriment impediments of divine law from those of ecclesiastical law is not the task of this work, nor is it an altogether simple undertaking. Nevertheless it seems proper concisely to indicate points of agreement and general parameters of differing views. Canons 1083 through 1094 list twelve different diriment impediments, some of which have various subdivisions. There appears to be agreement that the impediments of ecclesiastical law are: holy orders (c. 1087), public perpetual vow of chastity in a religious institute — with no distinction made as to whether the religious institute is of diocesan or pontifical right (c. 1088), abduction and detention (c. 1089), crimen (c. 1090 §§ 1-2), affinity (1092), public propriety (c. 1093), legal relationship arising from adoption (c. 1094). Im-

From a practical point of view, for the pastor of a parish the most important required condition in the *everything ready for the marriage case* may be that he cannot dispense from the impediment unless *the case* is an occult one. It is *the case*, the very existence of any impediment, which must be *occult*, that is, in fact, not publicly known.[50]

The *discovery* referred to in c. 1080 §1 is the discovery by the pastor or local ordinary that an impediment exists. The couple may have known of the existence of certain circumstances without knowing that those circumstances constituted an impediment. As a result the fact that an impediment exists may not become known to Church authorities until everything is ready

---

pediments of divine law are: antecedent and perpetual impotence (c. 1084 §1), bond of a previous marriage (c. 1085 §1), consanguinity in all degrees of the direct line (c. 1091 §1). The diriment impediment of age (actually non-age or insufficient age) as specified in c. 1083 §1 is of ecclesiastical law, but at the very least the age of actually reaching the use of reason would seem to be of divine law. Disparity of worship (c. 1086 §§1-2) in practice is an impediment of ecclesiastical law, but it has been argued that it would be of divine law in a case where the faith of the Catholic party would be *de facto* in danger. Consanguinity in the collateral line is proclaimed an impediment up to and including the fourth degree by c. 1091 §2, and c. 1078 §3 directs that a dispensation from the impediment of consanguinity in the second degree of the collateral line is never given, but whether or not that precise impediment is of divine or ecclesiastical law is an unsettled question. See P.C. AUGUSTINE, *The Pastor According to the New Code of Canon Law*, second edition, St. Louis, MO: B. Herder Book Co., 1924, pp. 129-130; and J.I. BAÑARES and J. MANTECÓN, "Impedimentos dirimentes en particular," Commentary on cc. 1083-1094, in *Comentario exegético*, vol. III/2, pp. 1161-1210.

50 Canon 1074 establishes: "An impediment which can be proven in the external forum is considered to be a public impediment, otherwise it is an occult impediment." Canon 1080, however, requires that "the *case* is an occult one" (italics added), not that the *impediment itself* be occult. Canon 1074 is a verbatim reproduction of c. 1037 of the 1917 Code and c. 1080 §1 uses substantially the same expression "dummodo casus sit occultus" as was employed on the same subject by c. 1045 §3 of the Code of 1917 "solum pro casibus occultis." The *fontes* for c. 1080 §1 include a reference to PONTIFICIA COMMISSIO AD CODICIS CANONES AUTHENTICE INTERPRETANDOS, Resp. III, 28 dec. 1927 (*AAS*, 20 [1928], 61), which interprets the "occult cases" of c. 1045 §3 to include not only matrimonial impediments which are by nature and in fact occult but also those which are by nature public and in fact occult. Also see DOYLE, "Marriage," in *CLSA Commentary*, p. 763; J. FORNÉS, "Diriment Impediments," in *Code Annotated*, pp. 673-674; KELLY, "Marriage," in *Letter & Spirit*, n. 2131, p. 597; J. FORNÉS, "Impedimentes en general," Commentary on cc. 1073-1082, in *Comentario exegético*, III/2, p. 1159.

for the wedding.[51] The condition set down in c. 1081 §1, "After all the wedding preparations are made," refers to the canonical preparations required by the Code itself and norms of the National Conference of Bishops set down in accord with c. 1067.[52] The final condition c. 1080 §1 required in an *everything ready for the marriage case* is "the marriage cannot be deferred without probable danger of serious harm until a dispensation can be obtained from competent authority." The serious harm which, for the validity of the dispensation must be truly probable but does not need to be certain, could involve a loss of reputation for the parties to the marriage and their family members, serious repercussions within the families of the bride and/or groom, substantial financial loss and similar *serious* problems.

---

[51] A question arises whether this dispensing faculty may be used on behalf of persons who deliberately and in bad faith withheld information about the impediment until everything was ready for the marriage. Commenting on that question with respect to c. 1045 §1 of the 1917 Code which treated the same matter, several canonists held that even such bad faith concealment by those to be married would not vitiate the power to dispense, as cited in T.L. Bouscaren and A.C. Ellis, *Canon Law: A Text and Commentary*, 2nd rev. ed., Milwaukee: The Bruce Publishing Company, 1951, p. 499, footnote 89; J.A. Abbo and J.D. Hannan, *The Sacred Canons: A Concise Presentation of the Current Disciplinary Norms of the Church* (=Abbo & Hannan, *The Sacred Canons*), rev. ed., St. Louis, MO: B. Herder Book Company, 1957, vol. II, p. 224; Woywod and Smith, *Practical Commentary*, p. 681; Doyle, "Marriage," in *CLSA Commentary*, pp. 762-763 appears to be making the same point, but seems to misnumber the 1917 canon as 1044 rather than 1045 §1; Kelly, "Marriage," in *Letter & Spirit*, n. 2129, p. 596 hints, without clearly taking the position, that if the parties deliberately conceal the impediment then c. 1080 §1 would not be applicable.

[52] As of 1993 a number of National Conferences of Bishops appear not to have acted on this matter, see *Code Annotated*, Appendix III, "Complementary Norms to the Code Promulgated by English-Language Conferences of Bishops," pp. 1309-1434 passim. The National Conference of Catholic Bishops of the United States determined: "Until a study is completed, the National Conference of Catholic Bishops authorized diocesan bishops to establish interim norms for pre-nuptial investigation for their own dioceses," as in *Code Annotated*, Appendix III, "Complementary Norms to the Code Promulgated by English-Language Conferences of Bishops," p. 1421.

4.3.4.2 — The pastor's faculty to dispense from or commute private vows

Canon 1192 establishes: "A vow is *public* if it is accepted in the name of the Church by a legitimate superior; otherwise it is *private*." Only a *public* vow can pose an impediment which would render a marriage null. In a *danger of death case* the pastor may dispense from the impediments posed by any vow (cc. 1079 §1 and 1088), but in an *everything ready for the marriage case*, the pastor cannot dispense from an impediment arising "from a *public* perpetual vow of chastity in a religious institute of pontifical right" (c. 1078 §1). Canon 1196 regulates dispensations from private vows and indicates that a pastor can dispense his own subjects as well as travelers[53] provided that the dispensation is from a *private* vow, that there is a just reason for dispensing *and* such a dispensation does not injure a right acquired by others.

A vow, even simply a private vow, is, after all, a deliberate promise made to God and so a just reason is required for granting a dispensation. Such just reasons would include, but not be limited to, a vow that was ill advised and should not have been made in the first place, a vow about something which was, or has become, physically or morally impossible, or could be injurious to others, or even to the person who made the vow, a vow which was not made freely — especially in a psychological sense, and other similar circumstances.

Depending on what is promised in a vow, other persons, physical or juridical, may acquire rights as a result of a vow or as a result of the person who made the vow having taken some

---

[53] A pastor's *own* subjects would be those for whom he is the *proper* pastor. Canon 107 §§ 1-3 establishes the pastor of the territory in which a person has a domicile or quasi-domicile is that person's proper pastor; if one has *no* domicile or quasi-domicile, or has *only* a diocesan domicile or quasi-domicile, that person's proper pastor is the pastor of the territory in which the person is actually staying. A Latin rite pastor's subjects might also include the faithful of Catholic Eastern rites who live within the territory of his parish, if no eparch of their own rite has jurisdiction over the same geographical area.

steps toward carrying out the vow. Since an acquired right is a legal construct, the existence of an acquired right in any given case should be demonstrable through a legal process. It would appear, therefore, that no person acquires a right as the result of what has been vowed to God unless the individual who made the vow has subsequently informed others of the terms of the obligation self-imposed by the vow. Thus, if a person vowed to God that he or she would do some particular work for a charitable cause, or make some financial donation to some worthy project, but never revealed the vow to anyone else, neither the charitable cause nor the worthwhile project would have an acquired right as a result of the vow.

Canon 1197 provides that a pastor can commute the work promised in a vow to a lesser good, provided the same circumstances exist as set forth in c. 1196, i.e. a private vow, a just reason, and no injury to a right acquired by others.

4.3.4.3 — The pastor's faculties to dispense from or commute obligatory Mass attendance on Sundays and feast days and the obligations of days of penance

Canon 1245 authorizes a pastor to dispense from or commute to other pious works "the obligation to observe a feast day or a day of penance" under several conditions. There must be a just reason for the dispensation or the commutation, the action must be in accord with the prescriptions of the diocesan bishop and the pastor can only act in individual cases.

The just reason for dispensing from or commuting the obligations of attending Mass on feast days (Holy Days of Obligation) or observing days of penance (fast and/or abstinence) cannot be capricious or idiosyncratic.[54] Where a diocesan bishop has

---

[54] This would appear to be especially true with regard to the obligation to attend Mass on Sundays and Holy Days of Obligation because of the importance of the community gathering together to worship God by carrying out their respective liturgical roles as the Second Vatican Council emphasized.

issued prescriptions which cover dispensing from or commuting these obligations, c. 1245 imposes an obligation on a pastor to obey such prescriptions. If there are no diocesan prescriptions about these matters, it would seem prudent for a pastor to follow whatever he may know to have been the diocesan bishop's general practice or wishes about such dispensations or commutations.

The pastor can dispense from or commute these obligations only in "individual cases (*singulis in casibus*)."[55] An individual case may, however, encompass far more than one person, even everyone in a parish, depending of the facts of the case.[56] Since the obligations of Sundays and Holy Days of Obligation and of fast and abstinence exist for important reasons, the course of prudence in many, if not most, cases might be to commute the obligation to some other specific good work, rather than simply to dismiss the obligation by way of dispensation.

4.3.5 — The pastor's obligations to keep records

The work of record keeping may be dull, repetitive and boring, but it is extremely important. Records of the reception of sacraments are records of the status of persons in the Church. Records kept in response to civil requirements may prove indispensable to lay employees in matters of government programs to assist those injured or disabled at work (or the families of employees killed on the job), to those who, perhaps years later,

---

[55] Canon 1245.

[56] R. Browne, "Sacred Times," Commentary on cc. 1244-1253, in *Letter & Spirit*, n. 2462, pp. 699-700. The more restrictive words of c. 1245 of the 1917 Code "singulos fideles singulasve familias" and draft c. 43's "sive singulis fidelibus, sive singulis familiis" (for individual faithful or individual families) was deliberately dropped by a 4 to 2 vote of the consultors on the committee during the formulation process of the 1983 Code so that, the other conditions being fulfilled, a pastor would be in a position to dispense even the entire parish if necessary. *Communicationes*, 12 (1980) p. 358.

will need proof to establish their right to government retirement programs and/or Church pension plans.[57] Records may also be necessary for the parish to prove ownership of property and/or payment of bills. In some civil jurisdictions also, Church baptismal and marriage records are as acceptable as civil records of birth, or marriage, or death. The indispensability of such records for spiritual concerns and for matters of justice and equity renders the keeping of those records a serious moral obligation as well as a grave canonical obligation.

Canon 535 §§1-5 deal with parish sacramental, adoption and death records, which records need to be kept, and how the registers containing them should be protected.[58] Canon 788 §1 directs that the names of those admitted to the catechumenate "are to be registered in a book destined for this purpose."[59]

Canon 958 §1 requires pastors to have a special book to record Mass stipends, the number of Masses involved, the intention and the date of celebration; c. 1307 §2 orders that a similar book be kept to record the fulfillment of obligations arising from a pious foundation. Canon 1306 §2 prescribes that a copy of the terms of a pious foundation is to be "securely filed in the archive" of a parish which has accepted a pious foundation. Canon 1284 §2, 7° requires that the administrator, i.e. the pastor of the parish, keep "well ordered books of receipts and expen-

---

[57] Canon 231 §2 does not mention record keeping, but it calls to the pastor's attention the rights of lay employees of the Church to "their pension, social security and health benefits"; in many civil jurisdictions, to ensure those rights the employer-parish will need to have thorough employment records.

[58] In connection with baptismal records, c. 877 §2 places an obligation on the pastor that he be one of three witnesses to an unmarried father's declaration that he is the father of a child who is to be baptized and that he wishes his name to be inserted into the baptismal register.

[59] This requirement of c. 788 §1 is interesting because of its location in the Code in Book 3, Title II, *Missionary Activity of the Church*. Liturgical law of the Roman Rite whether for missionary territories or otherwise has required that there be such a register since 1972. See SACRA CONGREGATIO PRO CULTU DIVINO, *Rituale Romanum ex decreto Sacrosancti Oecumenici Concilii Vaticani II instauratum auctoritate Pauli PP. VI promulgatum, Ordo initiationis christianae adultorum*, 1972, Typis polyglottis Vaticanis, n. 17, p. 18. English translation *Documents on the Liturgy*, pp. 300-302.

ditures"; in addition, the same canon in §2, 9° requires a suitable and secure archive for all documents and deeds which establish the legal rights of a parish; it also requires that the Diocesan Curia be supplied with authentic copies of such legal instruments. Canon 1307 §1 establishes that there is to be retained in an obvious place a list of obligations arising from pious foundations so that the obligations will be fulfilled and not neglected.

Other canons repeat or reinforce the general requirements of c. 535: Baptism, cc. 877 §1; Confirmation, cc. 895; Holy Orders, c. 1054; Marriage, cc. 1121 §1. Among the canons which mandate record keeping, there are some which confer an implicit right on certain pastors by imposing on those who have administered or witnessed a sacrament an explicit obligation that they inform the pastor of the parish in which the person receiving the sacrament was baptized; c. 878 requires this with respect to a Baptism unknown to the newly baptized's pastor; c. 896 orders the same concerning a Confirmation unknown to a person's pastor. Canons 1121 §§2-3, 1122 §§1-2 oblige certain witnesses under various circumstances, to inform the pastor of the parish in which a marriage took place, and to inform the pastors of the parishes of baptism of the spouses, if either is different from the parish of marriage. Canon 1123 requires, without specifying who is required, that if any marriage is convalidated, annulled or legitimately dissolved other than by death, the pastors of the parish of the marriage and of the baptism of each spouse are to be informed "so that a notation may be duly made in the marriage and baptismal registers." Canon 1081 places an obligation on pastor, priest or deacon who dispenses from matrimonial impediments to immediately inform the local ordinary.[60]

---

[60] READ, "Parishes, Parish Priests and Assistant Priests," in *Letter & Spirit*, n. 1061, p. 297, also suggests that there is a need to preserve the dossier of marriage preparation and celebration documents and data called for in cc. 1066-1070. Presumably the explicit requirements that data and documents be gathered implies that they are to be retained even after the marriage.

Finally c. 535 §3 may suitably be noted here. This third paragraph of c. 535 does not concern keeping records, but imposes the obligation that each parish is to have its own seal, which is to be used in conjunction with the signature of the pastor or his delegate, to authenticate "documents which are issued to certify the canonical status of the Christian faithful as well as all acts which can have juridic importance." As a result, the pastor is obliged to have such a seal and to sign certificates himself unless he delegates someone else to sign in his place.

4.4 — MINISTRY OF GOVERNING: THE PASTOR'S CARE OF PARISH TEMPORALITIES

Since the Church and its pastors are to carry out their work in the world, the reality of temporalities, both ecclesiastical and civil, touches the parish just as it touches almost every other human community. Many canons which regulate the handling of temporalities apply not only to pastors and parishes but to other ecclesiastical administrators and institutions as well. For clarity of focus in treating most of those canons, references will be made simply to *pastor(s)* or *parish(es)*, not in any way to deny that other church administrators and/or other juridic persons are also subject to the same canons, but because such other administrators and entities do not for the most part impinge on the topic at hand.

In accord with c. 532, the pastor has the obligation and right to administer the temporalities of a parish as required by canon law.[61] In addition, as noted earlier "The pastor represents the parish in all juridic affairs in accord with the norm of law" (c.

---

[61] In addition to c. 532, the same conclusion is reached by considering that c. 1279 §1 stipulates that the individual who immediately governs a juridic person has the responsibility to administer its goods and c. 519 establishes that the pastor has the duty of governing his parish.

532).[62] Every legitimately erected parish is a juridic person (c. 515 §3), as a juridic person each parish is capable of acquiring temporal goods by every just means of natural or positive law[63] and retaining, administering and alienating[64] temporal goods in accord with the law (c. 1255).[65] With due respect for the right of the Pope, temporal goods rightfully belong to the juridic person which acquires them (c. 1256).

Probably the most basic and concise direction the pastor has with respect to the administration of the parish's temporalities is presented in c. 1254 §2: "The following ends are especially proper to the Church: to order divine worship; to provide decent support for the clergy and other ministers; to perform the works of the sacred apostolate and of charity, especially towards the needy."

The pastor's obligations and rights will be considered under the four canonical *Titles* of Book 5 of the Code, *The Temporal Goods of the Church*. These treat respectively: Acquisition, Administration, Contracts and Alienation and both Pious Dispositions in general (contributions or gifts with specified conditions) and Pious Foundations (or trusts). Under the first three of those titles the obligations and rights imposed or conferred by the canons

---

[62] As representative of the parish in all juridic matters, from time to time a pastor may have to answer for obligations and/or exercise rights which belong, not to himself as pastor, but to the juridic person of the parish and which have become elements of some specific legal (canonical or civil) action. Such obligations and rights are not within the focus of this book.

[63] Canon 1259.

[64] "*Alienation* simply means the transfer of the ownership of property from one person to another.... In this context, however... it includes... 'any transaction whereby the patrimonial condition of the juridical person may be jeopardized' (Can. 1295)... such as mortgage, lien, option... any act whereby Church property would be subjected to either a permanent or long-term burden as e.g. in the case of borrowing money... included also... the dissipation of so-called immovable goods, e.g. a fund, for a purpose other than that for which it was donated or designed... the disposal of objects of a worth which is special by reason of their market value or their artistic, historical, consecrated or votive nature," F.G. MORRISEY, "The Temporal Goods of the Church," Commentary on cc. 1254-1310, in *Letter & Spirit*, n. 2572, p. 732.

[65] Also see cc. 1254, 1258 and 1259.

will be developed and treated by detailing six specific points: (a) the existence and effect of particular law; (b) permissions the pastor must obtain; (c) the duty to carry out the intention of the contributor/donor; (d) the requirements of vigilance and reporting; (e) the existence and effect of civil law; (f) other significant material. The final section concerning the administration of contributions or gifts with specified conditions or which establish pious foundations or trusts, imposes obligations more directly on the parishes as juridic persons than directly on pastors; that section will be treated in a more general way.

4.4.1 — Acquisition of parish temporalities

(a) *The existence and effect of particular law.* All temporal goods belonging to a parish are ecclesiastical goods and are regulated by the canons of Book 5 (c. 1257 §1). In addition to the canon law on temporalities, it is likely that there may be both particular law, diocesan regulations, and in a number of cases an unwritten, but publicly known, diocesan *practice,* perhaps even a custom properly so called, with regard to collections and fund raising. Canon 1265 §2 directs that the "conference of bishops can determine norms on fund-raising, which must be observed by everyone." If the conference of bishops has produced norms, the pastor is obliged to follow them. In virtue of c. 1266, the local ordinary may require parish churches to take a special collection "for specific parochial, diocesan, national or universal projects." There is no requirement that either the diocesan finance council or the pastoral council be consulted by the ordinary before requiring such collections. If the requirement is issued, the parish is again obliged to cooperate.[66] Canon law does

---

[66] The consultors formulating the Code intended that the local ordinary would use the authority to call for such special collections in a moderate manner. See MORRISEY, "The Temporal Goods of the Church," in *Letter & Spirit,* n. 2507, pp. 714-715 and p. 715, footnote 1 re: *Communicationes,* 12 (1980), p. 405 at c. 8.

not set any particular limit to the number of collections which may be taken up at any particular liturgy or other gathering, but often a diocese will have norms or customs which can guide a pastor in that matter.

Just as a parish has a right and a necessity to acquire finances for its own existence, its buildings, its operating expenses, its present programs and projects, and its future plans, so also a diocese has a right and a necessity to fund its needs. Canon 1263 directs that a diocesan bishop has the right to tax a parish to fund diocesan needs with a tax that is both *moderate* and *in proportion to the income* of each particular parish. This tax can only be *validly* imposed after the diocesan bishop has heard the diocesan finance council and the presbyteral council on the matter.[67]

Canon 1264, 2° provides a general rule about the establishment of stole fees for instances in which the Code has not set forth specific regulations.[68] The general rule is that a meeting of the bishops of a province is responsible for establishing stole fees. If stole fees have not been established either by canons of the Code or by the bishops of a province, it would then be proper for pastors to act in accord with the custom of the diocese in which they serve.[69]

(b) *Permissions the pastor must obtain.* With regard to all permissions required in matters relating to ecclesiastical temporal goods the pastor/administrator is well advised to keep in mind the following: cc. 128 and 1296, which in substance call for a recompense to persons, physical or juridic, who are injured by the

---

[67] Canon 1263 together with c. 127 §2, 2°. Canons 1504, 1505, 1506 of the 1917 Code which cover somewhat the same material as does the 1983 Code's c. 1263 did not require that the diocesan bishop consult with any council before levying taxes nor that taxes be proportionate to the income of the one taxed.

[68] J.J. Myers, "The Temporal Goods of the Church," Commentary on cc: 1254-1310, in *CLSA Commentary*, p. 867. Also see cc. 945-958 for laws regarding Mass stipends in general. Canons 945 §2, 947, 948, 950, 952 §§1-3 and 1181 have reference to the actual amount of the Mass stipend offering.

[69] Morrisey, "The Temporal Goods of the Church," in *Letter & Spirit*, n. 2504, p. 714.

failure of others to observe "required canonical formalities"; c. 1375, which permits a just penalty to be imposed for impeding "the legitimate use of sacred goods or other ecclesiastical goods"; c. 1377, which mandates a just penalty for "one who alienates ecclesiastical goods without the prescribed permission"; and c. 1741, 5°, which lists among "…the reasons for which a pastor can be legitimately removed from his parish… poor administration of temporal affairs with grave damage to the Church whenever this problem cannot be remedied in any other way."

In addition to any permissions which particular law may require, c. 1267 §2 mandates that offerings made to a parish: "may not be refused without a just cause and, in matters of greater importance, without the permission of the ordinary… permission of the same ordinary is required to accept those gifts to which are attached some qualifying obligation or condition."[70] A just cause for refusing a donation could arise from a question about whether the donor is the rightful owner, the good faith of the donor, the purpose for which it is to be donated, the circumstances of the donor, the nature of the object being offered, where it comes from, what it looks like or depicts.[71]

(c) *The duty to carry out the intention of the contributor/donor.* Canon 1267 §3 requires: "The offerings given by the faithful for a definite purpose can be applied only for that same purpose." This rule is stressed consistently in the Code[72] and is one of the

---

[70] This translation departs from that of the CLSA, which concludes with the words "a condition or a modal obligation." The words "qualifying obligation or condition" are taken from the *CLSGBI Code of Canon Law*, English Translation, c. 1267 §2.

[71] Morrisey, "The Temporal Goods of the Church," in *Letter & Spirit*, n. 2512, pp. 715-716; M. López Alarcón, "The Temporal Goods of the Church," Commentary on cc. 1254-1310, in *Code Annotated*, p. 783; D. Tirapu, "Adquisición de los bienes," Commentary on cc. 1259-1272, in *Comentario exegético*, vol. IV/1, p. 90.

[72] See cc. 950, 955 §1, 1294 §2, 1300, 1301 §2, 1302 §2, 1303 §2, 1304 §1, 1305, 1306 §1, 1307 §§1-2, 1308 §2. There are some exceptions provided for in cc. 1308, 1309 and 1310 and they are usually based on changing circumstances as the years pass after a donation has been made and/or the donor has died.

reasons why the permission of the ordinary is required for acceptance of donations which have qualifying obligations or conditions attached. The ordinary needs to be sure that the parish involved can foreseeably fulfill such obligations or conditions before he gives the parish permission to accept a donation.

(d) *The requirements of vigilance and reporting.* Although particular law may impose obligations on pastors with respect to reporting acquisitions, cc. 1259-1272 in that title of the Code do not do so explicitly. By implication however, since c. 1263 establishes that a lawful tax on a parish must be proportionate to its income, it appears incumbent on the pastor that he present to the diocesan bishop a canonically acceptable proof of what, in fact, the income of a parish amounts to.

(e) *The existence and effect of civil law.* Clearly, civil law varies from jurisdiction to jurisdiction, as does particular law. Whenever and in whatever circumstances the law of the Church gives to civil law the force of ecclesiastical law, to such a *canonization* of civil laws a proviso is always attached "insofar as they [the civil laws] are not contrary to divine law and unless it is provided otherwise in canon law."[73] The canons on acquisition do not explicitly extend canonical acceptance or authority or consequences to civil law in this matter. The pastor should, however, be alert to any existing civil laws regarding various types and methods of fund raising, or the transfer of title to equities, real estate or personal goods, or the type of archives needed to establish in civil law that obligations attached to offerings have been carried out, or records which may be required to assist contributors with respect to possible tax deductions or write-offs.

Canon 1268 establishes that property and freedom from obligations in regard to temporal goods are subject to *prescription* as provided in cc. 197-199. In turn, c. 197 mandates that with some exceptions, "the Church accepts prescription as it exists in the civil legislation of the respective nations...." In practice the

---

[73] Canon 22.

most practical application of prescription with respect to a parish would have to do with acquiring real property, or a right of way, or valuable objects, or, conversely and lamentably, losing them.[74] Since the pastor is responsible for the administration of parish goods, he would have an obligation to act prudently with respect to the local civil laws regarding prescription, which would at least involve consulting a civil attorney about whether any dangers are posed to parish real estate, rights of way or other goods by the circumstances of the parish and whether the conditions exist in which the temporal goods of the parish might be enlarged by prescription in accord with cc. 197 and 198. Whether the provisions of cc. 1269 and 1270 regarding public ecclesiastical persons would have any recognition in any given civil jurisdiction is questionable, but that is a question for a civil attorney.

(f) *Other significant material.* Canons 222 §1 and 1260 through 1262 set down that the Christian faithful are required to provide whatever is necessary to accomplish the purposes of the Church, that the diocesan bishop is to admonish the faithful about that obligation and encourage them to fulfill it following the norms established by the conference of bishops. The pastor has a right to expect that adequate offerings will be made to provide the support to which the parish has a right as it carries out its apostolic works.

Canon 1267 §1 mandates a rule for pastors: "Unless the contrary is established, the offerings given to... [the pastor of a parish] are presumed to be given to that juridic person."[75] Canon 531 provides a similar regulation with respect to offerings given to

---

[74] Prescription can involve either the acquisition or loss of temporal goods and usually, if not always, requires the passage of a substantial period of time. As a result, it seems that cc. 1268-1270 would fit more logically under the title *The Administration of Goods* than in their present location.

[75] A particular application of c. 1267 §1's general principle is found in c. 510 §4: "Any alms which are given to a church which is at the same time parochial and capitular are presumed to be given to the parish unless otherwise evident."

anyone who performs a parochial function; c. 551 explicitly applies c. 531 to offerings received by a parochial vicar on the occasion of his pastoral ministrations. The thrust of this canonical requirement is to assure that the intention of the donor be carried out with regard to any donation which the Church accepts. If the donor clearly indicates that a donation is a personal gift to a particular minister, then that is what it is; lacking such explicit direction, however, it becomes the property of the parish.

Where parochial benefices still exist in the strict sense, their pastors have the obligation of accepting and cooperating with the conference of bishops in the conference's supervising and management of the benefice — but not the pastoral care — of the parish "through appropriate norms which are agreeable to and approved by the Apostolic See," as required by c. 1272. The pastoral care of the community of the parish/benefice is the obligation and right of the pastor under the authority of the diocesan bishop.

4.4.2 — Administration of parish temporalities

(a) *The existence and effect of particular law.* Canon 1276 §1 establishes that it is the "responsibility of the ordinary to supervise carefully the administration of all the goods which belong to [a parish] subject to him." While he is the *supervisor of administration*, the ordinary is not the *administrator*. In accord with c. 1279 §1, the *pastor* who governs the parish is the *administrator* of the goods belonging to the parish, but the ordinary has the right to "intervene in case of negligence by an administrator." It is not surprising then, that c. 1276 §2 directs: "Ordinaries are to see to the organization of the entire administration of ecclesiastical goods by issuing special instructions within the limits of universal and particular law with due regard for rights, legitimate customs and circumstances." Wherever particular law or special instructions are in force a pastor has the obligation and right to know of such laws and to obey them.

Canon 1281 §2 authorizes a diocesan bishop to determine, after he has heard his finance council, limits and procedures of ordinary administration, which according to c. 1281 §1, a parish pastor is not to exceed without written authority from the ordinary. Since c. 1281 §1 and §2 does not require a particular law to establish "limits and procedures of ordinary administration," the diocesan bishop can oblige pastors by means of diocesan regulations, guidelines or operating procedures in these matters.

Canon 1284 §3 "strongly recommends" that particular law "issue regulations concerning... budgets and to determine more precisely how they are to be presented."[76] Where such particular law exists, it establishes a real obligation for the pastor. In addition, since in the text of c. 1284 §3 the preparation of annual budgets is "strongly recommended" by the universal law, the pastor would need a strong reason to decide that he would not prepare a budget even if there were no particular law requiring that he do so.[77]

(b) *Permissions the pastor must obtain.* A pastor, if he is to act validly, is required by c. 1281 §1 to obtain written authority from the ordinary before placing acts which go beyond the limits and procedures of ordinary administration. Such limits and procedures may differ from diocese to diocese, but would often place a limit on how large an expenditure of parish funds a pastor can authorize on his own for a particular operating or capital project.[78] Canon 1284 §2, 6° requires that the pastor have the

---

[76] It is interesting to observe that c. 1284 §1 requires that administrators fulfill their office with "the diligence of a good householder," while in paragraph §3 of the same canon even the preparation of an annual budget is only a vigorous recommendation. A diligent householder who does not have a budget two or three or more years into the future seems almost a contradiction in terms.

[77] Canon 1028 §§1-3 of the *CCEO* is substantially the same as c. 1284 §§1-3 of the *CIC*.

[78] Although a requirement to seek written permission has certain confining aspects to it, written permission actually affords a pastor protection in the matter at hand since it is proof that the pastor followed diocesan regulations and that the ordinary regarded the permitted action as proper.

ordinary's consent to invest excess parish funds; c. 1288 requires the pastor to have written permission of the ordinary to enter into or to contest a *civil* lawsuit on behalf of his parish. Canon 1289 implies that permission of the competent ecclesiastical authority is required before a pastor may relinquish his administrative duties; c. 1289 also explicitly provides that any administrator who acts irresponsibly "is bound to restitution" if the parish is harmed as a result.[79]

(c) *The duty to carry out the intention of the contributor/donor.* Canon 1284 §2, 3° and 4° respectively require the pastor to "observe the prescriptions of both canon and civil law or those imposed by the founder, donor or legitimate authority," and "...apply them [revenues and income] according to the intention of the founder."

(d) *The requirements of vigilance and reporting.* Canon 1284 §2, 8° requires pastors "to draw up a report on their administration at the end of each year," without, however, directing what is to be done with the report. Canon 1287 §2 sets down that there should be norms of particular law according to which pastors "are to render an account to the faithful concerning the goods offered by the faithful to the Church, according to norms to be determined by particular law." If there is no such particular law, the diocesan bishop appears to be called upon by c. 1287 §2 to provide the apposite legislation. In the absence of the required particular law a pastor should follow a set diocesan practice or instruction or custom, if such exists, although his obligation to do so would not be as strong as to obey particular law.

In accord with 1287 §2, the "goods offered by the faithful," concerning which a report is to be made, would not of itself require a full financial accounting reporting on temporal goods

---

[79] Canon 187 indicates that anyone who wishes to resign an ecclesiastical office needs to have a just cause for doing so; c. 189 §1 mandates that for validity a resignation must be submitted to "the authority who is responsible for the provision of the office"; in turn c. 189 §2 directs that "the authority is not to accept a resignation which is not based on a just and proportionate cause."

acquired and/or alienated by the parish in other ways, e.g., interest income, income from payment received in settlement of insurance claims, activities which raise funds by providing some service, instruction or entertainment, rather than simply by requesting that temporal goods be offered to the parish.[80] It is also interesting to note that c. 1287 §2 does not specify a time frame for the report, leaving that matter to particular law.

(e) *The existence and effect of civil law.* Canon 1286 requires pastors "to observe meticulously the civil laws pertaining to labor and social policy." Such laws in various civil jurisdictions may include providing a safe and harassment free work place, anti-discrimination law in hiring and firing, minimum wage requirements, contract law, unionization, withholding taxes, unemployment insurance, workers compensation coverage, social security tax payments, possibly mandated medical and dental programs, etc.[81] Both points 1° and 2° of c. 1286 are specifications of c. 231 which sets forth in general the obligations and rights of lay employees of the Church and c. 281 concerning clerics.

The requirements of cc. 1284 §2, 8°, 1287 §§1-2 with respect to reporting about administration, and of c. 1284 §2, 3° and 4° concerning the carrying out the intentions of founders, donors and other legitimate authority, may be paralleled by civil law requirements for the filing and/or publication of reports, even certified financial reports, by religious, charitable, not-for-profit

---

[80] Z. COMBALÍA, "Administración de los bienes," Commentary on cc. 1273-1289, in *Comentario exegético*, vol. IV/1, p. 144; MORRISEY, "The Temporal Goods of the Church," in *Letter & Spirit*, n. 2565, p. 730; LÓPEZ ALARCÓN, "The Temporal Goods of the Church," in *Code Annotated*, p. 799. With due regard for the particular law which might exist in any given diocese, c. 1287 §2 would not seem to require a report on real estate or other property bought, sold or leased by the parish unless such activity were to take place in the same reporting period during which the temporal goods involved were given by the faithful.

[81] See J.A. ALESANDRO and A.J. PLACA, "Church Agents and Employees: Legal and Canonical Issues," in *CLSA Proceedings*, 58 (1996), pp. 35-82, especially pp. 55-58; CANON LAW SOCIETY OF AMERICA, "Canonical Standards in Labor-Management Relations," in *The Jurist*, 47 (1987), pp. 545-575; T.E. MOLLOY and J.J. FOLMER, "The Canonization of Civil Law," in *CLSA Proceedings*, 46 (1984), pp. 43-65.

groups, which in some civil jurisdictions may also be civil corporations, or enjoy a tax exempt status, etc.[82] Canon 1284 §2, 2° calls on the pastor to protect the ownership of ecclesiastical goods through civilly valid means; 3° requires the pastor to observe prescriptions of civil law and "especially be on guard lest the Church be harmed through the non-observance of civil laws"; and c. 1288 requires the ordinary's written permission to file or defend against a suit in *civil* court on behalf of a juridic person.

(f) *Other significant material.* Canon 537 requires that each parish is to have "a finance council which is regulated by universal law as well as by norms issued by the diocesan bishop."[83] The purpose of the finance council according to c. 537 is to provide the pastor with the assistance of the Christian faithful in the administration of parish goods. As with the parish council, which is a consultative body only,[84] it appears that c. 537 expects that the pastor will be communicative and cooperative with the finance council members as he exercises his leadership role with respect to parish temporalities. The *Instruction on Certain Questions Regarding the Collaboration of the Non-Ordained Faithful in the Sacred Ministry of Priest* directs that parochial finance councils "enjoy a consultative vote only and cannot in any way become deliberative."[85] In view of c. 1276 §2, the ordinary would be the competent authority to issue statutes for all parish finance councils in a diocese, or, if he deemed it more prudent, to allow parishes to submit draft formulations of their own which he might then approve for use in those parishes.

---

[82] See Morrisey, "The Temporal Goods of the Church," in *Letter & Spirit*, n. 2565, p. 730.

[83] Canon 537 concerned with parishes in particular is far more specific than c. 1280 which concerns juridic persons in general and requires that each juridic person have a finance council or at least two advisors.

[84] Canon 536 §2.

[85] *Ecclesiae de mysterio*, art. 5, °2. English translation *Certain Questions Regarding Collaboration*, p. 16.

Canon 1286, 1°-2° requires that the pastor very carefully follow "Church principles in the employment of workers," paying "a just and decent wage so that they may provide appropriately for their needs and those of their family." Whatever canonical obligations those stipulations impose, it is more important still that they constitute moral obligations which bind in justice.

Canon 1282 binds pastors to fulfill their duties in the name of the Church and in accord with the norm of law[86]; c. 1284 §1 mandates that "All administrators [pastors] are bound to fulfill their office with the diligence of a good householder." Canon 1283, 1° requires that before taking their office pastors must "take an oath before the ordinary or his delegate that they will be efficient and faithful administrators."[87] In pursuit of this efficiency, c. 1283, 2°-3° requires the pastor to "prepare, sign and subsequently renew an accurate and detailed inventory" of all of the parish's goods, with descriptions and appraisals, to retain a copy in the parish archives with another copy in the diocesan curia and to keep such lists up to date. Canon 1284 §2, 1° lays upon pastors the obligation to see to it that "none of the goods entrusted to their care is in any way lost or damaged and to take out insurance policies for this purpose." Depending on the economic circumstances of the country and the applicability of its legal system, the diocesan bishop, acting in accord with c. 1276 §2, is to oblige pastors to cooperate with the bishop's efforts to assist the parishes and other diocesan entities by centralizing and coordinating the purchase of materials and services in order to

---

[86] For pastors both c. 537 and 1280 provide more, but not taxative, specification.

[87] Canon 1741, 2°, 4° and 5° enumerates failure to be an efficient and faithful administrator as being in substance among the principal reasons for which a pastor can be removed from office. It may be noted here that nothing prevents a pastor from delegating general administrative operations to a *business manager*; it may even be prudent to do so. Nevertheless, as in cases of delegating a school principal or a person to organize and supervise Religious Education, the pastor remains responsible for the careful administration of the temporalities of a parish and to that end the pastor must supervise and evaluate the performance of a business manager to praise or admonish, to discharge and replace as an objective evaluation may suggest.

achieve more economical group rates and more commercial bargaining leverage. Canon 1284 §2, 5° specifies two particular obligations of good pastoral administration, paying interest on a mortgage when due, and retiring any capital debt in due course. Perhaps particular mention of these two duties was made because they also involve payments which are due in justice and on which the good reputation of the Church in a particular area may stand or fall.

Canon 1285 sets down rights and obligations with respect to pastors making pious or charitable donations with parish funds. Two important conditions are imposed: the donations must be within the limits of ordinary administration and from movable goods which are not part of the parish's stable patrimony. The limits of ordinary parish administration would be established by the ordinary in accord with c. 1276 §2. If those limits are exceeded without written authority from the ordinary, such donations or gifts would canonically be *invalid* in accord with c. 1281 §1. Stable patrimony would include real estate, structures, whole crops or herds and fixed assets.

4.4.3 — Disbursing, contracting and alienating parish temporalities

(a) *The existence and effect of particular law.* Canon 1295 sets down that the requirements of cc. 1291-1294 are to govern not only alienation but any transaction which can adversely affect the patrimony of any juridic person.[88] Canon 1291 refers to following "the norm of law." Depending on the status of the ju-

---

[88] Although c. 1284 §2, 1° is not included along with cc. 1291-1294, from a practical point of view it is essential to be aware that the patrimony of a parish can be seriously worsened in an instant and without the permission of *a competent ecclesiastical authority* by the failure to have in force adequate insurance coverages for general public liability, fire, flood in some areas, theft, workers compensation, etc. and even business interruption where the parish may operate a school, nursery or summer camp, etc.

ridic person to whom the goods belong, the *law* involved may be canon law, the statutes of a public or private juridic person, proper law and/or particular law. Canon 1292 §1 calls for the conference of bishops to establish particular norms determining the minimum and maximum value limits for *ordinary* (as opposed to *extraordinary*) alienation. Canon 1293 §2 indicates that "other safeguards prescribed by legitimate authority are also to be observed." Since c. 519 prescribes that a pastor immediately governs a parish and c. 515 §3 sets down that a parish is a juridic person, c. 1279 imposes on the pastor the responsibility of the administration of the parish's ecclesiastical goods. The pastor of a parish, therefore, has a canonical obligation to be alert to any matters that could decrease, destroy or seriously encumber the patrimony of the parish. In practice he may need to seek advice from canon and civil lawyers.[89]

(b) *Permissions the pastor must obtain.* Canon 1291 requires that the pastor have the permission of the competent authority to validly take part in an alienation of parish goods worth more than the established minimum value and less than the established maximum value. Canon 1292 § 1 directs that "the diocesan bishop with the consent of the finance council, the college of consultors and the parties concerned [i.e. parties with rights in the matter]" is the competent authority to give the pastor of a parish permission for alienations of parish goods within the same established minimum and maximum values. Those minimum and maximum values of alienation are to be established by the conference of bishops for its region.[90] Beyond the maxi-

---

[89] Canon 1279 §1.

[90] In cc. 638 §§1-2 and 1281 §§1-2, the Code distinguishes "the limit and manner of ordinary administration" and the concept of "extraordinary administration"; c. 1292 §1 dealing specifically with "alienation" mentions "the range of the minimum and maximum amounts [of the value involved in an act of alienation] which are to be determined by the conference of bishops for its region"; c. 1292 §2 regulates a case which "exceeds the maximum amount." These three terms are interrelated and regulate *three different levels or spans of monetary values* of alienations of ecclesiastical goods. These spans are: (a) *the lowest span of regulated values*, (b) *the medium span of regulated values*, and (c) *the highest span of regulated values*.

mum value thus established, the permission of the Holy See is required for an alienation, as is also the case with goods donated to the Church through a vow and those which are especially valuable for artistic or historical reasons (c. 1292 §2).

Canon 1292 §3 also mandates that if the alienation is divisible, then for permission to be valid it is necessary that "parts which have previously been alienated must be mentioned in seeking the permission." Canon 1292 §4 establishes for those giving advice or consent in alienations the obligation and the right to be "thoroughly informed concerning the economic situation of the juridic person whose goods are proposed for alienation and concerning previous alienations." That obligation and right of theirs implies an obligation on the part of the pastor of a parish to be thoroughly candid and cooperative in supplying the necessary information to them. To alienate goods whose value is more than the minimum level established for the region, c. 1293 requires a just cause, an estimate in writing of the value of the object to be alienated from at least two experts and compliance with other safeguards which may be prescribed by legitimate authority so that the Church will not be harmed.

Before the (a) lowest span of regulated values can be determined in a region, the maximum and minimum of the (b) medium span of regulated values, referred to in c. 1292 §1, is determined by the conference of bishops for its region *and* the conference's determination must be reviewed by the Apostolic See before it is promulgated and achieves the force of law in accord with c. 445 §§1-2. For a parish the minimum and maximum limits of the (a) lowest span of regulated values are the "limits... of ordinary administration" mentioned in c. 1281 §§1-2. Those limits are established by the diocesan bishop. The pastor, with due regard for particular law, can operate on his own judgment up to the maximum allowed by the diocesan bishop. The maximum value the diocesan bishop can allow for the (a) lowest span of regulated values must be less than the minimum level for the (b) medium span of regulated values, because the diocesan bishop himself needs consent in accord with c. 1292 §1 in order to alienate regulated values between the minimum and the maximum of the (b) medium span of regulated values. For alienations in excess of the maximum limit of the (b) medium span of regulated values, which alienations would be in the (c) highest span of regulated values, the permission of the Holy See is required. The cash value amounts represented by each of those three spans will be likely to vary from one bishops' conference to another around the world and to be based on a *relative* judgment reflecting the local economy in any given area.

(c) *The duty to carry out the intention of the contributor/donor.* Strictly speaking canons 1290 through 1298 do not mention intentions of donors or contributors. Somewhat analogous to those concerns, however, is c. 1294 §2, which mandates that money acquired by means of alienations is to be "wisely expended in accord with the purposes of the alienation."

(d) *The requirements of vigilance and reporting.* These appear implied in c. 1292 §§1-2 and expressly stated in §§3-4 of the same canon and in cc. 1293 §1, 2°, 1294 §2, 1296 and 1298. All are treated *passim* in this section 4.4.3.

(e) *The existence and effect of civil law.* Pastors are obliged to observe local civil law on contracts and payments in accord with c. 1290, with the exception of civil laws which "are contrary to divine law or canon law."[91] Canon 1297 indicates that norms concerning the leasing of Church goods are the responsibility of the conference of bishops. Any prudent kind of leasing, however, will certainly involve a civilly enforceable contract which is *canonized* by c. 1290. In addition to the obligation of observing the local laws on contracts and payments, a pastor would also be bound by the norms from the conference of bishops, which might also include means of calculating charges to be made, types of insurance to protect the Church's interests with respect to properties to be leased, or to protect the Church when using property it has leased from others, etc.

As they administer parish property, pastors are obliged to follow canonical procedures and they may be appropriately pun-

---

[91] Canon 1290 concludes with a special reference to c. 1547 superseding civil law. Canon 1547 sets down that "proof by means of witnesses is admitted in every kind of case under the supervision of the judge." Thus if, subsequent to entering into a written agreement required by civil law about contracts or payments, the parties were to agree orally to different terms in the presence of witnesses, a civil court might hold that the written agreement remains in force, while a Church tribunal might decide in favor of the subsequent agreement as testified to by the witnesses. For example, confer c. 1299 §2. In any circumstances in which civil law might apply, a prudent pastor will consult a knowledgeable civil attorney.

ished for neglecting to do so. Canon 1296 establishes what is to be done when ecclesiastical goods have been alienated in a manner which violates canonical norms, but which is nevertheless civilly valid. Among the generally stated possible courses of action is the implication that the person(s) responsible might be subject to Church sanctions, as provided in Book 6 of the Code,[92] or *civilly* sued for damages.

(f) *Other significant material.* Canon 1294 §1 cautions that "Ordinarily an object must not be alienated for a price which is less than that indicated in the estimate." Reference to an *estimate* is also found in two other canons. In c. 1283, 2° it refers to the value of goods in an inventory which an administrator is required to compile before taking up his or her duties. In c. 1293 §1, 2° an estimate is required for the alienation of goods, the value of which exceeds the minimum sum above which the diocesan bishop needs to consult and obtain consent from his finance council and college of consultors. Canon 1295 directs that the requirements in cc. 1291 through 1294, treated above, are to be observed in all transactions "through which the patrimonial condition of a juridic person can be worsened." This poses a number of obligations for a pastor, since the parish he governs is a juridic person. Canon 1298 obliges pastors not to sell or lease an object of any importance which belongs to the parish either to himself or to close relatives[93] without "special written permission of the competent authority."

---

[92] Both cc. 1375 and 1377 allow for a just penalty in such circumstances and depending on the facts in any given case several of c. 1741's causes for legitimate removal of a pastor might be found to be present.

[93] Specifically up to the fourth degree of consanguinity (blood relatives) or affinity (in-laws).

4.4.4 — Administration of contributions or gifts with specified conditions, or which establish pious foundations, or trusts, accepted by the parish

A pastor's contact with cc. 1299 through 1310 is based on some contributors attaching conditions to their donations.[94] Canons 1300 and 1303 §2 provide that, once accepted, conditions attached to gifts and contributions are to be carried out most diligently. These canons concern the handling of such *conditioned* offerings, trusteeships and/or pious foundations. The first obligation of the pastor of a parish receiving an offer of any sort of conditioned contribution is to inform the ordinary and obtain permission *before* accepting the conditioned contribution. Canon 1267 §1 requires such permission with respect to general donations and c. 1304 §1 requires the ordinary's written permission for a parish to accept a foundation. By analogy with both of those canons plus c. 1302 §1, which directs that "a person who accepts the role of trustee… must inform the ordinary of this trust," it appears that the ordinary's permission should be sought by the juridic person of a parish even before accepting a trusteeship.[95]

If the parish receives the requisite, or prudently sought

---

[94] Canon 1299 §2 does not impose an obligation specifically on a pastor, but if a pastor is the only one who knows that the formalities of civil law were not observed with the result that the will of a deceased person for the good of the Church cannot be enforced, he would be obliged by this canon to see to it that the heirs are advised of the decedent's wishes in the matter. Considering the possible civil law ramifications of such an action in various civil jurisdictions, the pastor might be well advised, by analogy with c. 1288, to consult his diocesan bishop before acting.

[95] Canon 285 §4 forbids a cleric, who does not have his ordinary's permission, to assume a secular office which entails an obligation to render an account. A parish is not a physical person in sacred orders as a cleric is, but a parish is a juridic person which by accepting a trust, may, depending on the nature of the trust and local civil law, become involved in civil requirements of rendering accounts about the trust to the state. Although the parish is not a cleric, the ordinary might have even more serious reasons for judging that a parish should not become involved in such civil regulations, especially if the state is clearly hostile to the Church. It would seem prudent for a pastor to consult the ordinary *before* accepting a trust in the parish's name as its legal representative.

permission and accepts the *conditioned* contribution, pious foundation, or trusteeship, then the pastor has the obligations and rights which arise from the document directing how the contribution is to be used or establishing and governing the goals and operation of the trust or pious foundation.[96]

Canons 1308 and 1309 do not impose obligations or confer rights on pastors, but they concern the reduction and/or transfer of Mass obligations and may, therefore, involve the Mass obligations arising from stipends received from whatever source by the juridic person of the parish governed by the pastor. A parish pastor needs to know that he does not have a canonical right to reduce or transfer Mass stipend obligations; if problems arise in these matters, the diocesan bishop is to be consulted. Canon 1310 provides for a similar situation which might arise with respect to contributions received for other pious causes or purposes and modifying or transferring the obligations they generate for the juridic person of a parish. Again, a pastor is not authorized to make any adjustments; such matters must be presented to the diocesan bishop.

Pastors must also take note that some of the trusts, foundations, last wills and testaments and other forms of *conditioned* gifts may be subject to civil laws which impose civil filings, financial reports, and/or administrative requirements. Compliance with such laws is a canonical obligation of the pastor in view of c. 532.

---

[96] Legal last wills and testaments are by their nature written documents. Canons 1306 and 1307 require that there be copies of terms and obligations of any foundation held by the juridic person involved and filed in the curial archives. There is no explicit canonical requirement that the terms and conditions of a trust be in a written document. Nevertheless c. 1302 §2 requires the ordinary to exercise on behalf of trusts the same vigilance required of by c. 1301 §2 for the execution of pious dispositions. The vigilance required by c. 1301 §2 includes "even… visitations, so that pious wills are fulfilled; other executors must render him an account concerning the performance of their duty," thereby implying that trusts should be set down in written documents, so that the ordinary may know what ought to be done and other executors can have a definite basis for the account concerning their performance. In addition, by analogy with cc. 1306 and 1307 a trust made orally should be put into writing and copies of the trust establishment, conditions and fulfillment be appropriately archived.

4.5 — SHARING FULFILLMENT OF OBLIGATIONS AND EXERCISE OF RIGHTS

The pastor's tasks of governance extend through a varied spectrum of activities. Some activities require the pastor to exercise the power of governance, specifically the executive power of governance, e.g. delegating to visiting priests or deacons the faculty to assist at marriages, dispensing or commuting vows or promissory oaths, dispensing from the observance of feasts and/or fasts. The pastor cannot share with lay persons any exercise of the executive power of governance except as c. 129 §2 provides "in accord with the norm of law," which does not seem to provide for sharing the executive power of governance in the case of the office of pastor.[97] In the broader and less exact manner of speaking of governance or administration, the pastor's obligations include, but are certainly not limited to, visiting poor families in a parish, preparing parish budgets which may range into the hundreds of thousands of dollars per year, determining dates for a parish lecture series on social justice, discharging an incompetent parish employee, mediating a disagreement about which parish society has the right to use the parish auditorium at a particular time, protecting parish interests in a potentially crippling lawsuit. Throughout this chapter consideration has been given to many of the ways in which others are able to share the burdens of a pastor of a parish as he carries out his work of governance or administration. Often the pastor will do so personally, but in various circumstances he may choose to share his authority, the exercise of his governing rights, by *delegating* others to help in fulfilling some of his obligations. Depending on the circumstances, his delegation may be either a precise canonical delegation of another priest or deacon or a simple act of administration.[98]

---

[97] The pastor has neither legislative power of governance nor judicial power of governance; as a result he has no authority in those areas to share with others.

[98] Delegation to assist at marriages would be canonical in accord with c. 1111 §1.

Since the pastor of a parish is able to share with others to some extent almost all of his governing and administrating obligations, except those which require the exercise of the executive power of governance, it may be more sufficient and practical here to make only two observations. The first has been noted before, but bears repetition. It is that the pastor cannot fulfill his obligations by simply appointing others to perform various administrative tasks. The obligations remain his and he must evaluate how others carry out their assignments under his authority. The pastor must provide that kind of effective supervision which may be necessary for the successful fulfillment of his obligations. Such supervision may include taking a particular assignment or appointment away from one individual and assigning the work to another, or completely replacing a person whose abilities are unequal to the task assigned.

Secondly, although the pastor is encouraged by the Code to govern in a cooperative, communicative and consultative manner, nevertheless the parish finance council required by c. 537, the parish pastoral council which may be mandated as described in c. 536 §1 and, by implication, any other group of parishioners who offer advice to the pastor "enjoy a consultative vote only and cannot in any way become deliberative structures."[99] It is the pastor who governs the parish[100]; he has the responsibility for the administrative decisions which are made.

CONCLUSION

As the pastor participates in the mission of Jesus, priest, prophet and king, the pastor truly governs the parish community entrusted to him. Recognizing that the pastor will need help in the

---

[99] *Ecclesiae de mysterio*, art. 5, °2. English translation *Certain Questions Regarding Collaboration*, p. 16; also see art. 5 *in toto*. English translation *Certain Questions Regarding Collaboration* pp. 15-16.

[100] Canon 519.

extremely complex and important work of governing, the Church in various canons calls on other clergy, the religious and the laity to cooperate with the pastor and assist him in different ways according to their state in life and expertise. Often some of the assistance will be spontaneous and supplied by volunteers who see one need or another and offer to assist the pastor, some will be organized by the pastor himself, some may come from *Third Orders* or other associations of the faithful, both formal and informal.

Formal assistance envisioned by the Church includes a parish finance council, a parish council and, depending on the circumstances of the parish, regular consultations among the clergy staff of the parish and their common endeavor in fulfilling the total parochial ministry.[101] Informal assistance may take place in the work of many *ad hoc* groups and through a personal, open, alert, caring that is mutual between the Christian faithful and their pastor within the parish community.

There are other canons which treat of the ecclesiastical office of pastor. Some of those canons regulate the stability of the office, touching its reception, retention and resignation by the pastor, or provision of the office, or transfer or removal of a pastor by competent Church authority. Other canons govern a type of pastorate which involves more than one priest, all endowed with the faculties of pastor caring for the same parish *in solidum*, a single pastorate accomplished as a team.[102] The obligations and rights of pastors in accord with those canons are treated in the next and final chapter.

---

[101] Canons 536 §1, 537, 545 §§1-§2, 548 §§2-3 and 550 §2 in conjunction with c. 280.

[102] In American English the terms in wide use are: *"co-pastorate"* and *"team pastorate."* It is important to distinguish *"a co-pastorate"* and *"a team pastorate,"* either of which can only include priests, from the term *"pastoral team,"* which may encompass a parish's entire professional staff of clergy and laity. For the same reason it is necessary to distinguish a *"parochial vicar"* from a *"pastoral assistant."*

CHAPTER FIVE

The Office of Pastor of a Parish

INTRODUCTION

Most of the obligations and rights of a pastor of a parish arise from the many and varied ways in which he serves by leading the people of his parish in their shared pilgrimage on earth. Those obligations and rights flow from the pastor's sharing in the threefold mission of Christ as the pastor teaches the true faith, celebrates sanctifying activities with and for his parishioners through his participation in the ministerial priesthood of Jesus and governs the Christian faithful within the parish community. The canons which express such obligations and rights point out to the pastor the work he is expected to accomplish within the Church.

Some other obligations and rights connected with the ecclesiastical office of pastor of a parish relate more to enabling the pastor to know what stability in office he may expect as pastor of a parish. The canons which establish those parameters regulate conferral and loss of the office of pastor, stability in office, resignation, removal, deprivation and transfer.

5.1 — CONFERRAL AND LOSS OF THE OFFICE OF PASTOR OF A PARISH

Various canons regulate the assignment of a priest to the office of pastor, taking possession of the office, stability in office, resignation, removal and transfer from office. Throughout the previous chapters a great deal has been written about the *good works* a pastor is obliged to try to accomplish and the right that he has to fulfill his duties. The canons treated here deal more frequently with a pastor's rights than with his obligations. Obligations are not lacking among these canons, however, since in some circumstances the pastor's right to do something imposes a practical, if not canonical, obligation to exercise the right or explain why he is not doing so. For instance, if his pastoral administration is challenged, the pastor has a right to respond, but if he does not exercise that right in a timely manner, he may expose himself to various consequences.

5.1.1 — Conferral of the office of pastor of a parish

How does a priest become a pastor? Canon 523 establishes that "the diocesan bishop is the person competent to provide for the office of pastor by free conferral unless some other person possesses the right of presentation or of election."[1] However, the same canon also calls attention to c. 682 §1 which sets down special rules for the appointment of a religious to any ecclesiastical office in a diocese. Canon 682 §1 determines that if an ecclesiastical office in a diocese is to be conferred upon a religious, "the religious is to be appointed by the diocesan bishop, following presentation or at least assent of the competent superior."[2] A

---

[1] In whatever manner a priest may be selected as a candidate for the pastorate, he must be able validly to assume the office in accord with c. 521 §1. For a vacant or impeded diocesan see c. 525 which regulates competence to install, confirm or freely confer a pastorate. Also see c. 148.

[2] Selection by *free conferral* is treated in cc. 157, 524, 525 and 682 §1; *presentation* is regulated by cc. 158-163 and 683 §1. Canon 159 mandates that "No one may be presented who is unwilling." In accord with c. 160 more than one candidate can be presented for the same office. Unsuitable candidates can be rejected under cc. 161 §1 and 162. If a suitable and willing candidate is presented, c. 163 indicates that he has a right to be installed; if there are several suitable and willing candidates, the person who has the right to install must install one of those candidates.

priest may be called to the pastorate by accepting a free conferral, or being deemed suitable as a presented candidate, or having been confirmed as an elected candidate (or admitted as a
postulated candidate). In any case, because a parish exists to
provide pastoral care for the parishioners,[3] c. 527 §1 directs that
a priest acquires the pastoral care of a parish and is bound to
carry it out "from the moment he takes possession of the parish." A priest does not become a pastor in full right, does not
have a *ius in re*, until by taking possession of the parish he simultaneously takes upon himself the care of the parish community and the duty to supply that care. So important is the care of
the people of the parish that c. 527 §3 directs the local ordinary
to set a definite duration of time within which the designated
priest must take possession of the parish or the local ordinary
can declare the parish vacant. When a parish is declared vacant
under such conditions, the local ordinary has not removed a
pastor, since the priest designated never took possession of the
office nor accepted its obligations. The local ordinary has merely
cleared the way for the appointment of a pastor who will provide pastoral care for the people of the parish.

The first obligation and right of the pastor of a parish appears to be that he formally take possession of the parish. Nevertheless, c. 527 §2 also allows that "for a just cause, however,
the same ordinary can dispense from… [a formal or usual in-
stallation ceremony]; in such a situation the dispensation com-

---

A single willing and suitable person presented would have a *ius ad rem* to the
office in question until he is actually installed in that office. *Elections* are treated
in cc. 164-179, and elections encompass a possibility of a postulation, which is
covered by cc. 180-183. Canon 523, especially when read in the light of *CD*, nn.
28 and 31, which are included among its *fontes*, implies that the election of someone as pastor of a parish would fall under the requirements of c. 179 as an election which requires confirmation and that the diocesan bishop would have both
the obligation and the right to judge the suitability of the candidate as provided
in c. 149 §1 and *CD*, n. 31 before giving his confirmation. *Postulation* is regulated
by cc. 180-183.

[3] Canons 515 §1 and 519.

municated to the parish replaces the formal taking of possession."[4]

One obligation of a priest at the beginning of his term of
office as pastor is to make a profession of faith as required in c.
833, 6°.[5] By the act of taking possession of the parish the pastor
becomes bound to carry out the pastoral care of the parish, as
required by c. 527 §1.

Also, in accord with c. 152, a priest appointed to be a pastor should resign any other ecclesiastical offices he may hold, if
they would be incompatible with his serving a parish community as its pastor.[6] Entering into the service of a particular parish also, as a general rule, requires that the pastor reside "in a
parish house close to the church" as prescribed by c. 533 §1. However, exceptions do exist. The same paragraph of c. 533 does allow the local ordinary to permit a pastor "to live elsewhere es-

---

[4] In the case of a team ministry only the moderator needs to be formally installed
as prescribed in c. 527 §2.

[5] If a local ordinary dispenses from formal taking possession in accord with c. 527
§2, when does the new pastor make the profession of faith required by c. 833, 6°?
The required profession of faith is to be made personally in the presence of the
local ordinary or his delegate at the beginning of a pastor's term of office. Canon
833, 6° requires only the presence of two persons, does not call for any particular
ceremony, and is not subject to a strict interpretation in accord with c. 18; in addition, c. 527 §2, although subject to a strict interpretation in accord with c. 18,
merely requires a just cause for granting a dispensation from formal taking possession. As a result, it does not seem that the words of c. 833, 6°, "at the beginning of their term of office...," need be taken to mean that the profession of faith
must be made on the exact day, hour and moment at which the pastor takes possession of the parish. If, then, the formal ceremony is dispensed, the local ordinary or his delegate and the pastor should agree on a mutually convenient time
and place, allowing for local travel conditions and distances involved, for the
profession of faith around the time of the pastor's taking possession of the parish.

[6] In addition, c. 149 §1 requires that "In order to be promoted to an ecclesiastical
office, a person must be in communion with the Church...." If a priest appointed
to be a pastor were to be or to become excommunicated, even *latae sententiae*, before taking possession of the parish, he is forbidden to take possession of it because he is forbidden to discharge any ecclesiastical office or take part in any public worship ceremonies (c. 1331 §1). In the extremely unlikely circumstance that
a bishop would appoint as a pastor a priest whose excommunication had been
imposed or declared, he could not *validly* acquire the office (c. 1331 §2, 4°).

pecially in a house shared by several presbyters, provided there is a just cause and suitable and due provision is made for the performance of parochial functions." The use of the word "else-where" (the Latin *"alibi"*) in c. 533 §1 leaves no doubt that such a legitimate residence could be outside of the parish boundaries.[7]

5.1.2 — Stability of the office of pastor of a parish

Canon 522 mandates that the pastor "ought to possess sta-bility in office and, therefore, he is to be named for an indefinite period of time." Canon 193 §1 directs that an individual who has been appointed to an office for an "indefinite period" cannot be removed from the office except for grave reasons and accord-ing to the procedure determined by law.[8] Nevertheless, c. 522 also authorizes each conference of bishops, for its own area, to permit by decree, that the pastor be appointed for a term of a

---

[7] Do pastors living outside of their own parishes become subjects of the pastor within whose parish boundaries they live? The canons of the Code do not ap-pear to take up this question specifically, yet c. 465 of the 1917 Code and c. 533 §1 of the 1983 Code authorize the local ordinary to allow the pastor to reside out-side of his parish. Also, the existence of personal parishes is acknowledged by c. 216 §4 of the 1917 Code and c. 518 of the present Code and pastors of personal parishes often live within the boundaries of territorial parishes of the same rite. It appears that there is a *lacuna legis* concerning the relationship of such pastors with the pastor of the territorial parish in which they reside. An argument might be made that since a pastor is the "proper shepherd of the parish entrusted to him," (c. 519), it would be lacking in canonical equity, or that an incompatibility would arise, if he is regarded as a member of the "definite community" (c. 515 §1) of another parish and/or a subject of the pastor of that "definite community" (c. 107 §1) simply because he resides within the boundaries of that other parish.

[8] Canon 193 §2 also protects those on whom an office has been conferred for a set period of time so that before the expiration of their term they can be removed only for the same "grave reasons and according to the procedure determined by law." In addition, c. 539 implicitly expresses a general right of a pastor to retain that ecclesiastical office even if, although prevented from exercising his office, he has not been removed or transferred from, or deprived of the office of pastor in accord with Church law; cc. 1747 §3 and 1752 express the same point explic-itly and specifically with reference to an administrative process of removal or transfer while recourse is pending.

certain period of time. Many National Conferences of Bishops, among them those of Canada, Ireland and the United States, have issued decrees authorizing a six year, renewable term.[9] The exact text of each such decree as reviewed and approved by the Holy See is very important, since it becomes particular law throughout the territory of the conference of bishops which issued it. The texts for Australia, Canada and the United States establish that pastors *may* be appointed for six year terms, that of Ireland holds an indefinite term as the norm but provides that on occasion in special circumstances a pastor may be appointed to a parish for a period of not less than six years, that of India leaves to the bishops the adoption of limited tenure for pastors. All of the those texts say that the diocesan bishops *may* appoint pastors for limited tenures, Ireland's text places a limitation on the practice, and India's seems to be the broadest. Since (a) none of the texts on their face bind any given bishop to follow limited tenure as the only procedure in his diocese, and (b) none of the texts specify an exemption from or derogation from c. 522, it appears that each diocesan bishop has a choice to make each

---

[9]   As reported in *Code Annotated*, Appendix III, "Complementary Norms to the Code Promulgated by English-Language Conferences of Bishops," pp. 1310, 1321, 1346, 1358, 1396, 1417, by 1993 the Conferences of Bishops of Australia, Canada, Gambia, Liberia, Sierra Leone, Ireland, the Philippines, and United States of America had decreed permission for a six year term as pastor, which could be renewed at the diocesan bishop's discretion. Interestingly, however, the Conference of Bishops of Ireland decreed that ordinarily pastors should be appointed for an indefinite period but that in special situations, on occasion, a pastor might be appointed to a term of not less than six years, renewable by the bishop; the Conference of Bishops of the Philippines decreed that the fundamental norm was for a pastor to be appointed for an indefinite period, but also allowed a term of six years renewable. Also, in conformity with c. 522 the Spanish episcopal conference has accepted the appointment "ad certum tempus" as a faculty which "the bishop can use when he considers it opportune to act in that way; but not as the only law." *Boletín oficial de la conferencia episcopal española* 1 (1984), p. 101 as quoted by A. MARZOA, "Remoción y translado de párrocos," Commentary on cc. 1740-1752, in *Comentario exegético*, vol. IV/2, p. 2168. The *Comentario exegético* also holds that *CD*, n. 31 and c. 522 favor the indefinite term as the norm for a pastor. See SÁNCHEZ-GIL, "Parroquias y párrocos," in *Comentario exegético*, vol. II/2, pp. 1240-1243 and MARZOA, "Remoción y translado de párrocos," in *Comentario exegético*, vol. IV/2, pp. 2165-2173, especially pp. 2167-2168.

time he appoints a pastor in that he may appoint one pastor for an indefinite period and another for the term and under the conditions decreed by the conference of bishops for his area. If a pastor is appointed for a definite term, then he loses the office *de iure* when two events take place (a) the period of time for which he was appointed comes to a close (c. 184 §1) *and* (b) from the moment that the competent authority communicates to him that he has lost the office by the expiration of the term (c. 186). At that time the diocesan bishop would seem to be free to reappoint the pastor or not to do so, for any additional term or terms allowed by the decree of the conference of bishops, or indefinitely as provided by c. 522.

In the case of a priest who is a member of a religious institute or a society of apostolic life the matter is quite different.[10] Canon 682 §1 requires that either the priest is presented by his religious superior or that the religious superior gives written consent to the appointment of the priest before the diocesan

---

[10] Canon 682 §§1-2 (and c. 671, a more general canon concerning religious accepting offices) use only the term "religious" and are in the section of the Code which deals with Religious Institutes; however, c. 537 specifies that c. 682 §2 applies to removal of pastors who are members of religious institutes or societies of apostolic life and c. 738 §2 specifically applies cc. 679 through 683 to members of societies of apostolic life. There appear to be two possibilities with respect to pastors who are members of secular institutes. A member of a secular institute who is incardinated in a particular diocese and appointed a pastor would serve under the same canons as any other diocesan priest. Nevertheless, c. 266 §3 establishes that clerics can be incardinated into a secular institute itself "by virtue of a grant of the Apostolic See." Canon 715 §2 provides that members incardinated in a secular institute "are appointed to particular works of the institute or to the governance of the institute, they depend on the bishop in a way comparable to religious." Such dependence would include regulations of c. 682 §§1-2 with respect to the appointment of religious to and/or their removal from ecclesiastical offices in a diocese. How does a member of a secular institute who has been legitimately incardinated into the institute itself, but is not appointed to particular works or the governance of the institute relate to a bishop who might wish to appoint him as pastor of a parish? There appears to be a *lacuna legis* on this point. Perhaps a proper application of c. 19 would establish that a priest in those circumstances should relate to the bishop as a religious, since (a) by incardination into the institute he is no longer a diocesan priest and (b) his *de facto* competent canonical superior would be another priest incardinated in the secular institute rather than any diocesan bishop.

bishop can appoint the priest a pastor. Canons 682 §2 and 738 §2 leave the removal of a priest member of a religious institute or of a society of apostolic life from an ecclesiastical office in a diocese to the discretion of either the authority who made the appointment or the superior. Canon 682 §2 also requires that prior notice of the removal be given to the other authority by the authority who is effecting the removal. Neither authority needs the consent of the other for such a removal from office, nor is either required by law to give reasons to the other.[11]

Stability in office also depends on the pastor himself, his health and his age. A pastor who has been appointed for a definite term may prolong his pastorate by serving and leading his community well and thus motivating the bishop to appoint him to an additional term or terms as pastor. A pastor whose term is indefinite, and whose health is good, may also prolong his pastorate by serving and leading well and in that way motivating his bishop to defer acceptance of such a pastor's resignation when it is offered as he completes his 75th year of age.[12]

---

[11] Among the canons concerning *Individual Decrees and Precepts*, c. 51 requires: "A decree should be issued in writing, giving, in the case of a decision, the reasons which prompted it, at least in a summary fashion." Either the bishop or the superior of the institute will presumably have made a decision as part of deciding on a change of a priest's assignment; the fact that there should be a written document explaining the reasons for the decision does not impose any obligation on the bishop or the religious superior to share those reasons with one another. However, the religious priest who is removed from a pastorate in accord with c. 682 §2, even though no longer a pastor, would appear in view of cc. 37, 51, 55, 220 and 221 §1 to have a right to be informed of the reasons which motivated the decision. In fact, unless the case involves most serious reasons for not doing so, c. 55 implies that the priest would be entitled to the written text of the decree; and c. 51 requires that the text of the decree should give "the reasons which prompted it [the decree], at least in a summary fashion." The appointment, transfer or removal of a pastor who is a member of a religious institute or a society of apostolic life is regulated by c. 682 §§1-2 rather than by cc. 523, 538 and 1740-1752. As a result, if a religious pastor wished to take recourse against his being transferred or removed, his recourse would be in accord with cc. 1732-1739, rather than cc. 1740-1752 to which he has no canonical right. See T. RINCÓN PÉREZ, "The Apostolates of Institutes," Commentary on cc. 673-683, in *Code Annotated* p. 463.

[12] Canon 538 §3.

A term of office whether indefinite or for a definite period can also be brought to a close by a pastor who chooses to resign, but he is required to have a just cause for resigning.[13] A pastor's resignation, however, does not become effective unless it is accepted by the diocesan bishop.[14] Canon 401 §1 provides that if a bishop "becomes less able to fulfill his office due to ill health or another serious reason…" he is "earnestly requested to present his resignation from office." By analogy a pastor laboring under the same difficulties ought to understand that the mind of the Church, although not one of its explicit laws, is that he too is earnestly requested to resign. Depending on how ill he might be, or how serious other reasons might be, a pastor might have a moral obligation to resign for the good of the people of the parish.[15]

Canon 538 §3 establishes that:

> When a pastor has completed his seventy-fifth year of age he is requested to submit his resignation from office to the diocesan bishop, who, after considering all the circumstances of person and place is to decide whether to accept or defer the resignation.[16]

Canons 354, 401 and 538 §3, treating respectively of retirement age for cardinals, bishops and pastors of parishes, establish that when they complete their 75th year (i.e. at midnight ending their 75th birthday in accord with c. 202 §1) they are requested by the law to present their resignations to the apposite

---

[13] Canons 187, 189 §2 and 538 §1.

[14] Canon 538 §§2-3.

[15] In connection with any *requested* resignation, the provisions of c. 188 should be borne in mind: "A resignation submitted out of grave fear, which has been unjustly inflicted, or because of fraud, substantial error or simony is invalid by the law itself."

[16] The translation of c. 538 §3 used here departs from that of the *CLSA* translation. The Latin *"rogatur"* is rendered "is requested" here. The *CLSA* translation used the words "is asked" here, but in translating cc. 354 and 401 on the same general topic of retirement, translates the same Latin verb with the word "requested."

authority.[17] Strictly speaking each of those canons is making no more than a true *request*. It is a request, however, which clearly generates a moral obligation on the part of each bishop and pastor who reaches the age of 75, that he objectively consider the good of the souls who have been committed to his care, realize that the Church regards his having reached 75 years of age as a just cause for him to retire, and weigh the guidance provided by c. 223 §§1-2.[18]

---

[17] READ, "Parishes, Parish Priests and Assistant Priests," in *Letter & Spirit*, n. 1072, p. 300.

[18] Considerable, although relatively recent, history suggests that the *requesting* remains simply a request, but a request to which the Church has manifested its expectation and administrative need of a positive and cooperative response. In *CD*, n. 31 pastors of advanced years who were no longer able to perform their duties fruitfully were called upon to offer their resignations spontaneously, or when the bishop requested it. In *Ecclesiae sanctae 1ᵃ* Pope Paul VI directed that all pastors were asked to present their resignations to the proper bishops not later than the completion of their 75th year of age. See POPE PAUL VI, Apostolic Letter, Motu Proprio, August 6, 1966, On the Implementation of the Decrees Christus Dominus, Presbyterorum ordinis and Perfectae caritatis *Ecclesiae sanctae 1ᵃ*, in *AAS*, 58 (1966), pp. 757-758, here at n. 20 (3), pp. 768-769. English translation in FLANNERY, *Conciliar and Post Conciliar Documents*, p. 603. Cardinals were also called upon to submit their resignations, but at the age of 80; see POPE PAUL VI, Motu proprio, Advancing Age and the Ability to Fulfill Certain Offices of Greater Moment *Ingravescentem aetatem*, November 21, 1970 in *AAS*, 62 (1970), pp. 810-813, here at n. I, pp. 811, requests cardinals to submit their resignations at 75. English translation in *CLD*, 7 (1968-1972), pp. 143-145. Some members of the Roman Curia were directed to resign at the *beginning* of their 75th year, POPE PAUL VI, Motu proprio, General Regulations of the Roman Curia *Regolamento generale della Curia Romana*, February 22, 1968, in *AAS*, 60 (1968), pp. 129-176, here at p. 161, art. 101 §1 directs: "…for prelate superiors, the limit [for retirement] is the *beginning* of their seventy-fifth year." English translation in *CLD*, 7 (1968-1972), p. 167. In 1978, still under the 1917 Code, the Pontifical Commission for the Interpretation of Decrees of Vatican II in a response directed that a diocesan bishop could not simply declare that a pastor who refused to resign upon the completion of his 75th birthday had ceased from office, but rather that the bishop would have to follow the procedures of a formal removal of a pastor for due cause (1917 CIC, cc. 2147, 2157-2161, which canons set procedure for the removal of a "removable pastor"). See PONTIFICIA COMMISSIO DECRETIS VATICANI II INTERPRETANDIS, response, July 7, 1978, in *AAS*, 70 (1978), p. 534; *CLD*, 9 (1978-1981), p. 997. Under the 1983 *CIC* even if it were to be argued that cc. 354, 401 and 538 §3 are tantamount to commands, c. 186 would continue cardinals, bishops and priests in their various ecclesiastical offices until "the moment when it [the termination of their possession of office by reason of age] has been communicated in writing by the competent authority."

In addition, the text of c. 538 §3 is a single (although compound) sentence, which sets out a three step process that the Church expects will take place when each bishop or pastor becomes 75 years old: submission of resignation at 75, consideration and acceptance or rejection of resignation by the diocesan bishop, suitable support and housing for the retired pastor. It seems not improbable, therefore, that the use of the word "requests" in c. 58 §3 is an application of the third principle of revision of the Code, "canonical norms are not to impose duties *where instructions, exhortations, persuasions and other helps,* by which communion among the faithful is warmly promoted, *seem sufficient to achieve the Church's goal more easily.*"[19] In this case the goal of the Church is the good of souls.

5.1.3 — Removal from, or deprivation of the office of pastor of a parish

Various circumstances exist which can adversely affect a pastor's stability in office. Sometimes the problem may be that a pastor's ministry has become detrimental or ineffective.[20] The ineffective ministry need not involve culpability on the pastor's part.[21] In grave cases the problem is handled through an administrative process which may result in the pastor's removal from

---

[19] *Communicationes,* 1 (1969), pp. 79-80. Emphasis added.

[20] *CD,* n. 31 had decreed that "the procedure for the transfer or removal of a parish priest should be reexamined and simplified so that the Bishop, while observing the principles of natural and canonical justice, may more suitably provide for the good of souls." A decision of the Supreme Tribunal of the Apostolic Signatura *coram* Agustoni on June 24, 1995, pointedly noted that "the good of souls is always to be sought as the supreme end to such extent that, the good of individuals, or the good of the parish priests themselves, gives way to the good of souls." See Supremum Signaturae Apostolicae Tribunal, *coram* Agustoni, in *Forum* 6 (1995)[2], pp. 117-122, here at 118.

[21] Canon 1741, 5° requires that efforts be made to assist, rather than to remove, an otherwise effective pastor whose poor temporal administration has caused serious harm to the Church.

office. At other times a serious action or actions culpably engaged in by a pastor may be punishable in Church law by deprivation of office.

The administrative process required for the removal of a pastor who is a member of a religious institute or a society of apostolic life differs from that for the removal of a diocesan priest, which is set forth in cc. 1742-1747. Those canons impose obligations on the pastor and some, by imposing precise obligations on the diocesan bishop, generate rights for the pastor that the bishop deal with him as each of the detailed obligations of the bishop require. These obligations and rights have to do with a particular administrative process, the removal of a pastor from office for specified and proven reasons. Church law, however, does not prohibit a bishop from simply asking that a pastor resign for any just cause. In various circumstances a bishop may make such a request and the pastor may agree or decline to do so. Even while an administrative process of removal is in progress, or, indeed, even after a decree of removal may have been properly issued, Church law still encourages efforts to reach an equitable and mutually acceptable solution in any dispute.[22] The administrative acts necessary for the removal of a pastor who is not a member of a religious institute or a society of apostolic life are set forth in cc. 1742-1747.

The steps which the diocesan bishop[23] must take in order to remove a pastor by administrative process are:

1. An inquiry must be conducted which proves to the bishop's satisfaction that the pastor's ministry has become "detrimental or ineffective for any reason, even through no grave

---

[22] Canons 1733 §1, and by analogy 1713-1716, 1446 §§1-3.

[23] Canon 134 §3 dictates that since the diocesan bishop has been specified only he, others equivalent to him in c. 381 §2, or, *only with a special mandate, either* a vicar general or episcopal vicar could act to remove a pastor from office in this way (or to transfer a pastor in accord with cc. 1748-1752, in which the implication is clear that the "bishop" referred to is the "diocesan bishop").

fault of his own...."[24] Even in the investigation of a penal matter, c. 1717 §2, which sets up rules for a penal procedure, directs that "care must be taken lest anyone's good name be endangered" by the cautious inquiry required in a penal procedure. Since the law requires the careful protection of a person's good name when a penal matter is under investigation, *a fortiori* and in accord with c. 220 and by analogy with c. 1717 §2, in an administrative process for the removal of a pastor, those conducting an inquiry about a pastor's ministry have an obligation not to endanger his good name by the manner in which the inquiry is carried out. Correlative to the investigators' obligation to obey the law, the pastor under investigation has a right that such investigators do *de facto* obey the law.

2. Canon 1742 §1 specifies that "the bishop is to discuss the matter with two pastors from the group permanently selected for this...." The group of *pastors* with two members of which the diocesan bishop is required to discuss the situation of a pastor whose ministry the bishop believes has been proved to be detrimental or at least ineffective, is to be a group "permanently selected for this by the presbyteral council after their being pro-

---

[24] Canon 1740. Because a priest is entrusted with the ecclesiastical office of pastor of a parish for the good of the faithful, to teach, sanctify and lead the parish community on its pilgrimage to God, the basic reason why a pastor may be removed from office is that his ministry "has become detrimental or at least ineffective" whether or not he is responsible for the problem. Canon 193 §§1-2 requires "grave reasons" for the removal from office of a person appointed for an indefinite period, or before the expiration of an appointment made for a definite period of time. By way of example, a non-taxative list in c. 1741 specifies five especially pressing grave reasons, more common sets of circumstances (such as would render a pastor's ministry detrimental or at least ineffective). Whether one of the enumerated reasons is appealed to, or some other reason is proposed, if a pastor is to be removed, it would be necessary that the reason alleged is, in fact, causing harm to the good of souls. It should be also be noted that among the reasons listed in c. 1741, 5° "poor administration of temporal affairs with grave damage to the Church whenever this problem cannot be remedied in any other way," seems to suggest that in the case of an otherwise good and effective pastor, other arrangements be made for temporal administration, and the pastor be left to carry out his other functions. See MARZOA, "Remoción y translado de párrocos," in *Comentario exegético*, vol. IV/2, pp. 2175-2182.

posed by the bishop…" (c. 1742 §1). In view of that explicitly detailed requirement, the diocesan bishop has an obligation to consult as directed and any pastor whose removal is sought by the bishop has a right that the bishop first have the requisite discussion with two members of this group, which group must have been selected according to the stipulations of c. 1742 §1.[25]

3. If, after the discussion, the bishop concludes that the pastor must be removed, "he is paternally to persuade the pastor to resign the pastorate *within a period of fifteen days*, after he [the bishop] has explained *for validity*, the reason and the arguments for removal."[26] Canon 1742 §1 does not specify whether the fifteen days are *continuous* time or *available* time; however, since the time in question is provided in order that the pastor may "exercise or pursue a right," the fifteen days would be *available* time in accord with c. 201 §2. Indeed, the Code is so concerned about providing the pastor enough time to reply that,

---

[25] M. THÉRIAULT, "Procedure for the Removal or Transfer of Parish Priests," Commentary on cc. 1740-1752, in *Letter & Spirit* comments in footnote 1, p. 968: "The requirement that the group be 'stably established' excludes a situation whereby such a group might simply be set up *ad hoc*, for individual cases. It is to be a permanent body and obviously should be known as such…" E. LABANDEIRA, updated by J. MIRAS, "The Procedure for the Removal or Transfer of Parish Priests," Commentary on cc. 1740-1752 in *Code Annotated* disagrees to some extent on p. 1076 by indicating that two pastors to be consulted are to be "…from the select committee or group appointed *ad hoc* by the council of priests." Since c. 1742 §1 specifically describes the group as "parochis e coetu… stabiliter… selectis," the mind of the legislator seems to favor a stable committee or group and not an *ad hoc* group. It also appears that if a diocesan bishop did not have a permanently selected group for this purpose, as c. 1742 §1 presumes he should have, the bishop would be better advised to set up the permanently established group required by the law, not only for the case he has at hand but for any other case which might arise in the future. In addition, THÉRIAULT, "Procedure for the Removal or Transfer of Parish Priests," in *Letter & Spirit* in footnote 2, p. 968 comments that if the vicar general or an episcopal vicar is also a pastor "…it would be against the spirit of the law that either be appointed to this group, since they are by their office committed to be of one mind with the Bishop (cf. can. 480): the thrust of this canon is that in this particularly sensitive situation the Bishop be given sound but independent advice."

[26] Canon 1742 §1. Emphasis added.

even if the pastor fails to meet the first deadline, the bishop is required to give him still more time.[27]

4. If, in accord with c. 1743 the pastor exercises his right to attach a condition or conditions to his resignation rather than simply to resign, the diocesan bishop must decide whether the condition or conditions specified can be accepted legitimately and, if so, whether he wishes to accept them.[28] If the pastor does present his resignation with or without conditions and the diocesan bishop accepts it *and* communicates this acceptance to the resigned pastor, the resignation is complete and the office becomes *de iure* vacant.

5. If the pastor does not answer within fifteen days of the bishop's paternal invitation to resign in accord with c. 1742 §1, then as required by c. 1744 §1 "the bishop is to repeat the invitation extending the available time for the response." Canon 1744 §1 leaves to the bishop the setting of the time limit for the pastor's response to the second invitation. Since a second invitation is required precisely because there has been no response to the first, the canon implies that the second period of time determined should be reasonably long in order to allow the pastor to reconsider the importance of responding.[29]

6. In accord with c. 1744 §2, the sixth step regulates what is to be done if (a) there is no response to the second invitation

---

[27] Canon 1744 §1. The time granted would also presumably be *available time* since it is still a matter of the pastor exercising or pursuing a right.

[28] With or without conditions, c. 189 §1 requires for *validity* that a resignation be submitted in writing, or orally in the presence of two witnesses. If conditions attached to a resignation are legitimate, but the bishop does not wish to accept them, he would be prudent to weigh the situation in the light of the teachings of c. 223 §§1-2 with respect to the conflict of rights and the common good. The bishop might also consider what effect a refusal on his part to accept a legitimate condition might have if the pastor takes recourse against an administrative decree removing him from office. The pastor in question would also be prudent to consider the applicability of c. 223 §§1-2 to his circumstances as he decides whether to resign, whether conditionally or simply.

[29] LABANDEIRA and MIRAS, "The Procedure for the Removal or Transfer of Parish Priests," in *Code Annotated*, p. 1077 opine: "...common sense indicates, though, that it should not exceed the time limit set out on c. 1742 §1."

and the bishop has *proof* that: the pastor has *received* the second invitation *and* the pastor has not been hindered from answering by any impediment, *or* (b) the pastor does respond, but *"refuses* to resign giving *no* reasons." When either set of circumstances can be established, "the bishop is to issue the decree of removal."

7. If the pastor rejects both the cause and its reasons (the grounds and the supporting proof) proposed for his removal, presenting his own argumentation which appears insufficient to the bishop, then, in order to act *validly*, the bishop must "invite the pastor to organize his challenges to removal in a written report, having inspected the acts; and also to offer proofs to the contrary."[30] The pastor's right is that he be *invited* to review the acts; if he refuses to do so, the process still continues and the pastor remains under the obligation of challenging the removal in a written report and presenting what proofs he may have for his position.

8. At this point in order to act *validly* the bishop must "consider the matter with the same pastors mentioned in can. 1742 §1 (step 2. above) unless others must be designated due to their inability...."[31]

9. In this final step the bishop must "determine whether or not the pastor must be removed and promptly issue a decree on the matter."[32] If the diocesan bishop does decree the removal of the pastor, the pastor may take recourse against the bishop's administrative decree as provided in cc. 1732-1739. In view of c. 1734 §3, 2° together with c. 1737 §1, when the bishop has decreed a pastor's removal from office, the pastor may make direct recourse to the Holy See, but *must* make such an appeal within a *peremptory* period of 15 available days, which run from the first day on which the decree of removal was published. In cases of

---

[30] Canon 1745, 1°.

[31] Canon 1745, 2°.

[32] Canon 1745, 3°.

this sort recourse is made specifically to the Congregation for the Clergy.

A recourse taken against a decree of removal from the pastorate does not have a suspensive effect, because c. 1747 §§1-3 regulates the matter specifically. As a result, a pastor who is the subject of such a decree of removal has in accord with c. 1747 §1 the obligation to "abstain from exercising the office of pastor, vacate the rectory immediately, and hand over all that pertains to the parish to the one to whom the bishop shall entrust the parish."[33] While a recourse is pending, the right of the removed pastor to the pastoral office is undecided and may yet be upheld. As a result, c. 1747 §3 mandates that the bishop is incapable of naming a new pastor during the recourse, but is to provide a parish administrator.[34]

Canon 538 §3 requires that if a bishop accepts the resignation of a pastor who retires at age seventy-five in the ordinary course of events, the bishop "is to provide suitable support and housing for the resigned pastor." Canon 1746 requires that the bishop is to provide for the pastor who is removed, and by implication *a fortiori* for the pastor who resigns at the bishop's request, "through assignment to another office, if he is suitable for this, or through a pension, as the case requires and circumstances

---

[33] Canon 1747 §2 does provide that if the pastor is sick and "cannot be transferred elsewhere from the rectory without inconvenience, the bishop is to leave the rectory even to his exclusive use while this need lasts." Since the word "inconvenience" is used it is clear that the bishop may exercise a benevolent latitude in judging the circumstances in each case. Presumably a pastor who is removed because his ministry has become detrimental or at least ineffective even through no fault of his own, would receive thoughtful consideration. A pastor who has been removed should take careful note that c. 1381 §2 establishes that "Illegitimate retention after deprivation or cessation of office is equivalent to usurpation" and c. 1381 §1 directs that "Whoever usurps an ecclesiastical office is to be punished with a just penalty."

[34] The Latin text is "...non potest novum parochum nominare...," which is simply a specific application of c. 153 §1: "The provision of an office which is by law not vacant is by that very fact invalid, and a subsequent vacancy does not validate the provision."

permit."[35] The administrative procedure of removal does not require that the pastor be proven to be guilty of any deliberate fault, nor does it generally have a tone of punishment about it and its principal purpose is to promote the spiritual welfare of the parishioners and not to punish the pastor. However there are also penal sanctions which can be inflicted on a pastor because of serious and culpable wrongdoing; removal from office is one such penalty. Removal as a sanction may result from a judicial procedure, or be imposed administratively; removal may be specified by law, it may a consequence of another penalty, it may arise *latae sententiae* or *ferendae sententiae*. Since the pastor has an office conferred for either an indefinite period or a definite period which has not expired, c. 193 §§1-2 provides that he cannot be removed except for grave reasons *and* "according to the procedure determined by law." In accord with c. 194 the law itself removes a pastor from office who (a) "has lost the clerical state" (cc. 290, 292, 1394); (b) "has publicly defected from the Catholic faith (c. 751) or from the communion of the Church (cc. 751, 1331)"; (c) "has attempted marriage even if only civilly" (c. 1394). Canon 194 also provides that in the case of (b) and (c) above, the removal "can be enforced only if it is established by the declaration of a competent authority."

If a pastor is charged before a Church tribunal with having committed a criminal act or a delict, c. 221 §1 establishes his right legitimately to "vindicate and defend" his rights "before a competent ecclesiastical court" in accord with each of the canons of Book Seven of the Code appropriate to his case, including especially the right to appeal a sentence.[36] His right that the law be *applied with equity* is set down by c. 221 §2, in addition,

---

[35] Canon 1746 precisely nuances the general requirements of cc. 195 and 281 §§1-2. It is interesting to note that in the 1917 *CIC* c. 2154 §2 dealing with similar matters stated: "All other considerations being equal, more favorable provision should be made for the pastor who resigns [when asked to do so] than for the one who is removed."

[36] Especially cc. 1717-1731 and 1628-1640.

his right that he not be punished with canonical penalties except as provided by law is confirmed by c. 221 §3. If the charges against a pastor are being handled by means of an administrative process, he has the right that the process must be carried out as prescribed by law[37] which stipulates that the administrative process could be used in addressing such charges. After a determination is reached administratively, the pastor would also have the right to an administrative recourse in accord with cc. 1732-1739.

Whether found guilty in a trial and removed from office, or removed from office by a decree resulting from a *penal* administrative procedure, the pastor has a right to appeal or pursue recourse, an action which has a *suspensive* effect in accord with c. 1353: "An appeal or recourse from judicial sentences or from decrees which impose or declare any penalty whatsoever has a suspensive effect."

It is, however, equally important to remember that according to cc. 1740-1747 removal of a pastor is *not a penalty*; even if there is a recourse, the decree of removal has immediate specific effects in accord with c. 1747.[38] Even though a recourse in a case

---

[37] Especially cc. 1341-1353.

[38] When a penal process has been begun against a pastor, even before it has resulted in the removal from, or deprivation of the *ecclesiastical office* of pastor, a pastor may be *physically removed from a parish* under the conditions set forth in c. 1722. Canon 1722 provides that: "To preclude scandals, to protect the freedom of witnesses and to safeguard the course of justice, having heard the promoter of justice and having cited the accused, the ordinary at any stage of the process can remove the accused from the sacred ministry or from any ecclesiastical office or function, can impose or prohibit residence in a given place or territory, or even prohibit public participation in the Most Holy Eucharist; all these measures must be revoked once the reason for them ceases; they also end by the law itself when the penal process ceases." This course of action does not settle guilt or innocence, nor affect the accused's possession of the ecclesiastical office of pastor. The actions authorized solely under the limited conditions specified are not actions of the judge in a judicial penal procedure, nor of the individual or committee instructing an administrative penal process, they are the actions of the ordinary. It appears that consultation with the promoter of justice is required in order to be sure that the ordinary has advice about such a delicate matter which involves a

of this sort does not have a suspensive effect, if the pastor is ill and "cannot be transferred elsewhere from the rectory without inconvenience" the bishop is obliged by c. 1747 §2 to allow the pastor to remain in the rectory "while this need lasts."

The pastor's canonical obligation with respect to any seriously culpable, punishable behavior, is extremely general and is implied by every other canon which imposes obligations on him as a member of the faithful, a priest and a pastor: he is obliged to avoid such reprehensible behavior and to give outstandingly good example and leadership by faithfully discharging all of his canonical obligations.

Another individual administrative act of a diocesan bishop which can result in a pastor losing his ecclesiastical office is the suppression of the pastor's parish. Suppression of a parish is directly regulated by c. 515 §2; the diocesan bishop alone is competent to make the decision but for *validity* he must first hear the presbyteral council. Such a suppression is a specific application of the general directive of c. 120 §1 with respect to the extinguishing of a juridic person.[39] The decree of suppression itself would be subject to Common Norms for Individual Administrative Acts, cc. 35-47, and the specific norms for Individual Decrees and Precepts, cc. 48-58 and cc. 124-128 which regulate Juridic Acts. By analogy with c. 1746, which deals with a pastor who has been

---

conflict of rights; the citation of the accused is required, perhaps so that the accused will have an opportunity to present a defense or offer some other possibilities for obviating the concerns expressed in the opening lines of c. 1722. Clearly the underlying purpose of c. 1722 is to provide for the good of souls, which is basically a responsibility of the ordinary. It is also to be noted that the "suspensive effect" provided by c. 1353 would not be applicable to an ordinary's decrees issued in accord with c. 1722, because, even if the citation necessary for the invocation of c. 1722 may be to a penal trial, the actions authorized by c. 1722 are not themselves "penal but preventive and prudential" as noted by F. Loza, "The Penal Process," Commentary on cc. 1717-1731, in the *Code Annotated*, p. 1063.

[39] If the act decreeing the suppression of a parish is also to include the church building being relegated "to profane but not sordid use," it would also be necessary for the diocesan bishop to follow the steps required by c. 1222 §2. It would seem prudent to administer the suppression of a parish and the disposal of its church building as the separate and distinct matters which they are.

removed from office, the pastor of a suppressed parish would have a right to another office or to a pension. By analogy with c. 1752, which treats of a pastor transferred against his will, the pastor of a suppressed parish would have a right to be treated with canonical equity.[40]

It should also be recognized that stability in the ecclesiastical office of pastor of a parish, does not always include full exercise of that office. Canons 539 through 541 mandate and regulate the appointment of a "parochial administrator," a priest who is to provide pastoral ministry to a parish which has become vacant or whose "pastor is prevented from exercising his pastoral office in the parish" as explained in c. 539. Five specific causes of such prevention are listed in c. 539, but then there follow the words "or some other cause." Two inferences from such a text appear legitimate: (a) any other cause should be on a par with the seriousness of those specifically listed and (b) the diocesan bishop is the judge of the presence and seriousness of any other cause. One commentary opines that as soon as the bishop receives word that a pastor is prevented from fulfilling his office, it would be fitting that, before taking the step of appointing a parochial administrator, the diocesan bishop, when he is able to do so, expressly state the cause which is impeding the pastor and the degree to which that cause is interfering with the pastor's exercise of his office.[41]

Canon 540 §1 authorizes the diocesan bishop to determine to what extent a parochial administrator "is bound by the same duties and enjoys the same rights as a pastor." It appears, then, to be within the competence of a diocesan bishop to decide that some reason is preventing a pastor from exercising his pastoral office, appoint a parochial administrator and entrust the admin-

---

[40] It does not appear, however, that the pastor of a suppressed parish would have any special right to be appointed a pastor elsewhere, since cc. 523 and 524 leave to the diocesan bishop's discretion selection of any qualified priest to serve as pastor for a vacant parish.

[41] SÁNCHEZ-GIL, "Parroquias y párrocos," in *Comentario exegético*, vol. II/2, p. 1299.

istrator with the complete administration of a parish. As a result, a pastor, while still technically incumbent in the office of pastor, might, in fact, be left with very little to do. If a pastor in such circumstances believes that the bishop's decisions and actions are incorrect, or unjust, or both, recourse against such an administrative decree is an option. Since, however, the appointment of a parochial administrator is not a penalty, a recourse would not have the suspensive effect provided by c. 1353.

5.1.4 — Transfer of a pastor

There are at least two fundamental differences between the transfer of a pastor and the removal of a pastor; one has to do with the abilities of the pastor himself, the other arises because he is to be transferred to another ecclesiastical office. To begin with, a pastor who is to be transferred is described by c. 1748 to be "governing usefully" the parish of which he is pastor. His ministry has not become detrimental or ineffective; c. 1748 notes further that a pastor to be transferred has the ability to serve the "good of souls or the need or advantage of the Church" as pastor elsewhere or in another ecclesiastical office (unlike the removed pastor who may need to be retired and pensioned).[42] In addition to the pastor's qualities, c. 153 §1 stipulates that if an office is not vacant according to law, any provision of such an office is invalid, and even a subsequent vacancy would not render a provision of that kind valid. Canon 153 §2 establishes one exception: provision for an occupied office can be validly made

---

[42] It is to be noted that cc. 538 §2 and 682 §§1-2 which deal directly with the appointment and removal of members of religious institutes and members of societies of apostolic life as pastors do not provide explicit directions for transferring such a priest from one pastorate to another. Applying those canons however, it appears that the diocesan bishop could remove the pastor from parish "A" on his own authority, but would need the agreement of the priest's competent superior to appoint the same priest to be pastor of parish "B."

within six months of the expiration of a term of an office which was conferred for a determined period of time.

Nothing seems to prevent the bishop, *per se vel per alios*, from first discussing the proposed transfer with the pastor involved. Such a preliminary discussion would also fit in well with the general teaching of the Second Vatican Council: "Therefore to ensure an increasingly effective apostolate, the bishop should be willing to engage in dialogue with his priests, individually and collectively, not merely occasionally, but if possible, regularly."[43]

Nevertheless, cc. 153 §§1-2 and 190 §1 set forth bases for the essential canonical step which must precede the initiation of the procedure for the transfer of a pastor that begins with c. 1748. The parish or the office to which the bishop wishes to transfer the pastor must be vacant by law. If there is a pastor in the parish *ad quam* who has either been appointed for an indefinite term of office or is not within six months of the end of his determined term of office, the bishop needs to obtain the resignation of that incumbent pastor of the *ad quem* parish before undertaking to transfer another pastor to be pastor of the *ad quam* parish. A definitive sentence of the Supreme Tribunal of the Apostolic Signatura, c. Agustoni, June 24, 1995 stated:

> It is necessary [*oportet*] that the parish *ad quam* is vacant *before* [*antequam*] the procedure for transfer begins, otherwise such procedure is illegitimate not because of the condition of the office from which the parish priest is being transferred but because of the condition of the office to which the priest is being transferred, that is because the transfer would be made to an office which cannot be conferred.[44]

---

[43] *CD*, n. 28. English translation in FLANNERY, *Conciliar and Post Conciliar Documents*, p. 580.

[44] See *Forum*, 6 (1995)², pp. 117-122, here at pp. 120-121; original Latin text and English translation are presented together.

The reasons why the office cannot be conferred are clear: (a) the parish *ad quem* is not vacant by law (c. 152 §1) and (b) since the parish is not vacant the bishop does not have the right to assign anyone as its pastor, since he is prevented from doing so by c. 190 §1. In addition, if, in such circumstances (the pastor has not resigned and is not within six months of the end of a term of specified duration) a bishop appointed another priest as pastor of that *ad quem* parish, that appointment would be — and remain — invalid even if the pastor of the parish *ad quam* did resign later (c. 153 §1). Even taking all of the foregoing conditions into account, nothing seems to prevent a bishop from discussing with pastors various hypothetical changes and transfers which he might be thinking about making.

The steps of the formal procedure for the transfer of a pastor are:

1. Canon 1748 establishes that "the bishop is to propose the transfer to him [the pastor] in writing and persuade him to consent to it for the love of God and of souls."[45]

2. If, after counsel and persuasion, the pastor intends not to cooperate, the pastor "is to explain his reasons in writing" in accord with cc. 190 §2 and 1749. The pastor should bear in mind that the bishop has already become convinced that the good of souls or the need or advantage of the Church requires the proposed transfer. When the pastor draws up his reasons for resisting a transfer, he needs to overcome or mitigate those judgments of the bishop, or any assertion that "a grave cause" exists which requires the transfer;[46] nothing prevents the pastor from also introducing additional considerations against the transfer if he wishes to do so.

---

[45] Marzoa, "Remoción y translado de párrocos," in *Comentario exegético*, vol. IV/2, p. 2198, points out that the transfer treated in cc. 1748-1752 pertains to a pastor who by definition "is governing usefully...." That kind of transfer has no relationship to the "penal transfer to another office" listed among other expiatory penalties in c. 1336 §1,4° the imposition of which would be regulated according to law by cc. 1717-1728 on *Penal Procedure* or by cc. 1341-1353 on *Application of Penalties*.

[46] Canon 190 §2.

3. If, after reviewing the pastor's reasons against the transfer, the bishop judges that the transfer should still be effected, c. 1750 directs that the bishop "is to discuss the reasons which favor or oppose the transfer with two pastors chosen in accord with c. 1742 §1."[47] As noted above in step 2 for the administrative removal of a pastor from office, c. 1742 §1 makes provision for the establishment of a group of pastors, with two of whom the bishop is to consult in the process of deciding whether to remove a pastor and, in accord with c. 1750, in the process of considering whether to transfer a pastor. If, after this consultation, the bishop concludes that the transfer is to take place, c. 1750 requires that the bishop "is to repeat the paternal exhortation to the pastor."

4. If, after the repeated exhortation, the pastor continues to refuse and the bishop "thinks the transfer must be made, he is to issue a decree of transfer stating that the parish [the parish of which the pastor refusing the transfer is still pastor] shall be vacant after the lapse of a predetermined time" as directed by c. 1751 §1.[48] The "decree of transfer" referred to in c. 1751 §1 must indeed require the same transfer to the same other parish or office originally proposed in the first step of this process, because no other transfer has been an element in the canonical procedure. Canon 1751 §2 then requires: "If this period of time has passed in vain, he is to declare the parish vacant."[49]

---

[47] The English translation used here departs from that of the CLSA, which reads in part "with *the* two pastors chosen in accord..." (emphasis added). The insertion of "the" is not supported by the Latin text and creates a lack of clarity, especially since c. 1742 §1 refers to "two pastors from the group permanently selected."

[48] That decree of transfer would be an individual precept, defined in c. 49 as: "a decree directly and legitimately enjoining a determined person... to do... something, especially concerning the urging of observance of a law." See MARZOA, "Remoción y translado de párrocos," in *Comentario exegético*, vol. IV/2, p. 2204.

[49] If the pastor reconsiders and obeys the precept he has been given within the time limit set, his taking possession of the new parish or some other ecclesiastical office will render his former parish vacant in accord with c. 191 §1, "unless the law provides otherwise or something else has been prescribed by the competent authority."

5. The pastor involved may take recourse as provided in cc. 1732-1739 against the bishop's administrative act of issuing the decree of transfer, or against the declaration that the parish is vacant when it is issued as required by c. 1751 §2. In view of c. 1752, however, the specific directions of c. 1747 §§1-3 are immediately effective even while the recourse is in process.[50] Also c. 1752 requires that in cases of transfer c. 1747 is to be applied "always observing canonical equity." That requirement becomes an obligation of the bishop who is enforcing the transfer, and, implicitly, it expresses a right of the pastor who refuses the transfer to be treated with canonical equity.[51]

---

[50] With respect to c. 1747 §2 being invoked, it does not seem likely that a bishop would be transferring a sick pastor to another pastorate, but it is not inconceivable that as the elements of cc. 1748-1752 develop in an individual situation a pastor might become sick and/or incapacitated. In any case, as noted above with respect to removal, the transferred pastor should also be aware that c. 1381 §2 establishes that: "Illegitimate retention after deprivation or cessation of office is equivalent to usurpation," which should be punished with a just penalty as directed by c. 1381 §1.

[51] Canonical equity is a complex concept encompassing legal principles, gospel teaching, practice and common sense. The concept arises from a realization that following strictly the letter of a usually just and effective law may, in some peculiar or extraordinary circumstances, not achieve justice nor exemplify the practice of Christian virtue. J.A. CORIDEN, "Rules For Interpreters," in *The Jurist*, 42 (1982), pp. 277-303, here at p. 283, states: "The concept [equity] is subtle, nuanced and sometimes obscure. It shares etymological roots with epiky, and some notable authors, e.g., St. Thomas and Suarez, did not distinguish the two notions. Equity encompasses two ideas: one, from Roman law, of perfect justice, that is, seeing that the ideal of justice is actually realized in practice, assuring the fair result, and the other from Christian sources of justice tempered with mercy, a softening of the rigor of the law under the influence of charity. The two ideas are combined in 'canonical equity' which places the legal notion in the context of a juridical system with a spiritual purpose." Also see LABANDEIRA and MIRAS, "The Procedure for the Removal or Transfer of Parish Priests," in *Code Annotated*, p. 1080, the reference to c. 1752 in the commentary on c. 1750, which suggests that there could be a question of canonical equity in the transfer of a pastor from one parish to a parish which is exceedingly inferior (the "non sit ordinis nimio inferioris" of c. 2163 of the 1917 CIC).

5.2 — THE OFFICE OF PASTOR IN UNUSUAL CIRCUMSTANCES

Canons 526 §1 and 517 §§1-2 establish three special arrangements for pastoral care which in unusual circumstances may be permitted by the diocesan bishop.[52] Since each of these canons "contain an exception to the law [they] are subject to a strict interpretation" in accord with c. 18.[53] The second clause of c. 526 §1 allows that "the care of several neighboring parishes can be entrusted to the same pastor due to a dearth of priests." With a different starting point and envisioning a different approach, c. 517 §1 also allows for the possibility of a priest to provide pastoral care for more than one parish at the same time as a member of a group of priests serving *in solidum*. Canon 517 §2 allows a deacon and or lay members of the Church to share in the exercise of the pastoral care of a parish, supervised by "some priest endowed with the powers and faculties of a pastor." Since that arrangement does not require either a canonical pastor or administrator, it constitutes an exception to c. 539.

With respect to the unusual conditions required for the

---

[52] Canons 526 and 517 §§1-2 also generate canonical questions concerning the traditional principle of the union between community and ministry and the nuances raised by those canons; whether those canons treat of *exceptions* to the law or *alternatives*; whether c. 517 §1, although using the words "*in solidum*," does not rather describe a collegiate form of pastoral activity, which conjures up the concept of a juridic person as pastor, which, in turn, is excluded by c. 521 §1; whether c. 517 §2 can be taken simply as a legitimate manner in which to develop the laity; how key concepts are to be correctly understood and then accurately translated into various modern languages. See Borras, *Les communautés paroissiales*, pp. 163-199. As important and interesting as those questions and the discussions surrounding them are, they do not fall within the focus of this work which addresses the obligations and rights of those who validly possess the ecclesiastical office of parish pastor according to the *CIC*. Possession of the office of pastor is clearest when one priest serves as pastor of one parish only, then when one priest serves as pastor of more than one parish concomitantly; incumbency in the ecclesiastical office of pastor becomes less clear in the cases of one priest among other priests all or none of whom may be canonical pastors simultaneously serving the same one parish or group of parishes.

[53] Borras, *Les communautés paroissiales*, p. 164, footnote 1.

application of these special arrangements for pastoral care, a shortage of priests is identified as the *only* basis for invoking c. 517 §2; c. 526 §1 can be acted upon because of a shortage of priests *or* "in other circumstances"; c. 517 §1 can be followed "when circumstances require it." Although the *circumstances* are not further specified, there seems to be an implication that they would have to be serious circumstances concerning good pastoral care of souls, since the good pastoral care of souls is the reason why exceptions to the common law of the Church are permitted.[54]

5.2.1 — One pastor for more than one parish

Canon 526 §1 first sets down the general norm that a pastor is to have the parochial care of only one parish, but allows that because of (a) a scarcity of priests, or (b) in other circumstances (c) several, (d) *neighboring* parishes can be entrusted to the same pastor. The *other circumstances* are not spelled out, but the text of c. 526 §1 implies that those circumstances would have to be on a par with the seriousness of a shortage of priests.[55] The wording of c. 526 §1, "the care of several neighboring parishes can be entrusted to the same pastor due to a dearth of priests," neither requires nor forbids that the pastor to whom the care of an additional parish or parishes is entrusted should receive specific canonical appointments as the pastor of each of those other parishes. An alternative would be for the pastor in question to be appointed administrator of the other parishes, or, more simply, to be directed by the diocesan bishop to provide pastoral care for the designated neighboring parishes in accord with c. 526 §1. A priest who legitimately holds the ecclesiastical office

---

[54] The *CCEO* has no canon which corresponds to either paragraph of c. 517 *CIC*.

[55] Borras, *Les communautés paroissiales*, p. 167 suggests population shifts and massive emigrations as other circumstances and notes that in the 1800's there were many small parishes established, the maintenance of which has now become a problem.

of pastor in more than one parish would have the canonical obligations and rights of a pastor with respect to each parish ministered to by him, with the exception that he would be "obliged
to apply only one Mass for all the people entrusted to him" in
accord with c. 534 §§1-2. The obligation of c. 533 §1 that the pastor reside in the parish would technically exist, but no one can
be bound to the impossible. Because the residence law seems
intended to make sure that the pastor is present to the people, it
would appear equitable for the pastor to arrange to be present
at some definite place in each of the parishes involved according to some published schedule, so that the people of each parish could easily arrange to meet with him.

In addition, cc. 526 §1 and 517 §§1-2 are silent about various administrative and procedural questions which could arise
during the course of everyday parish administration. Particular
law for a region, diocesan synodal law, diocesan statutes or diocesan policies dealing with such questions and establishing procedures could impose additional obligations and/or confer additional rights on pastors appointed under these canons.

The burden of caring for additional parishes would not add
to the pastor's precise obligations and rights as pastor of his own
parish; nevertheless the additional parish or parishes would un-
doubtedly increase a pastor's work load because of obligations
and rights with respect to supervision of pastoral care for the
good of souls in the other parish or parishes. Since that is the
case, the pastor would be under a serious obligation to determine before accepting such an appointment whether it would
be incompatible with his work as pastor of one parish. Canon
526 §1 certainly implies that the Church does not regard being
pastor of two or more parishes simultaneously as holding ecclesiastical offices which are *per se* incompatible. Nevertheless, if a
pastor were to reach the judgment that he could not pastor two
or more parishes at the same time, c. 152 would give him the
obligation and the right to decline the appointment to the additional parish or parishes. On the other hand, if a priest were
appointed canonical pastor of more than one parish and then

found the work to be too much for him, he could, in accord with c. 187, seek to resign from the office of pastor of one or more of the parishes to which he had been appointed.

5.2.2 — Priests *in solidum* providing pastoral care

Canon 517 §1 allows another approach to the pastoral care of one or more parishes. In accord with c. 517 §1 the pastoral care of (a) a parish, or (b) different parishes together can be entrusted to (c) several priests *in solidum*, (d) when circumstances require it and, (e) provided that one of the priests should direct their joint action (f) and answer to the bishop for it. The term *in solidum* usually means that each member of a group operating *in solidum* is personally responsible to see to it that all of the obligations of the group are fulfilled and has personally all of the rights arising from the obligations of the group and from membership in the group. The *in solidum* concept in c. 517 §1 is, however, a special canonical institute, unique in the Code of 1983, because only one of the priests has the obligation and right to direct their joint activity and the obligation and the right to answer to the bishop for their joint activity. As significant as they are, these two departures from the usual understanding of *in solidum* do not diminish in the slightest the personal responsibility of each priest in the group for every *other* required element of pastoral care. The Code does not use the term pastor (*parochus*) with respect to any of the members of the group working *in solidum*. There is a legitimate question concerning whether any member of an *in solidum* group as described in c. 517 §1 and cc. 542-544 possesses the ecclesiastical office of pastor of a parish.[56]

---

[56] For additional views and commentary see R. PAGÉ, *Les églises particulières*: Tome II: *la charge pastorale de leurs communautés de fidèles selon le Code de droit canonique de 1983*, vol. 4 of *Les institutions ecclésiales*, Montréal: Éditions Paulines & Médiaspaul, 1989, pp. 144-154; BORRAS, *Les communautés paroissiales*, pp. 169-179, especially 170-174; SÁNCHEZ-GIL, "Parroquias y párrocos," *Comentario exegético*, vol. II/2, pp. 1215-1216.

If they do not possess that ecclesiastical office however, they possess an ecclesiastical office very much like it, the prerequisites for which are identical and the obligations and rights of which are *for the most part* substantially the same, except as provided by c. 544 with respect to the conditions under which a parish or parishes they are serving would become vacant and the subsequent membership of the *in solidum* group when one or more members depart.

Canon 542 provides that each priest in the group must meet all the requirements of one who is to be appointed to be a pastor as set down in c. 521 §§1-3; each priest of the group must be appointed or installed in accord with cc. 522 and 524; the priest who is to coordinate their joint activity and answer to the bishop for that activity is to be placed in possession of the parish in accord with the prescriptions of c. 527 §2 (just as a pastor is ordinarily installed); for the other priests of the group "a legitimately made profession of faith substitutes for taking possession." As with pastors, their responsibility for pastoral care begins only with taking possession of the parish or parishes. Canon 543 §1, in addition to referring to canons which express a pastor's principal duties, directs that the members of the group are to arrange among themselves how they will carry out the duties and functions of the pastor, provides to each the faculty to assist at marriages and declares that each has all faculties granted to a pastor by the law itself; c. 543 §1 also repeats that they are to minister under the management of the priest who is to coordinate their joint activity. Canon 543 §2 establishes that the members of the group are bound by the obligation of residence, are by common counsel to arrange which of them will offer the Mass for the people as per c. 534; the priest coordinator of joint activity is designated as representative of the parish or parishes in juridic matters by c. 543 §2.

Canon 544 provides that if any member of the group ceases from office or becomes incapable of functioning, the parish or parishes do not become vacant. In such a case the bishop is directed to fill the vacancy and, if the priest coordinator is the one who is to be replaced, the senior priest of the group in terms of assignment is to fulfill that office in the meantime.

The obligations and rights of each of the priests ministering *in solidum*, would be almost the same as those of any pastor except in three instances. First, in accord with c. 543 §2, 2° only one of them would be obliged to offer the Mass for the people, which, if they are serving only one parish, would be an exception to c. 534 §1. Second, only the "moderator, *qui nempe actionem coniunctam dirigat*" of c. 517 §1 represents the parish in all juridic affairs in accord with c. 543 §2, 3°, which is an exception to c. 532. Third, only the "moderator, *qui nempe actionem coniunctam dirigat*" of c. 517 §1 directs their joint activity and answers for it to the bishop. Residence requirements and the possibility of additional obligations and/or rights arising from local legislation or policies would be the same as described for one pastor alone.

5.2.3 — Parish without a pastor

Canon 517 §2 stipulates that:

> If the diocesan bishop should decide that due to a dearth of priests a participation in the exercise of the pastoral care of a parish is to be entrusted to a deacon or to some other person who is not a priest or to a community of persons, he is to appoint some priest endowed with the powers and faculties of a pastor to supervise the pastoral care.

Canon 517 §2 does not employ the terminology *providing for the pastoral care of a parish without a pastor*, but explicitly describes a *participation* in the exercise of the pastoral care of a parish, which parish quite clearly does not have a pastor. One or more members of the faithful who are not priests will participate in the day to day requirements of pastoral care and a priest, who might be termed a *priest-moderator*, who is not pastor of the parish, will participate by supervising their activities. Canon 517

§2 is silent on the subject of whether the *priest-moderator* is required or expected to celebrate for the people of the parish those sacraments which only a priest can celebrate, or whether the member or members of the faithful, who are sharing the pastoral care of the parish, are required to recruit and engage another priest or priests for that purpose.[57]

Canon 517 §2 establishes that the *priest-moderator* is to be "endowed with the powers and faculties of a pastor." That "endowment" is accomplished by the normal process of Church law. The powers and faculties proper to the pastor of a parish are established by various canons of the Code. In addition, diocesan bishops acting within the limits of their own authority may establish other powers and faculties of the pastor of a parish within their dioceses. Ordinarily a diocesan bishop can confer the powers and faculties established in the Code as proper to a pastor by appointing a priest to either the office of pastor of a parish (c. 524), or the office of administrator of a parish (cc. 539-540 §1). Canon 517 §2 establishes a third office, described above as a *priest-moderator*, by appointment to which the diocesan bishop can cause a priest to be "endowed with the powers and faculties of a pastor." Nevertheless, the *priest-moderator* called for by c. 517 §2 does not become the pastor of the parish for which provision is being made. Because of a dearth of priests, such a parish simply does not have a pastor.[58]

---

[57] For any parish, with or without a pastor, c. 1248 §2 makes specific recommendations for prayerful activities of the faithful on Sundays and Holy Days of obligation where circumstances render the celebration of the Eucharist by a priest impossible. The member or members of the faithful participating in the pastoral care of a parish in accord with c. 517 §2 could exercise their ministry under such conditions. See *Letter & Spirit*, n. 1026, p. 287.

[58] Canon 517 §2 does not provide a pastor for a parish nor a precise delineation of the interaction expected between the *priest-moderator* and those members of the faithful whom he supervises; in addition, it is a course of action allowed for only one specific reason, "a dearth of priests." That canon seems, therefore, to regard what it stipulates as merely a temporary measure in a truly desperate situation, which the bishop must make every legitimate effort to ameliorate.

Canon 517 §2 does not provide detailed regulations for interaction among the *priest-moderator* and those supervised, nor a precise plan for implementing shared participation in the pastoral care of a parish.[59] At least one practical concern has arisen about the exact meaning and scope of "pastoral care" as used in c. 517 §2. Does that "pastoral care" include authority even for non-ordained faithful, to whom a participation in the pastoral care of a parish has been entrusted, to perform acts of administration on behalf of the juridic person of the parish? Could such administrative acts be exercises of the power of governance? Canon 129 §1 stipulates that: "In accord with the prescriptions of law, those who have received sacred orders are capable of the power of governance"; and c. 129 §2 sets down that: "lay members of the Christian faithful can cooperate in the exercise of this power in accord with the norm of law." Can c. 517 §2 be an instance in which the law would implicitly allow lay members of the Christian faithful to exercise the executive power of governance? Those questions do not fall precisely under the topic being treated here, both because they do not touch upon the obligations or rights of a pastor as such, and because they deal with circumstances which exist precisely because there is no pastor. Nevertheless such considerations seem inexorably involved with c. 517 §2.

A pastor could be affected under c. 517 §2 if a bishop wishes to appoint a priest, who is already pastor of another parish, to carry out the supervision of a parish being cared for under c. 517 §2. As noted above in section 5.2.1 concerning one pastor as pastor of more than one parish, the same question of incompatibility of the two offices might arise for the particular pastor who has been asked to do the supervising. He also could turn to c. 152 for his obligations and rights in those circumstances.

---

[59] B.A. CUSACK and T.G. SULLIVAN, *Pastoral Care in Parishes Without a Pastor*, p. x. These authors take the position that the law's lack of "a well-defined plan for applying and implementing this canon" is a good thing because: "Local culture, customs, concerns must help to shape the direction that implementation of canon 517, §2 will take."

CONCLUSION

The content of the canons about the office of pastor of a parish which have been considered in this chapter give evidence of the Church's deep concern for the people who make up parish communities and the individual priests who serve them as pastors. In addition, the adaptability and openness of Canon Law itself can be seen in those canons which address the special circumstances of parishes in areas experiencing a shortage of priests.

Before a priest may reasonably expect to be appointed a pastor he needs to have made use of the means available to prepare himself to serve others in that particular ecclesiastical office. He is expected to have a distinguished grasp of sound doctrine and be known to be living a good moral life and to be zealous for souls. Merely growing older in the priesthood is not a qualification for appointment as a pastor.

In the act of taking possession of a parish the pastor simultaneously takes on the responsibility of providing for the pastoral care of the parish community. The pastor not only accepts the obligation of living *for* the people of the parish, but normally of living *among the people of the parish.*

A pastor can expect a reasonable measure of stability in office, whether the term is indefinite, or for a specific duration with possible renewal in accord with particular law. The pastor can anticipate that during the term of his office he will neither be arbitrarily dismissed from office nor transferred to another office against his will and due process. The pastor and the parish are both protected by the canons applicable in such matters. A diocesan bishop cannot remove a pastor at will, but a pastor who is not properly caring for the good of the people cannot hold on to his office to their detriment if the bishop accurately carries out the process provided in cc. 1740-1747.

Mutatis mutandis a pastor can expect that during his term of office he will not be transferred to another office unless the diocesan bishop has proposed the transfer to him in writing and made an effort to persuade the pastor to accept the transfer.

Should the pastor remain unpersuaded, the bishop may still proceed with the transfer carefully applying the process stipulated in cc. 1748-1752.

While he serves the parishioners the pastor is ordinarily entitled to a month's vacation each year, time for a spiritual retreat, and perhaps a sabbatical in accord with particular law. A condition of those times away from the parish is that the needs of the parishioners will be provided for. Although a pastor may wish to continue ministering to his parish after he has reached the age of 75, he is expected to offer his resignation to the diocesan bishop, who, having considered all of the circumstances of person and place (which certainly must include the good of the parishioners and the good of the pastor), will accept or defer the resignation.

When a pastor's resignation has been accepted he has a right to suitable support and housing provided by the diocesan bishop, who is to consider the norms set down by the conference of bishops.

In those areas of the world where the Church must care for God's people with fewer and fewer priests, Canon Law acknowledges the problems and strives to adapt the law to the *de facto* circumstances. Provisions are made for (a) appointing one priest as pastor of more than one parish, (b) appointing more than one priest to serve *in solidum* to provide pastoral care for one or more parishes, and (c) parishes without a pastor to be served by a deacon or lay person supervised by a priest with the faculties of a pastor.[60]

In fine, the relationship between a parish and its pastor in both normal circumstances and in the challenges resulting from a dearth of priests or other particular circumstances is addressed by the canons with honesty, balance and flexibility.

---

[60] Canons 517 §§ 1-2, 526 §1, 542-544.

General Conclusions

The Second Vatican Council has infused new life into various Church institutions and that life generates a new light in which the theological and ecclesial elements of those institutions can be more clearly seen than before. Among those institutions the parish and the office of pastor of a parish, while retaining many of their historical features, are now perceived to be more dynamic, personal and communitarian than had been previously realized.

Led by the ecclesiology of Vatican II, Canon Law now presents a parish as a Eucharistic community of the faithful, clergy and laity together, honoring God by celebrating the liturgy with one another, each actively participating according to his or her own proper role, all living their day to day Christian lives in witness of their faith and aware that their community is a vital part of the particular and universal Church. The parish is seen to exist for the salvation of each soul and every person of the community. From a practical and juridical viewpoint, the parish remains, in fact, a useful administrative grouping in the Church and a source of support for the priests who minister to its members, even though these elements are no longer emphasized or regarded as primary. The pastor of a parish, both theologically and juridically, is at the center of a parish community.

The qualifications which a priest is required to have before being appointed a pastor of a parish are substantially the same as stated in the 1917 Code (c. 453) and in the 1983 Code (521). Nevertheless in theology and in the 1983 Code the pastor of a parish is clearly understood to be especially conformed to Christ by priestly ordination in order to serve God's people. The pastor is expected to do this by providing mutually respectful and cooperative leadership so that the lay faithful, sharing in Christ's priesthood through baptism, and the priest, sharing in Christ's priesthood in an essentially different manner through priestly ordination, work together to carry out the threefold tasks of Jesus as priest, prophet and king. The 1983 Code places a great emphasis on the obligation of the pastor to lead by example and persuasion. That emphasis reflects modification of the 1917 Code which, although it set down many obligations for the pastor to fulfill, appeared firmly to propose that the pastor had a right simply to direct the faithful to assist him by commanding them to do so.

A significant change can also be observed in the canonical expression of the pastor's obligations to provide Catholic education and religious instruction for all in his parish. There is no less insistence on the presentation of the intellectual content of the Catholic faith, but the Code makes it clear that such teaching, however successful it may be, is only one element of what is required of the pastor. The pastor is required to provide an education in the faith for the people of the parish in such a way that, as c. 773 put it: "the faith of the faithful becomes living, explicit and productive through formation in doctrine and the experience of Christian living." The Code also indicates the right of the pastor to call for and receive cooperative effort from the faithful in order to achieve that high goal.

With respect to the pastor's mission of sanctifying God's people, several shifts in perspective have taken place. The Church has not departed from teaching the *ex opere operato* efficaciousness of the sacraments *validly* celebrated. The Church has, however, called on pastors and parishioners alike to recognize their obligation and right to give honor, glory and praise to God as a parish community in and through the liturgical celebration during which the sacraments are *validly* made present and/or administered. Emphasis is placed on the fact that we are called by God to be a worshiping Eucharistic community. Canon 528 §2 places a specific canonical obligation on the pastor "to see to it that the Most Holy Eucharist is the center of the parish assembly of the faithful." He is also reminded of correlative obligations to prepare the people to knowingly and actively take their proper parts in the liturgy and to watch carefully to keep any abuses from entering into the liturgies celebrated within the parish community.

The theology of the Second Vatican Council acknowledged, or perhaps rediscovered, that the lay faithful have abilities, experience, expertise, gifts and charisms which can be utilized for the spread of the faith and the good of the Church. This awareness appears in the Code and raises new obligations for the pastor of a parish with respect to working with a parish finance council (c. 537) and a pastoral council (c. 536), if the diocesan bishop requires them to the established. The 1983 Code may not establish any greater right for the pastor to call upon the faithful to assist him as he exercises leadership in a parish, but those canons which call on the faithful to become more involved in the life and work of the Church, are likely to make a pastor less reticent about asking for help. Indeed, the Code advises and/or requires the pastor to cooperate with other members of the parish community.

All things considered, it appears that the Code, reflecting the teachings of the Second Vatican Council, establishes *Service in the Form of Leadership* as the principal obligation and the principal right of the pastor of the parish. The pastor is obliged and entitled to teach the faith so that it produces dynamic Christians; together with the faithful he is to plan and celebrate the liturgies through which they will offer public worship to God as a Eucharistic community; he is to govern the parish in a consultative manner aided and advised by the faithful in a relationship of mutual trust and respect. Various canons indicate the Church's awareness that the pastor will need the help of the faithful in order to fulfill many of his obligations, and that, even though he should prudently share some of his authority with others, he cannot delegate away his leadership responsibility.

Finally the focus of the Code, if not its exact words, ought to be reiterated. It is this: the obligations, rights and entitlements of the pastor of a parish exist principally and directly to provide for the good of parishioners' souls, the *salus animarum* of c. 1752.

Selected Bibliography

Sources:

Catechism of the Catholic Church, New York: Catholic Book Publishing Co., 1994.

Catéchisme de l'Église catholique, Paris: Mame, Nouvelles Éditions, 1992.

Code of Canon Law, Latin-English ed., translation prepared under the auspices of THE CANON LAW SOCIETY OF AMERICA, Washington, DC: Canon Law Society of America, 1983.

Code of Canons of the Eastern Churches, Latin-English edition, translation prepared under the auspices of THE CANON LAW SOCIETY OF AMERICA, Washington, DC: Canon Law Society of America, 1992.

Codice di diritto canonico: testo ufficiale e versione italiana, prepared under the sponsorship of the Pontifical University of the Lateran and the Pontifical Salesian University, (*Lateran-Salesian, Codice di diritto canonico*) Roma: Unione Editori Italiani, 1983.

Codex canonum Ecclesiarum orientalium, auctoritate Ioannis Pauli PP. II promulgatus, Romae: Typis polyglottis Vaticanis, 1990.

Codex canonum Ecclesiarum orientalium, auctoritate Ioannis Pauli PP. II promulgatus, fontium annotatione auctus, Libreria editrice Vaticana, 1995.

Codex iuris canonici, auctoritate Ioannis Pauli PP. II promulgatus, Libreria editrice Vaticana, 1983.

Codex iuris canonici, auctoritate Ioannis Pauli PP. II promulgatus, *fontium annotatione et indice analytico-alphabetico auctus*, Libreria editrice Vaticana, 1989.

Codex iuris canonici, Pii X Pontificis Maximi iussu digestus, Benedicti Papae XV auctoritate promulgatus, praefatione, fontibus annotatione et indice analyticio-alphabetico ab Emo Petro Card. Gasparri auctus, Romae: Typis polyglottis Vaticanis, 1933.

Congregatio pro Clericis, Pontificium Concilium pro Laicis, Congregationes de Doctrina Fidei, de Cultu Divino et Disciplina Sacramentorum, pro Episcopis, pro Gentium Evangelizatione, pro Institutis Vitae Consecratae et Societibus Vitae Apostolicae and Pontificium Concilium de Legum Textibus Interpretadis, *Instruction on Certain Questions Regarding the Collaboration of the Non-Ordained Faithful in the Sacred Ministry of Priest Ecclesiae de mysterio*, August 15, 1997, in *AAS*, 89 (1997).

_____, *Instruction on Certain Questions Regarding the Collaboration of the Non-Ordained Faithful in the Sacred Ministry of Priest Ecclesiae de mysterio*, August 15, 1997, Vatican City: Libreria editrice Vaticana, 1997.

Congregatio pro Clericis, *General Directory for Catechesis, Directorium Catechisticum Generale*, Città del Vaticano: Libreria editrice Vaticana, 1997. English translation United States Catholic Conference, *General Directory for Catechesis*, Washington, DC, 1998.

English Language Conferences of Bishops, *Complementary Norms to the Code Promulgated by English-Language Conferences of Bishops, Code of Canon Law Annotated,* Latin-English edition of the Code of Canon Law and English language translation of 5th Spanish language edition of the Commentary prepared under the responsibility of the Instituto Martín de Azpilcueta, Montréal, Wilson & Lafleur, 1993.

Flannery, A. (ed.), *Vatican Council II*, 2 vols.: vol. 1: *The Conciliar and Post Conciliar Documents*, New Revised Edition, Dublin, Ireland, Dominican Publications, 1992; vol. 2: *More Postconciliar Documents*, Collegeville, MN: The Liturgical Press, 1982.

GASPARRI, P. (ed.), vols. 1-6; J. SEREDI (ed.), vols. 7-9, *Codicis iuris canonici fontes*, Romae: Typis polyglottis Vaticanis, 1926-1939.

General Catechetical Directory, Washington, DC, Publications Office, United States Catholic Conference, 1971.

INTERNATIONAL COMMISSION ON ENGLISH IN THE LITURGY, *Documents on the Liturgy 1963-1979, Conciliar, Papal and Curial Texts*, Collegeville, MN: Liturgical Press, 1982.

JOHN XXIII, Special Allocution to the congregation at the Benedictine Monastery of St. Paul's Outside the Walls, after the celebration of Mass by His Holiness in the Patriarchial Basilica at Ostia, *Questa festiva*, January 25, 1959, in *AAS*, 51 (1959), pp. 65-69.

JOHN PAUL I, Sermon at the conclusion of the Mass celebrated with the Cardinals the day following his election to the papacy, *Ad gravissimum munus*, August, 27, 1978, in *AAS*, 70 (1978), pp. 691-699.

JOHN PAUL II, Apostolic Exhortation, "Catechesis in Our Time," *Catechesi tradendae*, October 16, 1979, in *AAS*, 71 (1979), pp. 1277-1340.

_____, Letter to all Bishops of the Church, On the Mystery and Worship of the Eucharist, *Dominicae caenae*, February 24, 1980, in *AAS*, 72 (1980), pp. 113-148.

_____, Apostolic Exhortation, "The Christian Family in the Modern World," *Familiaris consortio*, November 22, 1981, in *AAS*, 74 (1982), pp. 81-191.

_____, Apostolic Constitution promulgating the 1983 Code of Canon Law, *Sacrae disciplinae leges*, January 25, 1983, in *AAS*, 75 II (1983), pp. vii-xiv.

_____, Apostolic Letter, Motu proprio, *Recognitio iuris canonici*, January 2, 1984, in *AAS*, 76 (1984), pp. 433-434.

_____, Post-Synodal Apostolic Exhortation, *Pastores dabo vobis*, March 25, 1992, in *AAS*, 84 (1992), pp. 657-804.

KACZYNSKI, R., *Enchiridion documentorum instaurationis liturgicae*, Torino, Marietti, 1976. Work is numbered "I," but no other volumes have been published.

LAUER, A., *Index verborum Codicis iuris canonici*, Romae: Typis polyglottis Vaticanis, 1941.

Missale Romanum ex decreto sacrosancti oecumenici concilii Vaticani II instauratum auctoritate Pauli PP. VI promulgatum, editio typica altera, Libreria editrice Vaticana, 1975.

NEDUNGATT, G., *A Companion to the Eastern Code: For a New Translation of Codex canonum Ecclesiarum orientalium*, vol. 5 of G. NEDUNGATT, (ed.), *Kanonika*, Roma: Pontificio Instituto Orientale, 1994.

OCHOA, X., *Index verborum cum documentis Concilii Vaticani Secundi*, Roma: Commentarium pro Religiosis, 1967.

_____, *Index verborum ac locutionum Codicis iuris canonici*, 2nd complete edition, Città del Vaticano: Libreria editrice Lateranese, 1984.

_____, *Leges ecclesiae post Codicem iuris canonici editae*, vol. 1-5 (1966-1980), Roma: Commentarium pro Religiosis, vol. 6 (1987), Roma, EDIURCLA.

PAUL VI, Apostolic Letter, Motu proprio, *Ecclesiae sanctae*, August 6, 1966, in *AAS*, 58 (1966), pp. 757-787.

_____, Motu proprio, General Regulations of the Roman Curia *Regolamento generale della Curia Romana*, February 22, 1968 in *AAS*, 60 (1968), pp. 129-176.

_____, Motu proprio, "Advancing Age and the Ability to Fulfill Certain Offices of Greater Moment," *Ingravescentem aetatem*, November 21, 1970 in *AAS*, 62 (1970), pp. 810-813.

_____, Address to the judges and officials of the Tribunal of the Sacred Roman Rota, *Vivissima gioia*, February 8, 1973, in *AAS*, 65 (1973), pp. 95-103.

_____, Apostolic Exhortation, "Evangelization in the Modern World," *Evangelii nuntiandi*, December 8, 1975, in *AAS*, 68 (1976), pp. 5-76.

PIUS X, Encyclical Letter, "On Religious Education," *Acerbo nimis*, April 15, 1905, in *AAS*, 37 (1904-05), pp. 613-625.

PONTIFICIA COMMISSIO CODICI IURIS CANONICI AUTHENTICE

INTERPRETANDO, *Acta Commissionum*, in *AAS*, 79 (1987), p. 1249.

PONTIFICIA COMMISSIO CODICI IURIS CANONICI RECOGNOSCENDO, Schema *Legis Ecclesiae fundamentalis, textus emendatus cum relatione de ipso schemate deque emendationibus receptis*, Typis polyglottis Vaticanis, 1971.

_____, *Relatio complectens synthesim animadversionum ab em.mis atque exc.mis patribus commissionis ad novissimum schema Codicis iuris canonici exhibitarum, cum responsionibus a secretaria et consultoribus datis*, Typis polyglottis Vaticanis, 1981.

_____, *Codex iuris canonici schema novissimum iuxta placita patrum commissionis emendatum atque Summo Pontifici praesentatum*, Romae, Typis polyglottis Vaticanis, 1982.

PONTIFICIA COMMISSIO DECRETIS VATICANI II INTERPRETANDIS, response, July 7, 1978, in *AAS*, 70 (1978), p. 534.

PONTIFICIUM CONSILIUM DE LEGUM TEXTIBUS INTERPRETANDIS, *Acta et documenta Pontificiae Commissionis Codici iuris canonici recognoscendo: Congregatio plenaria diebus 20-29 octobris 1981 habita*, Typis polyglottis Vaticanis, 1991.

PONTIFICIUM CONSILIUM INSTRUMENTIS COMMUNICATIONIS SOCIALIS, Pastoral Instruction for the Proper Implementation of the Decree of the Second Ecumenical Council of the Vatican Concerning the Means of Social Communication *Communio et progressio*, May 23, 1971, in *AAS*, 63 (1971), pp. 593-656.

RICHTER, A.L. and A. FRIEDBERG (eds.), *Corpus Iuris canonici*, Graz: Akademische durck - u. verlagsanstalt, 1959, 2 vols., pars prior, *Decretum magistri Gratiani*, pars secunda, *Decretales Gregorii P. IX.*

The Rites of the Catholic Church. Revised by decree of the Second Vatican Ecumenical Council and published by authority of Pope Paul VI. English translation prepared by The International Commission on English in the Liturgy, New York: Pueblo Publishing Co., 1976.

The Roman Missal: The Sacramentary. Revised by decree of the

Second Vatican Council and published by authority of Pope Paul VI, approved for use in the Dioceses of the United States of America by the National Conference of Catholic Bishops and confirmed by the Apostolic See. English translation prepared by the International Commission on English in the Liturgy, New York: Catholic Book Publishing Co., 1974.

Sacra Congregatio pro Catholica Educatione, Instruction, *L'école catholique*, March 19, 1977, in *La documentation catholique*, 74 (1977) 7-21 août, pp. 705-716.

Sacra Congregatio pro Clericis, *Directorium catecheticum generale*, April 11, 1971, in *AAS*, 64 (1972), pp. 97-176.

Sacra Congregatio pro Cultu Divino, Instruction on Masses for Special Groups, *Actio pastoralis Ecclesiae*, May 15, 1969, in *AAS*, 61 (1969), pp. 806-811.

_____, *Rituale Romanum ex decreto sacrosancti oecumenici concilii Vaticani II instauratum, auctoritate Pauli PP. VI promulgatum, Ordo initiationis christianae adultorum*, 1972, Typis polyglottis Vaticanis.

_____, *Rituale Romanum ex decreto sacrosancti oecumenici concilii Vaticani II instauratum, auctoritate Pauli PP. VI promulgatum, De benedictionibus*, editio typica, Typis polyglottis Vaticanis, 1985.

_____, Third Instruction on the correct implementation of the Constitution on the Sacred Liturgy, *Liturgiae instaurationes*, September 5, 1970, in *AAS*, 62 (1970), pp. 692-704.

_____, Order of Blessing the Oils of Catechumens and of the Sick, and of Confecting Chrism, *Ordo benedicendi oleum catechumenorum et infirmorum et conficiendi chrisma*, December 3, 1970, in *AAS*, 63 (1971), pp. 728-730.

_____, *Rituale Romanum ex decreto sacrosancti oecumenici concilii Vaticani II instauratum, auctoritate Pauli PP. VI promulgatum, Ordo paenitentiae*, editio typica, Typis polyglottis Vaticanis, 1974.

_____, General Instruction on the Roman Missal, *Cenam*

paschalem, March 26, 1970, in *Missale Romanum ex decreto sacrosancti oecumenici concilii Vaticani II instauratum, auctoritate Pauli PP. VI promulgatum*, editio typica altera, Libreria editrice Vaticana, 1975.

_____, *Ordo professionis religiosae ex decreto sacrosancti oecumenici concilii Vaticani II instauratus, auctoritate Pauli PP. VI promulgatus*, editio typica, Typis polyglottis Vaticanis, 1975.

_____, Instruction on Certain Norms Concerning the Worship of the Eucharistic Mystery, *Inaestimabile donum*, April 3, 1980, in *AAS*, 72 (1980), pp. 331-343.

_____, Sunday Celebrations in the Absence of a Priest, *Directorium de celebrationibus dominicalibus absente presbytero*, June 2, 1988, in *Notitiae*, 24 (1988), pp. 366-378.

SACRA CONGREGATIO PRO DOCTRINA FIDEI, Instruction on Infant Baptism, *Pastoralis actio*, October 20, 1980, in *AAS*, 72 (1980), pp. 1137-1156.

SACRA CONGREGATIO RITUUM, Instruction on the Proper Implementation of the Constitution on the Sacred Liturgy of the Second Vatican Council, *Inter oecumenici*, September 26, 1964, in *AAS*, 56 (1964), pp. 877-900.

SACROSANCTUM OECUMENICUM CONCILIUM VATICANUM II, Constitution on the Sacred Liturgy, *Sacrosanctum concilium*, December 4, 1963, in *AAS*, 56 (1964), pp. 97-133.

_____, Decree on the Means of Social Communication, *Inter mirifica*, December 4, 1963, in *AAS*, 56 (1964), pp. 145-153.

_____, Dogmatic Constitution on the Church, *Lumen gentium*, November 21, 1964, in *AAS*, 57 (1965), pp. 5-67.

_____, Decree on Catholic Eastern Churches, *Orientalium Ecclesiarum*, November 21, 1964, in *AAS*, 57 (1965), pp. 76-85.

_____, Decree on Ecumenism, *Unitatis redintegratio*, November 21, 1964, in *AAS*, 57 (1965), pp. 90-107.

_____, Decree on the Pastoral Office of Bishops in the Church, *Christus Dominus*, October 28, 1965, in *AAS*, 58 (1966), pp. 673-696.

_____, Decree on the Up-To-Date Renewal of Religious Life, *Perfectae caritatis,* October 28, 1965, in *AAS,* 58 (1966), pp. 702-712.

_____, Declaration on Christian Education, *Gravissimum educationis,* October 28, 1965, in *AAS,* 58 (1966), pp. 728-739.

_____, Dogmatic Constitution on Divine Revelation, *Dei Verbum,* November 18, 1965, in *AAS,* 58 (1966), pp. 817-830.

_____, Decree on the Apostolate of the Laity, *Apostolicam actuositatem,* November 18, 1965, in *AAS,* 58 (1966), pp. 837-864.

_____, Decree on the Church's Missionary Activity, *Ad gentes,* December 7, 1965, in *AAS,* 58 (1966), pp. 947-990.

_____, Declaration on the Right of the Person and Communities to Social and Civil Liberty in Religious Matters, *Dignitatis humanae,* December 7, 1965, in *AAS,* 58 (1966), pp. 929-941.

_____, Decree on the Training of Priests, *Optatam totius,* October 28, 1965, in *AAS,* 58 (1966), pp. 713-727.

_____, Pastoral Constitution on the Church in the Modern World, *Gaudium et spes,* December 7, 1965, in *AAS,* 58 (1966), pp. 1085-1115.

_____, Decree on the Ministry and Life of Priests, *Presbyterorum ordinis,* December 7, 1965, in *AAS,* 58 (1966), pp. 991-1024.

_____, *Acta synodalia sacrosancti Concilii oecumenici Vaticani II,* Typis polyglottis Vaticanis, 1976, 4 vols., Indices and Appendix.

Societas Goerresiana (ed.), *Concilium Tridentinum: diariorum, actorum, epistularum, tractatuum nova collectio,* t. 8, *Actorum pars quinta, complectens acta ad preparandum concilium, et sessiones anni 1562 a prima (XVII) ad sextam (XXII),* collegit, edidit, illustravit S. Ehses, Friburgi Brisgoviae: B. Herder, 1919.

Supremum Tribunal Signaturae Apostolicae, *Sententia definitiva 24 junii 1995 coram Gilberto Card. Agustoni*, in *Forum*, 6 (1995)², pp. 117-122.

TANNER, N.P., (ed.), *Decrees of the Ecumenical Councils*, vol. 2, *Trent to Vatican II*, Washington, DC: Sheed & Ward and Georgetown University Press, 1990.

Books:

ABBO, J.A. and J.D. HANNAN, *The Sacred Canons: A Concise Presentation of the Current Disciplinary Norms of the Church*, rev. edition, St. Louis, MO: B. Herder Book Co., 1957, 2 vols.

AGIUS, L., *Summarium iurium et officiorum parochorum ad normam Codicis iuris canonici*, Naples: M. D'Auria, 1953.

ANDREWS, E.A. (ed.), C.T. LEWIS and C. SHORT [revisers, enlargers, in great part rewriters], *Harper's Latin Dictionary: A New Latin Dictionary founded on the Translation of Freund's Latin-German Lexicon*, Franklin Square, NY: Harper & Brothers, Publishers, 1891.

AUGUSTINE, P.C., *A Commentary on the New Code of Canon Law*, St. Louis, MO: B. Herder Book Co., 1921-1922, 8 vols.

_____, *The Pastor According to the New Code of Canon Law*, St. Louis, MO: B. Herder Book Co., 1924.

AYRINHAC, H.A., *Constitution of the Church in the New Code of Canon Law*, New York: Longmans, Green and Company, 1930, 5 vols.

BENDER, L., *De parochis et vicariis paroecialibus: commentarius in canones 451-478*, Rome: Desclée, 1959.

The Book of Blessings, approved for use in the dioceses of the United States of America by the National Conference of Catholic Bishops and confirmed by the Apostolic See, prepared by the INTERNATIONAL COMMISSION ON ENGLISH IN THE LITURGY, Collegeville, MN: The Liturgical Press, 1989.

BORRAS, A., *Les communautés paroissiales: droit canonique pastorales*, Paris: Les Éditions du Cerf, 1996.

BOUSCAREN, T.L., A.C. ELLIS, and F.N. KORTH, *Canon Law: a Text and Commentary*, 4th rev. edition, Milwaukee: Bruce, 1966.

BROWN, B.F., *The Canonical Juristic Personality with Special Reference to Its Status in the United States of America*, Canon Law Studies, No. 39, Washington, DC: The Catholic University of America, 1927.

BUETOW, H.A., *The Catholic School: Its Roots, Identity and Future*, New York: Crossroad, 1988.

CANON LAW SOCIETY OF AMERICA, *The Art of Interpretation: Selected Studies in the Interpretation of Canon Law*, Washington, DC: Canon Law Society of America, 1982.

CANON LAW SOCIETY OF AMERICA COMMITTEE ON PROCEDURES FOR THE PROTECTION OF RIGHTS OF PERSONS IN THE CHURCH, *Protection of Rights of Persons in the Church*, Washington, DC: Canon Law Society of America, 1991.

CAPARROS, E., M. THÉRIAULT, and J. THORN (eds.), *Code of Canon Law Annotated*, Latin-English edition of the Code of Canon Law and English language translation of 5th Spanish language edition of the Commentary prepared under the responsibility of the Instituto Martín de Azpilcueta, Montréal: Wilson & Lafleur Limitée, 1993.

CAPPELLINI, E. and F. COCCOPALMERIO, *Temi pastorali de nuovo codice*, Brescia: Editrice Queriniana, 1984.

CAPPELLO, F.M., *De administrativa amotione parochorum*, Rome: F. Pustet, 1911.

CARLEN, C., *The Papal Encyclicals: 1740-1981*, Wilmington, NC: Consortium Book, McGrath Publ., 1981, 5 vols.

_____, *Papal Pronouncements, A Guide, 1740-1978*, Ann Arbor, MI: Pierian Press, 1980.

CHIAPPETTA, L., *Il Codice di diritto canonico: commento giuridico-pastorale*, 2nd edition, Roma: Edizioni Dehoniane, 1996, 3 vols.

COCCOPALMERIO, F., *De paroecia*, Roma: Editrice Pontifica Università Gregoriana, 1991.

COGAN P.J. (ed.), *CLSA Advisory Opinions 1984-1993*, Washington, DC: Canon Law Society of America, 1995.

CONGRESSO INTERNACIONAL DE DERECHO CANÓNICO, *La norma en el derecho canónico, actas de III congresso internacional de derecho canónico, Pamplona 10-15 de octubre 1976*, Pamplona: Ediciónes Universidad de Navarra, S.A., 1979, 2 vols.

CONNOR, M., *The Administrative Removal of Pastors*, Canon Law Studies, No. 104, Washington, DC: The Catholic University of America, 1937.

CORIDEN, J.A., (ed.), *The Case for Freedom "Human Rights in the Church,"* Washington, DC: Corpus Books, 1969.

CORIDEN, J.A., T.J. GREEN, and D.E. HEINTSCHEL (eds.), *The Code of Canon Law: A Text and Commentary*, New York: Paulist Press, 1985.

————, *The Parish in Catholic Tradition: History, Theology and Canon Law*, New York: Paulist Press, 1997.

CUSACK, B.A. and T.G. SULLIVAN, *Pastoral Care in Parishes Without a Pastor: Applications of Canon 517, Section 2*, Washington, DC: Canon Law Society of America, 1995.

DEEGAN, A., *The Priest as Manager*, New York: The Bruce Publishing Company, 1969.

DEUTSCH, B., *Jurisdiction of Pastors in the External Forum: An Historical Synopsis and Commentary*, Canon Law Studies, No. 378, Washington, DC: The Catholic University of America, 1957.

DILLENSCHNEIDER, C., *La paroisse et son curé dans le mystère de l'Église*, Paris: Éditions Alsatia, 1965.

DOHENY, W.J., *Practical Problems in Church Finances: A Study of the Alienation of Church Resources and the Canonical Restrictions on Church Debt*, Milwaukee: The Bruce Publishing Company, 1941.

DONLON, J., *The Human Rights of Priests to Equitable Sustenance and Mobility: An Evaluation of Canon Law from the "Codex iuris canonici" to the Proposed Revision of the Code of Canon Law*, Canon Law Studies, No. 510, Washington, DC: The Catholic University of America, 1984.

FANFANI, L.G., *De iure parochorum ad normam Codicis iuris canonici,*

3rd edition, Rovigo: Instituto Padamo de Arti Grafiche, 1954.

FRANCK, B. *Vers un nouveau droit canonique? Présentation, commentaire et critique du Code de droit canonique de l'Église catholique latine révisé à la lumière de Vatican II*, Paris: Éditions de Cerf, 1983.

FROMMELT, H.A., *Church Property and Its Management*, New York: The Bruce Publishing Company, 1936.

GALVIN, W., *The Administrative Transfer of Pastors*, Canon Law Studies, No. 232, Washington, DC: The Catholic University of America, 1946.

GRESKO, G., *Stability of the Pastoral Office*, Rome: Pontificia Studiorum Universitas S. Thomae in Urbe, 1983.

HACK, M., *Stability of the Office of Parish Priest in the 1983 Code of Canon Law*, Ottawa, ON: Saint Paul University, 1988.

HUELS, J.M., *The Pastoral Companion: A Canon Law Handbook for Catholic Ministry*, 2nd edition, revised, Quincy, IL: Franciscan Press, 1995.

JOYCE, M.P., *The Ministry of the Priest in the Exercise of the Munus Sanctificandi as It Pertains to the Eucharist*, Canon Law Studies, No. 539, Washington, DC: The Catholic University of America, Ann Arbor, MI, UMI, 1992.

KELLY, B.M., *The Functions Reserved to Pastors*, Canon Law Studies, No. 250, Washington, DC: The Catholic University of America, 1947.

KOUDELKA, C.J., *Pastors: Their Rights and Duties According to the New Code of Canon Law*, Canon Law Studies, No. 11, Washington, DC: The Catholic University of America, 1921.

LARRABE, J., *Los nuevas parroquias: doctrina conciliar de la Iglesia*, Madrid: Studium, 1969.

MADRENYS, C., *La empericia y la enfermedad como causas de remoción del párroco*, Cuadernos 5, Pamplona: Unversidad Navarra, 1965.

MAGNIN, E., *Pastor and People: A Summary of the Canon Law*

Affecting Parish Priests, Curates and the Laity, J. SCANLON, trans., St. Louis, MO: B. Herder Book Co., 1929.

MAIDA, A.J. and N.P. CAFARDI, *Church Property, Church Finances, and Church Related Corporations*, St. Louis, MO: Catholic Health Association of the United States, 1984.

MANZANARES, J., A. MOSTAZA, and J.L. SANTOS, *Nuevo derecho parroquial*, Madrid: Bibliotheca De Autores Cristianos, 1990.

MANZANARES, J. (ed.), *La parroquia desde del derecho canonico: aportaciones del derecho comun y particular; X jondas de la Asociación Española de Canonistas, Madrid 18-20 abril 1990*, Salamanca: Universidad Pontificia, 1991.

MARCHANT, J.R.V. and J.F. CHARLES [revisers], *Cassell's Latin Dictionary*, New York: Funk & Wagnalls Company, no date.

MARZOA, A., J. MIRAS and R. RODRÍGUEZ-OCAÑA (eds.), *Comentario exegético al código de derecho canónico*, Instituto Martin de Azpilcueta Facultad De Derecho Canónico Universidad De Navarra, 2nd edition, Pamplona: EUNSA Editiones Universidad de Navarra, S.A., 1997, 5 vols.

McDEVITT, G.V., *The Renunciation of an Ecclesiastical Office*, Canon Law Series, No. 218, Washington, DC: The Catholic University of America, 1946.

MICHIELS, G., *Normae generales iuris canonici commentarium libri I Codicis iuris canonici*, second edition, Paris: Typis Societatis S. Joannis Evangelistae Desclée et Socii, 1949.

MICKELLS, A.B., *The Constitutive Elements of Parishes: A Historical Synopsis and a Commentary*, Canon Law Studies, No. 296, Washington, DC: Catholic University of America, 1950.

MORGANTE, M., *La parrocchia nel Codice di diritto canonico: commento giuridico-pastorale*, Milano: Edizioni Paoline, 1985.

MYERS, J., *The Qualifications of Clergy for the Office of Pastor*, JCL thesis, Washington, DC: The Catholic University of America, 1976.

NATIONAL COUNCIL OF CATHOLIC BISHOPS, *A Shepherd's Care:*

Reflections on the Changing Role of Pastor, Washington, DC: United States Catholic Conference, 1987.

O'Connell, P., *The Concept of Parish in Light of the Second Vatican Council*, Canon Law Studies, No. 470, Washington, DC: The Catholic University of America, 1969.

Oswald, R. et al., *New Visions for the Long Pastorate*, Washington, DC: The Alban Institute, 1983.

Pagé, R., *Les églises particulières*: Tome II: *la charge pastorale de leurs communautés de fidèles selon le Code de droit canonique de 1983*, vol. 4 of *Les institutions ecclésiales*, Montréal: Éditions Paulines & Médiaspaul, 1989.

Périsset, J., *Curé et presbytérium paroissial: analyse de Vatican II pour une adaptation des normes canoniques du prêtre en paroisse*, Analecta Gregoriana, vol. 227. Series Facultatis Iuris Canonici, Section B., n. 46, Rome: Università Gregoriana Editrice, 1982.

_____, *La paroisse: commentaire des canons 515-572*, Paris: Éditions Tardy, 1989.

_____, *Les biens temporels de l'Église: commentaire des canons 1254-1310* (Le nouveau droit ecclésial, livre V), Paris: Éditions Tardy, 1996.

Pfnausch, E.G. (ed.), *Code, Community, Ministry: Selected Studies for the Parish Minister Introducing the Revised Code of Canon Law*, 2nd rev. edition, Washington, DC: Canon Law Society of America, 1992.

Pinto, P.V. (ed.), *Commento al Codice di diritto canonico*, Studia Urbaniana, No. 21, Roma: Pontificia Universitas Urbaniana, 1985.

Pontificium Consilium de Legum Textibus Iterpretandis, *Ius in vita et in missione Ecclesiae: Acta symposii internationalis Iuris canonici occurrente X anniversario promulgationis Codicis iuris canonici diebus 19-24 aprilis 1993 in civitate Vaticana celebrati*, Libreria editrice Vaticana, 1994.

Pospishil, V.J. and J.D. Faris, *The New Latin Code of Canon Law and Eastern Catholics*, Brooklyn: Diocese of Saint Maron, 1984.

_____, *Eastern Catholic Marriage Law: According to the Code of*

Canons of the Eastern Churches, Brooklyn: Saint Maron Publications, 1991.

_____, *Eastern Catholic Church Law: According to the Code of Canons of the Eastern Churches*, Brooklyn: Saint Maron Publications, 1993.

PROVOST, J.H. (ed.), *Official Ministry in a New Age*, Permanent Seminar Studies No. 3, Washington, DC: Canon Law Society of America, 1981.

PRUSAK, B., *The Canonical Concept of Particular Church Before and After Vatican II*, Rome: Pontificia Università Lateranense, 1967.

SANTOSO, P., *The Rules of Interpretation According to Canon 17: Searching the Will of the Legislator Inside the Words of the Law*, Roma: Pontificia Studiorum Universitas a S. Thoma Aq. in Urbe, 1986.

SHEEHY, G., R. BROWN, D. KELLY, A. McGRATH et al. (eds.), *The Canon Law, Letter & Spirit: A Practical Guide to the Code of Canon Law*, prepared by The Canon Law Society of Great Britain and Ireland in association with The Canadian Canon Law Society, Collegeville, MN: A Michael Glazier Book, The Liturgical Press, 1995.

SHEKELTON, M., *Doctrinal Interpretation of the Law*, Canon Law Studies, No. 345, Washington, DC: The Catholic University of America, 1961.

SUTTON, T., *The Stability of the Pastoral Office*, JCL thesis, Washington, DC: The Catholic University of America, 1984.

SWEENY, E.A., *Catechetical Instruction: A Systematic Analysis of Canons 773-780 of the Revised Code of Canon Law*, Masters Seminar, Ottawa, ON: Saint Paul University, 1994.

THOMPSON, C.J., *The Simple Removal from Office*, Canon Law Series, No. 285, Washington, DC: The Catholic University of America, 1951.

VANN, K.W. and J.I. DONLON (eds.), *Roman Replies and CLSA Advisory Opinions 1994*, Washington, DC: Canon Law Society of America, 1994.

_____, (eds.), *Roman Replies and CLSA Advisory Opinions 1995*,

Washington, DC: Canon Law Society of America, 1995.

VEMEERSCH, A. and J. CREUSEN, *Epitome iuris canonici*, 7th edition, Malines: Dessain, 1949-1956, 3 vols.

WERNZ, F. and P. VIDAL, *Ius canonicum*, Rome: Apud Aedes Universitatis Gregorianae, 1928, 7 vols.

WOESTMAN, W.H., *Sacraments: Initiation, Penance, Anointing of the Sick: Commentary on Canons 840-1007*, Ottawa: Faculty of Canon Law, Saint Paul University, 1992.

WOYWOD, S. and C. SMITH, *A Practical Commentary on the New Code of Canon Law*, New York: Joseph F. Wagner, 1952.

WRENN, L.G., *Authentic Interpretations of the 1983 Code*, Washington, DC: Canon Law Society of America, 1993.

YZERMANNS, V.A. (ed.), *All Things in Christ*, Westminster, MD: Newman Press, 1954.

Articles:

ALESANDRO, J.A., "General Introduction," in J.A. CORIDEN et al. (eds.), *The Code of Canon Law: A Text and Commentary*, pp. 1-22.

_____, and A.J. PLACA, "Church Agents and Employees: Legal and Canonical Issues," in *CLSA Proceedings*, 58 (1996), pp. 35-82.

ANANDARAYAR, A., "Parish and Its Pastor in the New Code of Canon Law," in *Indian Theological Studies*, 22 1985, pp. 79-99.

AUBERT, J.M., "Droit et morale dans le nouveau Code," in *L'Année canonique*, 28 (1984), pp. 13-18.

AUSTIN, R., "The Stability in Office of a Parish Priest, Canon 522 in the 1983 Code," in *Australasian Catholic Record*, 62 (1985), pp. 283-292.

BEAL, J.P., "Administrative Leave: Canon 1722 Revisited," in *Studia canonica*, 27 (1983), pp. 293-320.

BELGIORNO, M., "L'ufficio parrochiale nel rinnovamento

postconsiliare," in *La norma en el derecho canónico, actas del III congreso internacional de derecho canónico. Pamplona, 10-15 de octubre de 1976*, vol. 1, Pamplona: Ediciónes Universidad de Navarra, S.A., 1979, pp. 951-958.

BONI, A., "Le fonti di diritto nella struttura del nuovo CIC," in *Apollonaris*, 56 (1983), pp. 370-398.

BONNET, M., "Prise de possession canonique et profession de foi pour le curé," in *Les cahier du droit ecclésial*, 1 (1984), pp. 151-163.

BROWN, B.F., "The Canonical Juristic Personality," in *The Jurist*, 1 (1941), pp. 66-73; 125-133.

CALVO, J., "De la ordenación interna de las iglesias particulares (cc. 515-572)," in LOMBARDIA et al. *Código de derecho canónico*, 5th edition, Pamplona: Ediciónes Universidad de Navarra, 1987, pp. 358-389.

_____, "Parishes, Parish Priests and Assistant Priests," Commentary on cc. 515-552, in E. CAPARROS, et al. (eds.), *Code of Canon Law Annotated*, pp. 377-401.

CANON LAW SOCIETY OF AMERICA, "Canonical Standards in Labor-Management Relations," in *The Jurist*, 47 (1987), pp. 545-575.

CAPPELLINI, E., "L'ufficio pastorale et presbitero nel Codice rinnovato," in *Monitor ecclesiasticus*, 109 (1984), pp. 76-99.

CARLSON, R., "The Parish According to the Revised Code," in *Studia canonica*, 19 (1985), pp. 5-16.

CASTILLO LARA, R.J., "De iuris canonici authentica interpretatione in actuositate pontificae commissionis adimplenda," in *Communicationes*, 20 (1988), pp. 265-287.

CENTER FOR APPLIED RESEARCH IN THE APOSTOLATE, "Team Ministry/The Hartford Plan," in *Origins*, 5 (1975-1976), pp. 194-202.

COCCOPALMERIO, F., "Il concetto di parrochia nel Vaticano II," in *La Scuola cattolica*, 106 (1978), pp. 123-142.

_____, "De persona iuridica iuxta schema Codicis novi," in *Periodica*, 70 (1981), pp. 369-400.

_____, "La parrochia nel nuovo Codice," in *Orientamenti pastorali*, 31:9-11 (1983), pp. 143-168.

_____, "De causis ad amotionem parochorum requisitis (can. 1740-1741)," in *Periodica*, 75 (1986), pp. 273-302.

CORA, G., "Team Ministry: Theological Aspects," in *The American Ecclesiastical Review*, 167 (1973), pp. 684-690.

CORIDEN, J.A. and M. MANGAN, "Team Ministry," in *CLSA Proceedings*, 34 (1973), pp. 70-75.

_____, "Rules for Interpreters," in *The Jurist*, 42 (1982), pp. 277-303.

_____, "Book III: The Teaching Office of the Church," in J.A. CORIDEN et al. (eds.), *The Code of Canon Law: A Text and Commentary*, pp. 545-589.

COUGHLIN, J.J., "Canonical Equity," in *Studia canonica*, 30 (1996), pp. 403-435.

CUNNINGHAM, R.G., "The Principles Guiding the Revision of the Code of Canon Law," in *The Jurist*, 30 (1970), pp. 447-455.

CUNNINGHAM, T., "The Canonical Position of the Pastor after Vatican II," in *Irish Ecclesiastical Record*, 106 (1966), pp. 54-55.

DANEELS, F., "The Removal or Transfer of a Pastor in the Light of the Jurisprudence of the Apostolic Signatura," in *Forum*, 8 (1997)[2], pp. 295-301.

D'AVACK, P.A., "Legittimità, contenuto et methodologia del diritto canonico," in *Il diritto ecclesiastico*, 89, I-II (1978), pp. 3-41.

DAVID, B., "La paroisse selon le noveau Code," in *Espirit et vie*, 14 (1985), pp. 204-207.

_____, "Paroisses curés et vicaires paroissuaux dans le Code de droit canonique," in *Nouvelle revue théologique*, 107 (1985), pp. 853-866.

DE PAOLIS, V., "De paroeciis Institutis religiosis commissis vel committendis," in *Periodica*, 74 (1985), pp. 389-417.

DORAN, T., "Rights and Duties of Pastors," in *CLSA Proceedings*, 45 (1984), pp. 182-192.

D'OSTILIO, F., "La provvista degli uffici ecclesiastici," in *Monitor ecclesiasticus*, 107 (1982), pp. 57-78.

DOYLE, T.P., "The Canonical Rights of Priests Accused of Sexual Abuse," in *Studia canonica*, 24 (1990), pp. 335-356.

ERDÖ, P., "Expressiones obligationis et exhortationis in CIC," in *Periodica*, 76 (1987), pp. 3-27.

FARIS, J.D., "Inter-Ritual Matters in the Revised Code of Canon Law," in *Studia canonica*, 17 (1983), pp. 239-259.

FELICI, P., "El Concilio Vaticano II y la nueva codificacion canónica," in *Ius canonicum*, 7 (1967), pp. 397-420.

_____, "Norma giuridica e 'pastorale'," in *La norma en el derecho canónico, actas del III congreso internacional de derecho canónico. Pamplona, 10-15 de octubre de 1976*, vol. 1, Pamplona: Ediciónes Universidad de Navarra, S.A., 1979, p. 19.

FOX, J., "The Homily and the Authentic Interpretation of Canon 767 §1," in *Apollinaris*, 62 (1989), pp. 123-169.

FUENTES, J.A., "Predicación de la homilia," Commentary on c. 767, in A. MARZOA et al. (eds.), *Comentario exegético al código de derecho canónico*, vol. III/I, pp. 113-115.

GARCIA, L.M., "La función del párroco en la preparación del matrimonio," in *Ius canonicum*, 39 (1989), pp. 527-544.

GAUTHIER, A., "Juridical Persons in the Code of Canon Law," in *Studia canonica*, 25 (1991), pp. 77-92.

GRIFFIN, B.F., "Canon 766, Lay Preaching," in *CLSA Advisory Opinions 1984-1993*, P.J. COGAN (ed.), Washington, DC: Canon Law Society of America, 1995, pp. 217-220.

HEINTSCHEL, D., "Alienation of Church Property Under the New Code of Canon Law," in *The Catholic Lawyer*, 31 (1987), pp. 150-155.

HERVADA, J., "The Obligations and Rights of all Christ's Faithful," Commentary on cc. 208-223, in E. CAPARROS et al. (eds.), *Code of Canon Law Annotated*, pp. 190-197.

HITE, J., "Church Law on Property and Contracts," in *The Jurist*, 44 (1984), pp. 117-133.

_____, "Property and Contracts in Church Law," in *The Catholic Lawyer*, 30 (1986), pp. 256-265.

HOWES, R., "Regional Pastor: Regional People," in *The Priest*, 36 (1980), pp. 19-24.

_____, "Parish Life and the New Code," in *Concilium*, 185 (1986), pp. 64-72.

_____, "Interpreting an Instruction Approved *in forma specifica*," in *Studia canonica*, 32 (1998), pp. 5-46.

HUFTIER, M., "Le Code de droit canonique: les curés dans le Code," in *Esprit et vie*, 94 (1984), pp. 286-287.

JANICKI, J.J., "Parishes, Pastors, Parochial Vicars (cc. 515-572)," in J.A. CORIDEN et al. (eds.), *The Code of Canon Law, A Text and Commentary*, pp. 414-449.

KEENAN, J.F., "Confidentiality, Disclosure and Fiduciary Responsibility," in *Theological Studies*, 54 (1993), pp. 142-159.

KELLY, D., "Baptism," Commentary on cc. 849-878, in G. SHEEHY et al. (eds.), *The Canon Law, Letter & Spirit: A Practical Guide to the Code of Canon Law*, pp. 469-484.

_____, "Marriage," in G. SHEEHY et al. (eds.), *The Canon Law, Letter & Spirit: A Practical Guide to the Code of Canon Law*, pp. 571-659.

KENNEDY, R.J., "McGrath, Maida, Michiels: Introduction to a Study of the Canonical and Civil-law Status of Church-related Institutions in the United States," in *The Jurist*, 50 (1990), pp. 351-401.

KRUKOWSKI, J., "Responsibility for Damage Resulting from Illegal Administrative Acts in the Code of Canon Law of 1983," in *The New Code of Canon Law, Proceedings of the 5th International Congress of Canon Law*, M. THÉRIAULT and J. THORN (eds.), Ottawa, ON: Saint Paul University, 1986, vol. I, pp. 231-242.

_____, "The Juridic Personality of the Church in Relation to the State," in *Studia canonica*, 14 (1980), pp. 231-242.

LABANDEIRA, E. and MIRAS, J., "The Procedure for the Removal or Transfer of Parish Priests," Commentary on cc. 1740-

1752 in E. CAPARROS et al. (eds.), *Code of Canon Law Annotated*, pp.1075-1081.

LOBINA, G., "Parrocchia e parroco nei nuovi orientamenti giuridici postconciliari," in *Apollinaris*, 49 (1976), pp. 418-449.

LOZA, F., "The Penal Process," Commentary on cc. 1717-1731, in E. CAPARROS et al. (eds.), *Code of Canon Law Annotated*, pp. 1059-1067.

LYNCH, J., "The Parochial Ministry in the New Code of Canon Law," in *The Jurist*, 42 (1982), pp. 383-421.

MARCHAND, J.-Y., "Les agents de pastorale: les perspectives offerts par le Code de 1983," in *Studia canonica* 20 (1990), pp. 181-196.

MARCHI, T., "Nuovo Codice di diritto canonico (CIC): note e problemmatica in materia amministrativa," in *L'Amico del clero*, 65 (1983), pp. 206-208, 225-233.

MARCUZZI, P.G., "Verso una nuova definizione giuridica di parrocchia," in *Salesianum*, 43 (1981), pp. 831-844.

MARQUES, J., "El concepto de pastor y funcción pastoral en el Vaticano II," in *Ius canonicum*, 13 (1973), pp. 13-69.

MARZOA, A., "The Blessed Eucharist," Commentary on cc. 897-958, in E. CAPARROS et al. (eds.), *Code of Canon Law Annotated*, pp. 578-408.

_____, "Remoción y translado de párrocos: Introducción," Commentary on cc. 1740-1752, in A. MARZOA et al. (eds.), *Comentario exegético al código de derecho canónico*, vol. IV/2, pp. 2165-2171.

MCAREAVEY, J., "The Blessed Sacrament," Commentary on cc. 897-958, in G. SHEEHY et al. (eds.), *The Canon Law, Letter & Spirit: A Practical Guide to the Code of Canon Law*, pp. 493-523.

MCGRATH, A., "Christ's Faithful," Commentary on cc. 204-367, in G. SHEEHY et al. (eds.), *The Canon Law, Letter & Spirit: A Practical Guide to the Code of Canon Law*, pp. 115-209.

_____, "Title VIII Power of Governance," Commentary on cc. 129-144, in G. SHEEHY et al. (eds.), *The Canon Law, Letter &*

Spirit: A Practical Guide to the Code of Canon Law, pp. 76-86.

Mc Intyre, J.P., "Lineamenta for a Christian Anthropology: Canons 208-223," in *Periodica*, 85 (1996), pp. 249-276.

McLean, B., "Church Funerals," Commentary on cc. 1176-1185, in G. Sheehy et al. (eds.), *The Canon Law, Letter & Spirit: A Practical Guide to the Code of Canon Law*, p. 6673.

Mendonça, A., "The Effects of Recourse Against the Decree of Removal of a Parish Priest," in *Studia canonica*, 25 (1991), pp. 139-153.

Meszaros, J.C., "Procedures of Administrative Recourse," in *The Jurist*, 46 (1986), pp. 107-141.

Miras, J., "El ejercicio 'in solidum' del ministerio parroquial," in *Ius canonicum*, 39 (1989), pp. 483-502.

Molloy, T.E. and J.J. Folmer, "The Canonization of Civil Law," in *CLSA Proceedings*, 46 (1985), pp. 43-65.

Moodie, M., "The Administrator and the Law: Authority and Its Exercise in the Code," in *The Jurist*, 46 (1986), pp. 43-69.

Morrisey, F.G., "The Spirit of Canon Law: Teachings of Pope Paul VI," in *Origins*, 8 (1978-1979), pp. 33, 35-40.

_____, "Pastors and Parishes According to the New Code of Canon Law," in *Pastoral Life*, 33 (1984), pp. 20-29.

_____, "Ordinary and Extraordinary Administration," in *The Jurist*, 48 (1988), pp. 709-726.

_____, "The Temporal Goods of the Church," Commentary on cc. 1254-1310, in G. Sheehy et al. (eds.), *The Canon Law, Letter & Spirit: A Practical Guide to the Code of Canon Law*, pp. 707-747.

_____, "The Ministry of the Divine Word," Commentary on cc. 756-780, in G. Sheehy et al. (eds.), *The Canon Law, Letter & Spirit: A Practical Guide to the Code of Canon Law*, pp. 421-431.

Orsy, L., "Vatican II and the Revision of Canon Law," in *The Clergy Review*, 53 (1968), pp. 83-100.

_____, "The Interpreter and His Art," in *The Jurist*, 40 (1980), pp. 27-56.

PAARHAMMER, J., "De applicatione conceptus 'in solidum' ad novam figuram officii parochi," in *Periodica*, 73 (1984), pp. 191-202.

PARIZEK, J.F., "Procedure in Removal and Transferral of Pastors (cc. 1740-1752)," in J.A. CORIDEN et al. (eds.), *The Code of Canon Law, A Text and Commentary*, pp. 1029-1045.

———, "Pastors on the Go: The Pastor's Rights in the Removal Process," in *CLSA Proceedings*, 48 (1986), pp. 126-138.

PEPERONI, S., "Persone fisiche e persone morali nel nuovo CIC," in *Antonianum*, 60 (1985), pp. 423-458.

PÉRISSET, J., "De officio parochi coetui presbyterorum in solidum concredito," in *Periodica*, 72 (1983), pp. 357-385.

———, "De applicatione conceptus 'in solidum' ad novam figuram parochi," in *Periodica*, 73 (1984), pp. 191-202.

PROVOST, J.H., "Recent Experiences of Administrative Recourse to the Apostolic See," in *The Jurist*, 46 (1986), pp. 142-163.

———, "Diocesan Guidelines for First Eucharist and Penance," in *CLSA Advisory Opinions 1984-1993*, pp. 281-283.

———, "The Reception of First Penance," in *The Jurist*, 47 (1987), pp. 294-340.

RAYER, T.A., "Alienation of Church Property Under the New Code of Canon Law," in *The Catholic Lawyer*, 31 (1987), pp. 156-161.

READ, G., "Parishes, Parish Priests and Assistant Priests," Commentary on cc. 515-552, in G. SHEEHY et al. (eds.), *The Canon Law, Letter & Spirit: A Practical Guide to the Code of Canon Law*, pp. 285-305.

ROBITAILLE, L., "An Examination of Various Forms of Preaching: Toward an Understanding of the Homily and Canons 766-767," in *CLSA Proceedings*, 58 (1996), pp. 308-325.

SÁNCHEZ-GIL, A.S., "Parroquias y párrocos," Commentary on cc. 528-529, in A. MARZOA et al. (eds.), *Comentario exegético al código de derecho canónico*, vol. II/2, pp. 1256-1263.

THÉRIAULT, M., "Procedure for the Removal or Transfer of Parish Priests," Commentary on cc. 1740-1752, in G. SHEEHY et al. (eds.), *The Canon Law, Letter & Spirit: A Practical Guide to the Code of Canon Law*, pp. 966-971.

THOMAS, R., "The Revised Code of Canon Law and the Parish Priest," in *The Priest*, 39 (1983), pp. 29-32.

TOCANEL, P., "Le persone fisiche e giuridiche nella chiesa. Novità, motivazioni e significato," in *Apollinaris*, 56 (1983), pp. 411-421.

URRUTIA, F.J., "Responsa pontificiae commissionis Codici iuris canonici authentice interpretando," in *Periodica*, 77 (1988), pp. 613-628.

VALDRINI, P., "Les procédures de recours contre les actes administratifs et contre les actes de révocation et de transfert des curés," in *L'Année canonique*, 30 (1987), pp. 359-366.

VEGA, A.M., "Forma de celebrar el matrimonio," Commentary on cc. 1118-1123, in A. MARZOA et al. (eds.), *Comentario exegético al código de derecho canónico*, vol. III/2, pp. 1470-1478.

VIANA, A., "El párroco, pastor proprio de la parroquia," in *Ius canonicum*, 29 (1989), pp. 467-481.

WARD, D.J., "Bequests and Gifts to the Church Under the Code of Canon Law," in *The Catholic Lawyer*, 30 (1986), pp. 276-285.

_____, "Trust Management Under the New Code of Canon Law," in *The Jurist*, 44-1 (1984), pp. 134-142.

WOJNAR, M.M., "Interritual Law in the Revised Code of Canon Law," in *The Jurist*, 43 (1983), pp. 191-198.

WULF, K., "Commentary on the Decree on the Ministry and Life of Priests," in *Commentary on the Documents of Vatican II*, H. VORGRIMLER (ed.), Freiburg, Herder, 1968, vol. IV, pp. 210-236; 267-287.

ZIELINSKI, P.J., "Pious Wills and Mass Stipends in Relation to Canons 1299-1310," in *Studia canonica* 19 (1985), pp. 115-154.

ST PAULS

This book was produced by St. Pauls/Alba House, the Society of St. Paul, an international religious congregation of priests and brothers dedicated to serving the Church through the communications media.

For information regarding this and associated ministries of the Pauline Family of Congregations, write to the Vocation Director, Society of St. Paul, P.O. Box 189, 9531 Akron-Canfield Road, Canfield, Ohio 44406-0189. Phone (330) 702-0396; or E-mail: spvocationoffice@aol.com or check our internet site, www.albahouse.org